CHRISTINE TODD WHITMAN

CHRISTINE TODD WHITMAN

THE MAKING OF A NATIONAL POLITICAL PLAYER

ART WEISSMAN

A Birch Lane Press Book
Published by Carol Publishing Group

A Birch Lane Press Book
Published by Carol Publishing Group
Birch Lane Press is a registered trademark of Carol Communications, Inc.
Editorial Offices: 600 Madison Avenue, New York, N.Y. 10022
Sales and Distribution Offices: 120 Enterprise Avenue, Secaucus, N.J. 07094
In Canada: Canadian Manda Group, One Atlantic Avenue, Suite 105, Toronto, Ontario M6K 3E7
Queries regarding rights and permissions should be addressed to Carol Publishing Group, 600 Madison Avenue, New York, N.Y. 10022

Carol Publishing Group books are available at special discounts for bulk purchases, sales promotion, fund-raising, or educational purposes. Special editions can be created to specifications. For details, contact: Special Sales Department, Carol Publishing Group, 120 Enterprise Avenue, Secaucus, N.J. 07094

Manufactured in the United States of America
10 9 8 7 6 5 4 3 2 1

Library of Congress Cataloging-in-Publication Data

Weissman, Art.
    Christine Todd Whitman : the making of a national political player/Art Weissman.
        p.   cm.
    "A Birch Lane Press book."
    ISBN 1-55972-352-1 (hardcover)
    1. Whitman, Christine Todd.   2. Governors—New Jersey—Biography.
I. Title.
F140.22.W45W45   1996
974.9′043′092—dc20
[B]   95-50074
                                                                        CIP

In memory of my father,
Edward Weissman,
1927–1995

Contents

Preface

For the last generation, the statehouse has been the busiest way station on the road to the White House. Three of the past four presidents—Bill Clinton, Ronald Reagan, and Jimmy Carter—were governors. By 1996, a fresh crop of moderate Republican governors, including Michigan's John Engler, California's Pete Wilson, and Massachusetts's Bill Weld, were cited as the next wave of probable presidential hopefuls.

None of those past presidents, or potential contenders, rose as quickly to the national stage as did New Jersey's Christine Todd Whitman. Reagan served as California's chief executive for eight years. Clinton had run Arkansas for more than a decade and chaired the National Governors Association before trying for president in 1992. Carter completed a term as governor and spent two years campaigning in Iowa and New Hampshire before he registered on the nation's political consciousness. By contrast, Whitman rose from ridicule and scorn to acclaim as a national political heroine in just over a year; she had been in office only 372 days when she became the first woman and first governor to deliver a State of the Union response. Her frankness, her tax cuts, and her role as the nation's only woman governor had been ideal ingredients for Republican kingmakers hoping to mold a winning ticket in 1996. Her withdrawal from the vice-presidential sweepstakes in March 1996 didn't dissuade her supporters. Instead, they noted that Whitman would not be seventy-two years old—Bob Dole's age as he campaigned for the White House that year—until after the presidential election of 2016.

Little about Whitman's rise fit conventional political norms. She lacked a network of national supporters; she alienated her party's powerful conservative wing with outspoken stances on abortion and other issues and initiated fiscal practices that many claimed risked New Jersey's financial health. Perplexed by her growing celebrity, political leaders of both parties asked the same questions again and again. How did Whitman make the leap from nearly losing a 1993 gubernatorial election (to a remarkably unpopular politician, at that) to national prominence and a start on the road to the White House? Why had she even been nominated for governor that year, when her biggest prior achievement was a narrow loss in a Senate race with Bill Bradley, the popular Democrat? Where were the accomplishments that justified such a meteoric rise? How had she jumped to the national scene ahead of other GOP governors with more impressive credentials? Simply, what was the secret of her success?

The following pages are not an attempt to provide a definitive history of the Whitman administration. With the governor less than three years into her first term, such judgments must be left to future historians. Rather, what follows is an objective view of her remarkable rise to power, based on journalistic observations and interviews with the governor, her family and friends, political experts, and her Republican allies and Democratic adversaries. This perspective hopefully fulfills a journalist's obligation to present the facts clearly and fairly, and gives the reader the opportunity to assess this emerging national leader.

Acknowledgments

A political campaign, a state government, a newspaper and a television newscast each share a common element with this book: none would be possible without the efforts of a long list of professionals. While I take full responsibility for the pages that follow, I am also indebted to many people for their assistance.

Jody Calendar, deputy executive editor of the *Asbury Park Press*, brought the idea for this project to life and transformed a rookie author's efforts into book form. The pages that follow reflect her determination and caring. Many thanks also to Carl Calendar for his input and advice.

E. Donald Lass, publisher of the *Asbury Park Press*, and W. Raymond Ollwerther, the executive editor, took the risk of backing this project, focusing on its potential and journalistic value. Their faith is much appreciated.

Many of my colleagues—notably Sue DeSantis, Jay Johnston, Tom Zolper, Greg Trevor, Lisa Colangelo, and Kay Lazar—took on additional responsibilities for three months, enabling me to concentrate on this project. Jessica Nesterak pitched in repeatedly with research and proofing assistance, and Stacie Servetah, Larry Arnold, and Dave Willis cheerfully helped in the final editing.

Three *Press* staffers deserve special thanks. Tom Costello spent long hours reviewing, cataloging, and selecting pictures. Lisa Consiglio's assistance as a researcher was invaluable, and Herb Jackson repeatedly offered his insight.

Thanks also to Marty Greenberg, who made this book a reality, and to Steven Schragis of Carol Publishing Group, who recognized the value in telling this story. My editor at Carol Publishing, Kevin McDonough, had unlimited patience and helped expand the book's perspective to a national stage; and Carrie Cantor helped produce it on an accelerated schedule.

Dozens of people in state government, media, academia, and politics graciously offered their recollections and perspectives through long hours of interviews for this project, and for our state-house coverage during the Whitman administration. Many are listed in the endnotes; many others preferred to speak on back-ground, and will remain there. Several people in the Whitman administration also provided special assistance or expertise, including Mike Heid, Ted Pilalides, Jason Volk, and Keith Nahigian. Joe Donnelly of the Assembly Democratic office provided insight and perspective.

To my friends and family, thank you. Bob Karlin and Dave Blomquist provided constant support and guidance. Phil Weissman, my brother, undertook countless family tasks to give me time to complete this book. My father-in-law, Robert Otterbourg, offered insight on the life of an author, and my mother, Helaine Weissman, provided support.

Finally, my loving thanks to my wife, Laura. She was my inspiration and my sounding board, providing constant encouragement and overlooking the mounds of interview transcripts, yellowing clips, and video tapes that littered our home. She is also my partner and best friend—and this book would not have been possible without her.

CHRISTINE TODD WHITMAN

1

A Bold Move

We do not believe that Ms. Whitman herself . . . believes
in this plan. . . . In short, we think it's an intentional
fraud perpetrated by a desperate candidate.
　—*Philadelphia Inquirer* editorial, September 24, 1993

TO CHRISTINE TODD WHITMAN, SELF-CONFIDENCE CAME NATURALLY.
It was part of her, perhaps from the sense of determination she
learned from her parents. In their world—now her world—of
rough-and-tumble politics, any self-doubts or nervousness were to
be left behind, certainly never to be shown to the outside. But on
an afternoon in late September 1993, as she tried to sell an unprecedented proposal to a roomful of reporters, signs of uncertainty
were coming through.

The proposal she was unveiling was solid, Whitman believed.
New Jersey's economy had been reeling for the past three years
from the weight of the huge $2.8 billion state tax increase, the

1

largest increase in state history, pushed through in 1990 by Democratic governor Jim Florio, who was now seeking reelection. Cutting the state's income tax would put money back into the economy, in turn creating badly needed jobs and enhancing New Jersey's reputation as a good place to do business. Whitman believed in parts of supply-side economic theory, even if most reporters seated before her in a Ramada Inn conference room clearly didn't. The team that crafted her proposal featured solid supply-siders, including Malcolm "Steve" Forbes Jr., a longtime friend who was the publisher of *Forbes* magazine, and Lawrence Kudlow, the chief economist at Bear Stearns and Company, who was Ronald Reagan's first deputy budget director. They hoped they had anticipated every question the reporters might throw at her.

There was just so much depending on this. Her three years of hard campaigning, fund-raising, and shaking more hands than she could possibly count, brought her to this moment. Everyone in the room knew the stakes. Her older brother and campaign manager, Dan Todd, and the campaign cochairwoman, Hazel Frank Gluck, a former cabinet member, both paced nervously along the side, while a half-dozen GOP officials wondered whether she would make it through the press inquisition to come. If she lost, following her close 1990 defeat to Senator Bill Bradley, she'd be a two-time loser. Political leaders, particularly in a state that was often unkind to vanquished candidates, didn't like two-time losers.

"It was a major initiative and it was something that was very different from what anyone expected. We'd run all the numbers to the best of our ability, and I felt very comfortable with where we were going, but it was a major policy . . . and I expected a great deal of cynicism," Whitman said. "We were going to make it or not on how well I could stick to it and how credible I was in selling it."[1]

The usual poise and self-assured manner deserted her, almost from the start. Whitman customarily maintained steady eye contact and a firm gaze, conveying a sense that she cared about what she was saying or hearing. At five-foot-eight, she usually didn't have to worry about looking too far up or down in any discussion, and her

2

dark blond hair, cut short in a contemporary style, wasn't long enough to fall over her eyes. Reporters accustomed to politicians who evaded eye contact—often as they spoke with obvious insincerity—sometimes found Whitman's eye-to-eye assurance almost unsettling. They didn't have to worry on this particular afternoon. Whitman's dark brown eyes darted around the room as she began the opening pitch, a sure sign of her uncertainty and discomfort.

Her opening statement went smoothly enough. Whitman quoted John F. Kennedy, hardly a GOP stalwart but popular with voters and reporters, about the importance of tax cuts. She also borrowed a line from another Democrat, Treasury Secretary Lloyd Bentsen, to sting Florio. "I can safely say, Governor, you're no John Kennedy."[2]

She continued her attack on Florio's economic failings for a few more moments, citing the state's declining bond rating, the growing number of business failures, and the soaring jobless rate. Finally, she came to the economic plan she had kept from reporters, the public, and even top Republicans. "I am proposing a 30 percent tax rate reduction in state income taxes—10 percent per year for the next three years."[3] Joint filers with taxable income up to $80,000 would receive the full cut; taxpayers with higher incomes would receive a smaller though still substantial cut, she added.

Reporters were stunned by the proposal and skeptical about the numbers. The secret of the 30 percent cut had been well kept. The state's top Republican lawmakers, Assembly Speaker Garabed "Chuck" Haytaian and Senate President Donald DiFrancesco, had been briefed only a few days before. Even one of Whitman's campaign chairmen, New Jersey congressman Richard Zimmer, had been stymied in his effort to get details at a closed-door strategy session three days earlier at the campaign headquarters in central New Jersey.

Whitman's staff had delayed the press conference until midafternoon to keep the Florio reelection team guessing as long as possible. Releasing the plan early in the day would have given Florio's top staffers enough time to get their assuredly negative reaction to reporters in time for evening newscasts and early newspaper deadlines. But the reporters needed no partisan prodding to unleash their barrage of doubts.

"Suppose it doesn't work?" shouted Jim Goodman, the craggy *Trenton Times* reporter. Whitman loyalists felt that he clearly favored Florio; an anti-Florio group had even produced a bumper sticker proclaiming ANNOY JIM GOODMAN, DUMP FLORIO—though his open skepticism of all politicians was well known.

"It's going to work," she immediately shot back.

Goodman yelled over her reply, "No, suppose these savings in one year don't materialize."

"They will. I have the authority and the ability as a governor," Whitman said, holding her ground, as Goodman shouted yet again. "Suppose they don't."

"I am not going to take that supposition, Jim," Whitman replied, exasperated and glancing around the room for another question. "It's going to work."[4]

It didn't become any easier. Reporters wanted to know how she would save enough to pay for the tax cuts, which would cost more than $1.4 billion. She told them to look in their handouts. A moment later, Herb Jackson, then of the Associated Press, pointed out that the numbers did not add up properly. Reporters armed with calculators showed that the management reforms carefully listed by Whitman's economic team, supposedly totaling $500 million, actually totaled $430 million.[5]

Nothing was going well. Standing to the side, the candidate's husband, John Whitman, knew she was uncomfortable. As an expert in corporate finance and investment banking, he had been a fundamental part of the team that put together the tax-cut plan. Macroeconomics just wasn't her strong point, he knew. He was the businessman, she was the politician. As his wife of nineteen years struggled to articulate her vision, he wondered whether she could cope with the hostile questions about the tax cut's potential impact on job growth, interest rates, and much more.

"Her understanding of economics and so on was that it was a mile wide and an inch deep," he later reflected. "And at that mo-

4

ment, she knew what she wanted to do and she knew why, but she wasn't sure she could answer all the ancillary questions that came along with it. But she also knew she couldn't turn to Steve Forbes or Larry Kudlow or to me and ask them to answer those kinds of questions because she had to do it herself."[6]

Whitman tried desperately to sound convincing, but lacked the credibility she needed to convince the reporters or the public. Earlier in the year, Whitman had twice ridiculed Democrats for talking about an election-year tax cut, contending that the idea "insults the intelligence of New Jerseyans and shows contempt for their finances."[7] Now Whitman was unveiling what she had attacked as a political gambit in a floundering campaign. With six weeks to go before the election, reporters concluded that she was placing her chances for victory solely on the tax-cut plan. "It just looked so transparent for what it was," said Michael Aron, chief political reporter for New Jersey Network.[8]

Whitman insisted, again and again, that the tax-cut proposal reflected a policy decision about the best way to restore the state's economy rather than a political choice about the best way to be elected. But no one was listening. Politics aside, the plan appeared far too ambitious to be believable. No state had ever cut its income tax by 30 percent, and yet Whitman also promised to eliminate income taxes for the poorest residents, end the state's corporate tax surcharge, and repeal Florio's extension of the sales tax to include telephone calls and his creation of a gasoline surcharge on out-of-state truckers.

Besides the sheer size of the tax cuts, Whitman's proposal contradicted the latest thinking in government finance. Just a month before, President Clinton and the Democratic-controlled Congress had pushed through a tax package that resembled the Florio program in many ways. The federal proposal and the Florio plan both increased income taxes on upper-income residents and raised more regressive taxes that would be paid by low- and moderate-income residents. Following supply-side theory, Whitman insisted that her tax cuts could create 450,000 new jobs in New Jersey. Meanwhile,

Clinton was making similar claims about job creation based on tax *increases* designed to reduce the federal deficit.

Convinced that the off-year New Jersey election would be a bellwether for the future of Clinton's budget plans and a referendum on his first year in the White House, both parties brought out their biggest weapons. The president and his wife, Hillary Rodham Clinton, planned to campaign for Florio in the fall. Clinton had already appeared with Florio in New Jersey earlier in the year and campaigned with him several times during his 1992 presidential bid.

Republicans also were sending in their stars. In the weeks before Whitman's tax-cut announcement, Bob Dole, the Senate minority leader, and Jack Kemp, the former U.S. secretary of Housing and Urban Development, each appeared at Whitman fund-raisers. Ed Rollins, who ran Ronald Reagan's 1984 reelection bid and briefly directed Ross Perot's 1992 presidential campaign, and Lyn Nofziger, a longtime political confidant to Reagan and Richard Nixon, were both advising her campaign, along with Forbes and Kudlow.

"This is the important election this year, because there are those in Washington who will say Bill Clinton can do in Washington what Jim Florio did in New Jersey: raise taxes early and then win reelection," Forbes said.[9]

Whitman did not fully believe in the whole range of supply-side theories pushed by Forbes, Kudlow, and other GOP conservatives. She was convinced, however, that Florio's tax increases were destroying New Jersey's economy by driving businesses to other states and draining jobs from New Jersey, which in the Florio years was not a very attractive place, at least from an economic standpoint. Pessimism ran high, fed by the realities of layoffs and business failures. Just being elected wouldn't mean much if she couldn't reverse the state's financial decline, Whitman thought. Maybe no one would believe she really felt that way, since it sounded so self-serving. Still, it was the criterion she laid out to the small group, led by Forbes and Kudlow, that came up with the tax-cut proposal.

6

Her requirements were simple. "What's it going to take to make a difference? What's it going to take to really send a signal and to be enough that it would have a significance that would change mindsets and people's attitudes towards the state and change business, its feelings about New Jersey and its commitment?"

She understood that many factors influencing the state's economy were beyond any governor's control. "There's a whole other part of it that's really psychological. If people believe there is a real commitment to change, then they will make their decisions based on that. But we were looking at what threshold is big enough to do that and yet not so big that it is going to put a permanent crimp in your ability to manage government."[10]

Ostensibly her program was created by a campaign Council on Economic Recovery, chaired by Kudlow and Forbes, that held public hearings on the state's economic malaise. However, any open meetings were mere window dressing. Only a handful of sessions really counted. All were private, by invitation only, and far from nosy reporters.

She held the first meetings before formally announcing her candidacy, learning from Kudlow about economic projections and how the state could attract business. The hard decisions were hashed out months later, in August and September, in three sit-downs at Pontefract, the Whitman family home in the exclusive hills of Somerset County, where Whitman was raised and where she and her husband moved after her mother died in 1990. The core group consisted of Whitman her husband, Todd, Kudlow, Forbes, Rollins, Carl Golden, her press secretary, and Mike Murphy, her young Washington, D.C.–based media adviser. Other friends and strategists, such as former Republican governor Tom Kean, occasionally joined the debates in the late-summer heat— most rooms at Pontefract, an eighteenth-century farmhouse, did not have air-conditioning.

No one in that inner circle ever doubted that the plan would be broad-based. No tinkering with small cuts or expanded income-tax deductions until the economy could rebound. The "political side," as Whitman called her campaign team, wanted to somehow cut New Jersey's onerous local property tax, while the economic gurus fought for a large income-tax reduction.

The suggestions approached a level of tax cutting never attempted in American government. While the proposals were audacious, Whitman trusted Forbes and admired his intellect and grasp of American economics. They had grown up together, both attending the Far Hills Country Day School. While they had different interests, they had always kept in touch.

Forbes knew that Whitman would seriously consider his supply-side ideas, at least up to a point. She opposed his proposal for a flat federal income tax with no deductions of any type, not even for home mortgages or charitable contributions, and would not consider calling for a flat state income tax. Instead, the group talked about a potential 40 percent income-tax cut, along with a possible 50 percent cut for low-income residents. Forbes also suggested a 30 percent cut over two years. Retaining the current structure while cutting rates, he reasoned, could be sold to voters. "She's come a long way . . . in the sense of examining issues and coming to conclusions that she might not have reached before. She's not afraid to change her mind or examine the evidence," Forbes said.[11]

The entire discussion was a marvelous experiment in pure supply-side economic theory. Forbes and Kudlow would be the scientists, with New Jersey as their laboratory. "My prescription was a big-think, big-bang solution," Kudlow said. "This was not going to be tinkering around the edges. I've always been interested in the last couple of years to see if the Republicans can sell this message successfully."[12]

Their suggestions scared Whitman's political operatives, who knew the burden of selling it to the press and public would fall to them. Forbes and Kudlow didn't have a politician's perspective. They dealt in projections and statistics, not voter reaction and media scrutiny.

"We were arguing over what is a politically acceptable number, not what's right," said John Whitman. "The politicos used to say,

'Oh, promise 15 [percent]. Say you're going to try for 30.' All this kind of hedge your bets. Don't go the whole way."[13]

There was another obstacle: the Whitmans' wealth was likely to become a political liability. In 1990 alone, they earned $4 million. Florio was likely to portray any proposal for income-tax cuts as a windfall for rich folks like Forbes and the Whitmans.

The final decision, they all knew, would be made by the candidate. It was her campaign, and it would be her program to implement. With no access to Florio's figures, they were guessing at the amount of waste they might find to pay for the cuts; there was no way to be sure. "It might not be credible, but I was looking at it from, what would it do to the state? What impact was it going to have on the economy?" Whitman said. "I looked at the numbers and John looked at the numbers and the rest of us looked at them, and we were comfortable that it was doable."[14]

No one thought it would be an easy sell. But by the end of the hour-long press conference, "there was a big sigh of relief that we just got through it," John Whitman said.[15] Clearly, it had not gone well.

The press reaction, which was so negative during Whitman's press conference, did not improve in the following days. Columnists and editorial writers—except for the *Wall Street Journal*, the *Home News of New Brunswick*, and a few other small New Jersey newspapers—almost universally lampooned the proposal.

"You are late making mortgage payments. The credit card bills are backing up. You have already canceled this year's vacation to Disney World because of the financial stress. So, to solve the problem, you decide to take some time off from work without pay. Huuuuhhh? Incredible, right? Yet that's pretty much the formula offered by Republican gubernatorial candidate Christine Todd Whitman to resolve New Jersey's financial problems," the *Philadelphia Inquirer* said in an editorial headlined IT'S A FRAUD.[16]

To Whitman, the *Inquirer*'s accusation "was pretty darn nasty."[17] Few editorial writers, though, were gentle in their descriptions of the widespread disappointment. "Whitman has fallen way short of the high expectations with which she entered the fall campaign," wrote the *Asbury Park Press*. "She had the luxury of time—three years' worth—to come up with a compelling alternative for governing. Instead of dazzling us with a vision, she has run a lackluster campaign, highlighted by a proposal for a 30 percent tax cut over three years that justifiably has become the object of ridicule."[18]

Even supposedly sympathetic columnists who liked tax cuts and supply-side theory criticized Whitman for failing to defend the plan to their satisfaction. "The candidate kept the Kudlow-Forbes plan, but wilted under ridicule," complained Robert Novak, the nationally syndicated conservative writer for the *Chicago Sun-Times*. "Talking to me last week, Whitman sounded apologetic: 'It's the right thing to do. I don't want to walk away from it.' "[19]

The friendly fire also came from Republican lawmakers who refused to promise they would vote for her plans, and from leaders like DiFrancesco who endorsed the proposal but did not hide their fears about its risks. "I felt all the editorials would be against her and say it was a phony thing, a campaign thing. It was obviously a campaign thing. And . . . I felt another pretty valid point was that Jim Florio was known to the people of New Jersey as the guy who wants to raise taxes. You don't have to propose a tax cut in late September," DiFrancesco said.[20]

For Florio, Whitman's proposal offered the chance to finally grab the economic offensive and deride someone else's fiscal policies. His term had been difficult; he saw that reelection victory would vindicate his policy decisions and silence the critics. By extension, a Florio victory could also vindicate Clinton's federal tax increase. He considered Whitman's tax-cut proposal to be nothing more than a political gimmick, which offended his sense of responsible government. "For three years they've been calling me the anti-Christ, now it's my turn," Florio said after Whitman unveiled her plan.[21]

His initial public reaction came at a staged media event at Rutgers University, where the state was modernizing an aging football stadium. It was an ideal television setting, which showed Florio speaking to construction workers in blue and yellow hard hats. "She's talking, and we're doing. . . . This two-page plan isn't about getting New Jersey through the next four years, it's about getting Christie Whitman through the next six weeks."[22]

Florio could be convincing, especially when talking about policy. At each campaign stop, he repeated the same phrases about the proposal, brandishing the two pages that Whitman gave to reporters. "Ladies and gentleman, here is her plan," Florio would say, pulling the sheets from an inside jacket pocket and holding one in each hand for all to see, as if the crowd could read the small print. "Two pages, on one side, two years in the making. And the numbers don't add up. That's her plan."[23] By Election Day, the pages were badly creased; aides joked that Florio would hang them in his office, framed, during his second term.

After three years of good coverage, Whitman and her staff knew that her campaign could be destroyed by failing to meet the press's expectations. As Whitman slipped in the polls following the presentation of the tax-cut plan, the press began telling voters that it was fashionable again to support Florio.

"Three years ago, I would stop off at my local 7-Eleven, and people never referred to him as Governor Florio. It was always that 'beeping Florio,' " said David Rebovich, a Rider College political science professor often consulted by statehouse reporters. Now Rebovich saw Florio supporters holding their heads high again, giving Democrats hope. "There is still resilient resentment against him, but now it's socially acceptable to say you're going to vote for Jim Florio."[24]

After a lifetime in Republican politics, Whitman needed no pundits or newspaper stories to tell her that the campaign was floundering. She knew the signs too well. Crowds were small, and shrinking. At stops in South Jersey, Florio's core territory, Whitman aides had to coerce local politicians to stand by her side for pictures. Florio's piercing attack commercials, claiming she wanted to soften the state's drunk-driving laws and end his popular ban on semiautomatic assault weapons, were resonating with voters. Fundraising was sluggish, and her own internal polls largely jibed with press accounts that Florio's lead was growing.

"The expectations were that she was going to waltz through this campaign and have some landslide victory in the fall. I think it was a serious mistake on the press's part," Golden said. "There were reporters who basically had Christie Whitman inaugurated by July 4th. All of a sudden things were happening that were not necessarily consistent with that notion."[25]

She refused to become discouraged, bucking up the small cadre of young aides who were living at Pontefract and the dozens of downcast supporters she saw every day. She knew that New Jersey voters traditionally waited until the final moment to make their choices. Perhaps they wanted to see the intense barrage of commercials everyone knew would soon fill the airwaves of New York and Philadelphia television stations, or the negative, accusatory pamphlets that would soon flood mailboxes. She also realized that New Jersey voters tended to favor the middle of the road and to base their selection on the candidate rather than the party. She lived in a swing state that could go either way: Since World War II, Democrats had won seven gubernatorial elections, compared to six for Republicans; the GOP usually carried the state in presidential contests, while Democrats had a slight edge in the congressional delegation. The state's largely suburban character also transcended traditional party affiliations, attracting Democrats who once lived in New York or Philadelphia and Republicans moving out of farming communities to be closer to the cities.

To her staff, to voters, and to the press, Whitman was determined to maintain a confident front. Her self-discipline and Presbyterian upbringing forbade displays of discouragement or dismay to anyone outside the family—and she believed in her late father's doctrine that if "you were always a pessimist, then you were never disappointed."[26]

2

Republican Roots

By all rights, Florio should be heading for the unemployment line rather than cruising toward a second term. . . .
But Florio is winning because his political consultants, led
by the Mephistophelean James Carville, have successfully
portrayed Whitman as a rich bitch from horse country.

—*Boston Globe,* October 13, 1993

FOR WHITMAN, REMEMBERING HER PARENTS' LESSONS CAME EASILY.
She was living in Pontefract, the house where she had been raised,
and was following through with the political heritage that had
been a major part of her parents' lives. For close to four decades,
Webster B. Todd and Eleanor Schley Todd were powerful forces in
national Republican politics, espousing a caring, compassionate
philosophy that typified the more moderate Rockefeller wing of
the party. They were also pragmatic politicians, who knew that no
one can govern without first winning an election.

13

Her father, known as Web, became wealthy as a construction contractor before retiring at age fifty to devote himself full-time to government and politics. His firm's projects ranged from the restoration of colonial Williamsburg to the construction of New York City's Rockefeller Center and Radio City Music Hall; years later, Whitman's family became regulars at the Radio City Christmas Show. The family's true devotion, though, was politics. Web Todd was state campaign director for his friend Dwight Eisenhower, state party chairman in the 1960s and 1970s, and a national party leader and fund-raiser for several decades. In 1953, Eisenhower appointed him economic emissary to NATO, which sent the family to Paris for two years.

Eleanor Todd was no typical 1950s housewife. She was a potent political force on her own as president of the New Jersey Federation of Republican Women, vice chairwoman of both the Republican National Committee and the state Commission on Higher Education, and an official at every GOP National Convention from 1940 until 1976. She was even mentioned by the highly regarded *Newark News* in the 1950s as a possible gubernatorial candidate, in an era when women did not become state chief executives; she was a generation too early.

"My parents were both very, very involved, and they were wonderful role models. They cared deeply. They were very partisan people, but they always cared about what happened, the outcome, more than they did about partisan politics. I mean, good government was the best politics, as my father was very fond of saying. . . . And he also felt strongly, as did my mother, that if you cared and were concerned and complained but didn't get involved, you lost your right to complain."[1]

Christine—Christie to her friends and family—was the youngest of four children in a household that devoured party politics. It was the preferred topic at Pontefract, where political luminaries regularly came calling. "The people who came into the house were economically, socially, and politically prominent, and the matters of the day were discussed as a matter of course," her brother Dan Todd recalled.[2]

14

His description fit many of the family's Somerset neighbors, including Douglas Dillon, Eisenhower's ambassador to France and Kennedy's treasury secretary; Nicholas Brady, U.S. senator and treasury secretary under George Bush; Millicent Fenwick, the pipe-smoking longtime congresswoman; and, of course, Malcolm Forbes Sr., founder of *Forbes* magazine, flamboyant multimillion-aire and frustrated New Jersey gubernatorial candidate. The Todds fit right in. Indeed, Eleanor Schley Todd's family was one of the earliest to settle in the region; a Somerset County route bears the name of Schley Mountain Road.

In their political discussions, the Todd children were taught that public service offered a virtuous way of life. The oldest child, Katherine Todd Beach, served as U.S. deputy treasurer in the Bush administration, and Dan Todd held posts in both the federal government and the New Jersey assembly. Another brother, John Todd, who built architectural models, died in 1988 of heart disease. Christie, born in 1946, started her political indoctrination early. At age five, with young Steve Forbes, she was picked during the 1952 presidential campaign to give dolls to young Tricia and Julie Nixon. She attended her first Republican National Convention in 1956, at age nine, presenting Eisenhower with a leather golf-tee holder as he left the podium after accepting renomination. In the 1964 and 1968 primary battles, she worked for Nelson Rockefeller, riding with the New York governor in a Garden State motorcade in his 1968 campaign against Nixon. Nearly three decades later, Whitman still called herself a "Rockefeller Republican," espousing the late governor's socially inclusive views.

The Rockefeller faction of the party grew largely from the split in the 1950s and 1960s between Easterners' emphasis on civil rights and the more conservative view coming from Western leaders like Reagan and Barry Goldwater. Web Todd, always the pragmatic politician, largely stayed out of the battle. He remained neutral as state party chairman, for example, during the 1964 skirmishes between Goldwater and Rockefeller. From a fiscal perspective, Whitman opposed Rockefeller's belief in large government and the extensive social services that sent New York state

15

taxes soaring. By the 1990s, much of the movement's core philosophy had also shifted: while Rockefeller Republicans favored aggressive government action to combat civil rights abuses, contemporary moderates opposed government intervention in social issues, such as abortion. To Whitman, Rockefeller's fundamental appeal was not a specific policy. Rather, it was "his social inclusion aspects . . . and his ability to relate to people, and how people related to him."[3]

Her belief in Rockefeller also contributed to the allure of public office, specifically serving as governor. While there was no grand, twenty-five-year plan to reach that level, it was always an attractive goal. "In New Jersey, the governor is really the focal point," she said. "I knew that I wanted to be involved in politics, and obviously one facet of that is elective office. . . . The legislature was not the preferred side for me, the executive was where I'd like to be. Governor was the ultimate goal, if there was ever to be a goal."[4]

She started in staff positions, as a special assistant in the U.S. Office of Equal Opportunity and as an intern to U.S. Senator Clifford Case of New Jersey, a strict adherent to the principles of Rockefeller Republicanism. She also designed a project in 1969 for the Republican National Committee to discover why so many people—especially African Americans and students—were rejecting the GOP in the late 1960s. It took her to places and people she had not encountered in Paris, or at the private prep schools she had attended, or at Wheaton College in Massachusetts, from which she graduated in 1968. In Chicago's East Ward, members of a tough African-American gang tried to intimidate her with street talk, not realizing she had grown up with two older brothers on a working farm and had heard plenty of rough language in the fields. Soon she convinced the gang kids that their bluster wasn't working, and "we got into a very interesting discussion about the role gangs played in their lives."[5]

She also worked at a Peace Corps desk job before marrying John Whitman in 1974, at the Oldwick church where she had worshiped as a child. They had known each other casually for years

16

and started dating after she invited him to escort her to Nixon's second inaugural ball: he had a reputation as a good dancer, and she liked to dance. He too had an impressive political resumé. His grandfather, Charles Whitman, had been governor of New York before World War I, and his father was a New York State judge. He was a Yale graduate and had received two Bronze Stars for valor in combat in Vietnam. It was a marriage of political society, complete with a ride in a horse-drawn carriage between the church and the reception at Pontefract. "Our marriage vows could have said in sickness and in health and in politics, given Christie's family tradition and mine," John Whitman said.[6]

As newlyweds, he climbed corporate ladders as an investment banker in New York, she taught English as a second language in Spanish Harlem. While he expanded his financial expertise, in both the United States and for two years in London, she stayed in touch with Republican party leaders and was appointed to the Somerset County college trustee board. In 1982, the party asked her to run for the so-called women's seat on Somerset County's board of freeholders, the governing body of New Jersey county government. She easily won election in that predominantly Republican county and then was reelected three years later, gaining notice for her social initiatives and serving a term as freeholder-director.

Near the end of her second freeholder term, Governor Tom Kean, an old family friend, appointed her president of the state Board of Public Utilities, a largely anonymous panel that regulates garbage routes and electricity, gas, and telephone rates. It put her in the cabinet, albeit on the second tier, expanding her contacts and political possibilities. In early 1990, she offered to run a presumably token campaign against two-term Democratic senator Bill Bradley. With no one else willing to sacrifice himself in such an apparently hopeless cause, party leaders gratefully accepted the offer. Kean, however, advised her to stay away from the race. To run, she would have to resign from the Public Utilities board. "If she lost by a lot, and conventional wisdom said she would, she'd be dead politically. I told her to wait until a congressional seat came

17

up," said Kean, who had publicly predicted Bradley would be unbeatable.[7]

At age forty-seven, Bradley had already been a Hall of Fame basketball player with the New York Knicks, a Rhodes scholar, an All-American athlete at Princeton, an Olympic gold medalist, a bestselling author, and a widely touted presidential prospect. Given his $12 million campaign war chest and strong approval ratings, both parties assumed his reelection was a formality. Whitman had never run for office outside Somerset County. Her designated role, in the view of party leaders, was to help other Republicans on the statewide ticket by avoiding a rout and to bolster the perception that women had a place in the party. With just $1 million to spend, Whitman could not run commercials on the expensive New York and Philadelphia stations until just before Halloween—giving her less than a week to reach millions of viewers. Even Whitman assumed she had no chance to win, assuring her two children, Kate and Taylor, then twelve and ten, that they wouldn't be moving to Washington.

But predictions were completely upended by Jim Florio's $2.8 billion tax hike, signed into law just after the senatorial primary. During his 1989 campaign for governor, Florio told voters, "I'm convinced there is not a need for new taxes."[8] Frustrated by local property taxes that ranked among the nation's highest, voters believed in his message and backed Florio in a near landslide. Their faith was short-lived. Five months into his term, a Democratic-controlled legislature reluctantly approved Florio's proposal to double the state income tax for upper-income residents and raise the sales tax for everyone. Florio, an unabashed advocate of a proactive government, pointed to a large deficit left behind by Kean as justification for the unpopular move and made little effort to sell his rationale, beyond a few staff buttons proclaiming BLAME IT ON KEAN.

"I know what the headlines are going to say tomorrow," Florio predicted as he signed the budget in July 1990. "Florio Signs Biggest Tax Increase."[9]

The anger at Florio's perceived betrayal was more intense than anyone had anticipated. Thousands of angry residents mobbed the front of the statehouse on a sticky Sunday in July, throwing rolls of toilet paper that symbolized the household products that were suddenly subject to sales tax. Bumper stickers boldly proclaiming FLORIO FREE IN '93 became a part of the New Jersey landscape. A Trenton-based radio station with an all–New Jersey news and talk format seized upon the voter anger as its cause célèbre. WKXW-FM, owned by the parent company of the *Asbury Park Press* and known as "New Jersey 101.5," publicized anti-Florio rallies and provided a statewide forum for his opponents, simultaneously increasing both voter anger and its own ratings. The station and a local newspaper, the *Trentonian,* also became conduits for the organization of a new antitax group, Hands Across New Jersey. Eventually the station's anti-Florio, pro-Republican stance became so pronounced that one leading Democrat dubbed it "Radio Free Whitman."[10]

In the suburban, commuter culture of New Jersey, radio was a powerful and often overlooked medium. Program hosts, fighting for ratings, knew they could attract listeners and callers by attacking Florio. The Florio-bashing soon became a way of life; banners opposing the governor were even displayed at football games at Giants Stadium.

While much of the voters' anger grew directly out of their having to pay higher taxes (though most of the burden fell to upper-income residents), more of the negative emotion was generated by what the voters perceived as Florio's arrogance in ramming through tax hikes with no explanation or apology. He had made a promise and then broken it, engendering the same type of voter reaction George Bush had encountered when he raised taxes in 1990 after his famous "read my lips, no new taxes," pledge at the 1988 Republican Convention.

Convinced that the tax increases were needed, Florio had done little to quell the voter anger, refusing suggestions from Democratic officials to soften either his image or his stance. His approval rating dropped steadily until it set a modern low of 18 percent in

October 1990. Unable to get back at Florio until 1993, voters would take their hostility out on Bradley.

"Whitman very effectively told the voters how they could register their discontent: vote against Bradley," said Roger Stone, a prominent political consultant. "Senator Bradley made a tragic error in refusing to answer questions. . . . It is the height of arrogance not to tell the voters where you stand."[11]

Again and again, Bradley ducked the tax question. Although he admired Florio's determination to balance the state's budget, he felt taxes had been raised too high, too quickly, and without enough explanation. At the same time, he owed Florio a political debt for supporting his first Senate run during the 1978 Democratic primary. Rather than take a wishy-washy stance, Bradley and his strategists decided, he should stick to the line that he could not reverse Florio's policies. "I think people recognize we have different responsibilities. I represent New Jersey in the Senate in Washington, he is the governor. We have different roles and different responsibilities," Bradley said.[12]

For Whitman, Bradley's silence was political gravy. Just as 1974 had been a great time to be a Democrat in the post-Watergate era, New Jersey was a wonderful place in 1990 to run as a fiscally conservative Republican. And Whitman worked harder than most expected a token candidate to work, even receiving a primer on foreign policy from former president Richard Nixon, a Saddle River, New Jersey, resident, before her debate with Bradley.

Still, the state's press corps and pollsters never imagined Whitman could win. A *Star-Ledger*/Eagleton poll, conducted by Rutgers University's Eagleton Institute of Politics with the state's largest newspaper, put Bradley's lead at 55 to 27 percent in late October. Similarly, the final poll by the *Record* of Hackensack estimated Bradley's lead at 54 to 22 percent.

Years later, Bradley wrote that "not until October did I realize that the public had linked me to the governor." He had been preoccupied by Senate business for weeks and did not even begin full-time campaigning until just before the election. "I knew I was in trouble when I stood outside Giants Stadium before a football game in late October, and then at the Port Authority bus terminal a week before the election, and instead of hearing affection, as I had on the eve of the 1984 election, I heard anger and resentment directed toward me—words and looks that refuted the latest poll."[13]

On Election Night, Whitman edged ahead of Bradley with just under half the vote counted. By the end of a long, tense evening, large Democratic margins in Essex and Hudson counties helped Bradley squeak out a victory with a 50,000-vote margin out of almost 2 million cast; in 1984, he had won by almost 900,000 votes.

It would not be the last time that the state's newspaper polls underestimated Whitman's appeal. They weren't alone, though. Internal polls for both parties also failed to grasp just how angry voters were with Florio and his party, and the gloomy forecasts had convinced GOP leaders to refuse Whitman's plea for cash to pay for more commercials. In the campaign's final weeks, they had even reneged on an original promise to spend $600,000 her race, holding back the final $200,000 when the polls looked hopeless.

"They wanted a candidate, a sacrificial lamb against Bradley who wouldn't embarrass them, but they didn't want the financial commitment," said Greg Stevens, a GOP analyst with Ailes Communications in Washington, D.C., who believed that another $750,000 could have produced a new Republican senator in a huge upset victory.[14]

Who knows? Retrospective predictions are impossible to evaluate. How would voters have responded to a late round of Whitman attack ads? Certainly, the diminished expectations created and repeatedly reinforced during the fall by the polls hurt Whitman's fund-raising and her chances for victory; expectations of a Bradley romp probably held down Democratic turnout as well.

Whitman's strong finish put her in the forefront of potential 1993 Republican New Jersey gubernatorial candidates. While Bradley groped for answers, Republican leaders raced to anoint their new heroine.

Whitman kept her options open. The day after the election,

making her first appearance on ABC's *Nightline,* she told Ted Koppel that "I don't rule anything out. I'm going to stay around New Jersey and stay very active in politics. That's what my whole life has been in."[15] Some hours earlier, at a statehouse press conference, she told reporters, "If, one year ago, someone had said to me that I would be running against Bill Bradley, I would have said you're crazy. There's just no way you can make that kind of prediction. I just know that I want to stay involved."[16] The only plans she would disclose involved a vacation with her children and her husband.

Despite her reticence, Whitman knew that a run for the governorship was her best option. It was also the only top-level target on the horizon: she would have to wait four years to run again for the U.S. Senate, her district already had an incumbent Republican congressman, and New Jersey is unique in having only one elected state official. (The only other constitutionally mandated positions, treasurer and secretary of state, are appointed by the governor, making New Jersey's chief executive the most powerful state official in the country, at least from a legal standpoint.)

She faced potential primary opponents, such as W. Cary Edwards, who had been Kean's chief counsel and attorney general. The day after Bradley's victory, Edwards warned that Whitman's "got to beat me" if she wanted to be governor.[17] Another half dozen top Republicans, including most of the GOP congressional delegation, also loomed as possible challengers.

Despite the competition, reporters and GOP leaders immediately called it Whitman's race to lose. That the anti-Florio sentiment of voters was not abating was clear during the state's 1991 legislative elections. Democratic incumbents tried desperately to distance themselves from Florio, but their efforts largely fell short. Across New Jersey, Republican newcomers replaced the Democrats, handing the GOP a stunning veto-proof majority in both the assembly and the state senate.

With no official duties or financial concerns as a distraction, Whitman quickly set out to sell herself to the state's Republican rank and file. Her single-minded determination helped her endure endless handshakes and smiles at local events. Moving from table to table, she would introduce herself and exchange pleasantries, as an aide jotted down names and numbers for future mailings. She also funneled contributions and policy research to local candidates through the Committee for an Affordable New Jersey, a political action committee (PAC) created to promote her candidacy. Her name recognition was constantly bolstered through her radio program on 101.5 and a newspaper column in the *Bridgewater Courier News.*

She brought in big names to raise money, including Nixon and Massachusetts governor William Weld, a tax-cutting progressive who had gained national attention as part of a new breed of Republican governors. "On my best days, I may be a male Christie Whitman," Weld joked at a 1992 fund-raiser.[18] She campaigned for Republican candidates in every corner of the state, making personal appearances and taping radio and television endorsements. It was grassroots party politics that was not widely covered by the mass media.

Publicly Whitman refused to admit her plans to run for governor, despite mischievously asking for a phone number of 704-1993 for her PAC's office. "I think it's a real mistake to get into gubernatorial politics at this date," she said in late 1991. "We ought to be using this year and next to build a base and convince people we can win the state no matter who the candidate is. It's critically important, credibility is critically important, proving that you can win."[19]

"She did virtually everything right in the years between the end of the Senate campaign and the beginning of the gubernatorial campaign," said William Palatucci, a GOP consultant who managed Whitman's 1990 Senate bid. He knew New Jersey's Republican politics, having also managed Reagan's New Jersey reelection bid in 1984, Bush's 1992 state campaign, and Kean's landslide 1985 reelection victory. Now, three years after working with Whitman, he was advising Edwards—and he knew, only too well, how much Whitman had accomplished among the state's Republican rank and file. "I've dealt with a lot of candidates who hate getting in the car and going to small events, [thinking] that it was a drain on their psyche. But she'd think it was important and want to go," Palatucci said. "She'd be so comfortable at any Republican function. She knows the lingo, she knows the pecking order."[20]

Edwards formally launched his campaign in December 1992; Whitman was days away from her own formal announcement a month later when Edwards launched the first salvo of their primary campaign. Quietly, an aide alerted statehouse reporters on January 22 that Whitman had employed illegal aliens and failed to pay their Social Security taxes. The issue was hot: Zoe Baird, President Bill Clinton's first choice for attorney general, had withdrawn her nomination the day before, for almost identical reasons.

While the facts about Whitman's employees were simple, their implications were devastating. Whitman hired a Portuguese couple in December 1986 to care for nine-year-old Kate and seven-year-old Taylor, then tried for almost five years to secure their green cards. They started paying their Social Security taxes in 1991, when they were given legal immigrant status. Now Whitman apologized for the oversight and pledged to pay the back taxes immediately, stating, "At the time I was clearly acting more like a parent in search of capable child care than as a candidate for elective office."[21]

Explanations had not saved Baird's nomination on Capitol Hill, and they appeared likely to capsize Whitman's campaign. Statehouse humorists quipped that Clinton probably nominated Baird to force Whitman out of the race to help his friend and political ally Jim Florio. Florio and Edwards were already gearing up to attack Whitman as an out-of-touch heiress, and the illegal-alien controversy fit perfectly into their plans. Many Republicans assumed that a woman would be unable to take the bruising hits to come, and most considered her damaged goods. Reporters predicted her quick withdrawal. But the state's political community—reporters, lobbyists, party leaders, elected officials—knew little of Whitman's determination. For her, the front-runner, dropping out just wasn't an option. Why should she quit? She made a mistake and corrected it, she explained with a little sheepishness. It's time to move on, she added. "The difference between Zoe Baird and this is that hers was an appointed office. In this case, the people will get to make the ultimate judgment as to whether this is the critical issue, or if there are other things more critical, like the state's economy," she said.[22]

She faced the crisis with her sense of humor intact, joking about Beltway households facing similar green-card problems. "There's gonna be a lot of high grass and dirty windows in Arlington, Virginia, this summer."[23]

Her display of iron will surprised even strong supporters like Hazel Gluck, a former cabinet official who was Whitman's campaign cochairwoman. It was the first crisis of Whitman's political career, so she had never before needed to withstand such a media frenzy. "The woman was absolutely amazing," Gluck said. "I'd never seen anything like it."[24]

Whitman also benefited when Edwards confessed that he had a similar problem. Back in 1989, Edwards had hired a part-time Portuguese housekeeper who worked for his father-in-law before his death. Like the Whitman workers, she did not have a green card, and Edwards did not pay Social Security taxes until she received it eighteen months later. He, too, pledged to pay any back taxes owed.

For Whitman, Edwards's mistake eliminated the potential of being portrayed as a tax cheat running against an unblemished state attorney general. She still had more to endure, however. Whitman's liability for back taxes, interest, and penalties came to almost $25,000, compared to about $2,300 for Edwards, and because she was the Republican front-runner, most Democratic salvos targeted her, with state party chairman Raymond Lesniak calling her "the Leona Helmsley of New Jersey."[25]

"Whitman will be the one to pay the higher price," mused David Rebovich. "She has positioned herself as a new outsider, a progressive Republican who will come to Trenton to clean up the mess. For the Whitman campaign, personality and character is so important because there is no political experience there."[26]

Columnists enjoyed ridiculing both candidates. "I laughed out loud when I opened the papers Saturday morning. 'Oh, this is amazing,' I called to my wife. 'Both Republican candidates for governor did what Zoe Baird did. Both of them. Can you believe it?' " asked Jim Ahearn, a veteran political columnist. "The details were marvelously grisly. Politically, it was a double train wreck."[27]

Adrian Heffern, a longtime *Asbury Park Press* columnist, was also amused: "Employing illegal aliens is no laughing matter. At least it wasn't until the issue became embroiled in New Jersey's race for governor." Whitman and Edwards, Heffern wrote, "attained high visibility without spending a dime on commercials. All they had to do was reveal they once employed foreigners who lacked green cards. This earned them a full week of headlines. Who needs publicists when they have illegal aliens going for them?"[28]

Reporters desperately searched for other candidates—several writers had already confidently forecast Whitman's demise—but the only new contender was Jim Wallwork, a long-retired, little-known former state senator. Disclosures of similar illegal-alien problems by officials around the country, including Florio's policy chief, gradually reduced the sting. Perhaps most important, former governor Tom Kean, the high chieftain of Garden State Republicans, proclaimed that Whitman should stay in the race.

"She's starting out in a hole when for a while, it looked like people were ready to hand her the nomination after she almost beat Bill Bradley," Kean observed. "But if she gets through this, she will be a much better general election candidate because of it."[29]

Yet Nannygate was just the first in a long string of missteps and embarrassments that would plague Whitman's campaign. She survived each one, but together they reinforced Florio's portrayal of Whitman as an aloof aristocrat from the privileged hills of Somerset County. By contrast, Florio depicted himself as a child of the common class. Born in Brooklyn, he dropped out of high school to join the navy, worked his way through college and law school, and—according to political legend—owned one set of silverware and one pair of shoes while in Congress. While Whitman's father built skyscrapers, Florio's father had painted ships in the docks of Brooklyn and Hoboken.

Given the contrasts, Whitman's blunders might have been scripted by the Democrats. A Florio favorite was April 20, when Whitman introduced her education proposals but skipped voting in her local school board election. After all, her children went to a private school. Yet her absence might not have been noticed had the voting not resulted in a 207–207 tie. "Her single vote might have made the difference," Edwards said. "If Mrs. Whitman had taken the time to live up to the standards she called for in her own plan for education, the tie would have been avoided."[30]

A week earlier, reporters examining Whitman's state income tax return had discovered that she had not contributed to the state campaign finance fund, from which she was receiving more than $1 million. Florio strategists also seized on an ill-advised Whitman remark that "funny as it seems, $500 is a lot of money to some people," repeating it throughout the state.[31] Her campaign released a radio commercial in April incorrectly claiming that the staff for Florio's wife, Lucinda, cost taxpayers $1 million per year. And the Florio and Edwards campaigns repeatedly harped on Whitman's taking advantage of a regulation that qualified her for a sizable property tax break on Pontefract and the surrounding 222-acre farm.

One or two embarrassments could be dismissed as oversights. But the constant missteps created the impression that Whitman's campaign was being run by the Keystone Kops. "It was attributable to some of the people there who just had not been exposed to this before," said Carl Golden, who had been Kean's communications director and then a state supreme court spokesman before joining Whitman after the primary. "Just some folks who just simply did not appreciate what had to be done to run a statewide campaign. They had never done it before, and it was just tough."[32]

Florio's campaign aides exploited each gaffe, under the direction of former Clinton campaign guru James Carville, whose presence lent credibility to the notion that Florio might be reelected. Carville was riding a long streak of come-from-behind victories: he had helped reelect New Jersey Democratic senator Frank Lautenberg in 1988 and directed Harris Wofford's stunning upset victory in Pennsylvania's 1991 Senate race. A quick-talking, sarcastic, shoot-from-the-hip Louisiana native, the "Ragin' Cajun" had little personal rapport with the intense, policy-driven Florio, though they shared a progressive, proactive philosophy of government. Carville knew he wasn't in New Jersey to be Florio's drinking buddy. His job was to get him reelected, and many people thought he was the one person who could pull it off. "I'm left with a good feeling. I'm a longtime admirer of the guy," said John Currie, the Passaic County Democratic chairman, after a meeting with Carville. "He gives me that extra enthusiasm and trust that this thing is doable."[33]

Edwards hardly mattered to Carville. His attacks were reserved largely for Whitman. "Trying to get a position out of Mrs. Whitman is like trying to nail Jell-O to a wall," Carville quipped; he called her the "let them eat oat-bran candidate."[34]

Despite the mistakes, Whitman's years of selling herself to the GOP rank and file paid off with a seven-point victory over Edwards in the primary, with Wallwork a distant third.

While the Florio campaign marched through the summer virtually mistake-free, Whitman's kept stumbling. As Florio focused on her wealth, she spent a week in July mountain-biking in Idaho with John and the kids rather than mixing with voters along the Jersey Shore. While Florio blasted her as a friend of the gun lobby, she visited a Jersey City gun shop—aptly named "Gun-O-Rama." And despite three years of complaining about Florio's tax hikes, she still had no plan for the state's economic recovery.

In August, she suffered through racism charges for hiring Larry McCarthy, a Republican media expert who helped create the infamous, racially charged Willie Horton commercial that wounded Michael Dukakis's 1988 presidential bid. The Florio campaign's rapid-fire researchers found the connection just hours after McCarthy's hiring. New Jersey's African-American leaders quickly screamed for McCarthy's ouster, and reporters once again wrote stories questioning Whitman's competence. McCarthy's abrupt resignation—he was in her campaign less than twenty-four hours—did little to improve Whitman's image.

"A year ago, everyone was burying Jim Florio. Two things have happened. One is that Florio has begun to make a comeback. . . . Second, his opponent, Christine Whitman, has made a lot of mistakes and is no longer running in a vacuum, so that the race is essentially even," Jack Germond, a *Baltimore Sun* columnist, said on CNN.[35]

While Whitman was confident that she could regain momentum in the weeks before the election, she had even further to fall. Six days after her tax plan's release, while Democrats and editorial writers were lampooning her proposal, the *New York Times* released a poll showing Florio ahead by a 51 to 30 percent margin, by far the largest of the campaign. The underlying numbers were even worse. Asked which candidate had more honesty and integrity, 61 percent said Florio, while 35 percent chose Whitman. Forty-nine percent said Florio "did the right thing" by raising taxes in 1990. In a separate question, 36 percent said their taxes would rise under Whitman, but only 10 percent believed their taxes would drop.

"She needed to fill the airwaves with support for her plan, but she didn't," said Janice Ballou, Eagleton's polling director. "So there was nothing to fill the void but all the negative reaction to it, with the result that so far, it may have turned out to be more a minus than a plus."[36]

Whitman's internal polls showed Florio's lead at about ten percentage points, despite the larger margin of the *Times* poll, but "because it was the *New York Times*, people sort of thought that that made it sacrosanct, it was going to be absolutely right," she said. She could insist that the campaign was still viable, though most people were inclined to discount her claims. It wasn't quite as bad as screaming in an empty forest, but "you expect the candidate to always be the one who is beating the drum. . . . So it's hard to maintain credibility."[37]

Fund-raising dropped off even more, sparking fears that there would not be enough money to pay for all the commercials planned for late October. "I mean, it's a little hard to convince people to open their wallets when your candidate is twenty points behind," Golden said.[38]

After nearly three years of work, there were thirty-five days until the election—and a huge gap for Whitman to close.

"This campaign must fundamentally change the way it has operated in virtually every aspect, and it will have to do it overnight," advised Jay Severin, a Republican consultant. "It's not just that she is behind at this point. That's the easy part. It's why she's behind."[39]

3

Florio Free

JOHN McLAUGHLIN: Who's the winner in the New Jersey race, and margin? Freddie?

FRED BARNES, *New Republic:* . . . Florio, the Democrat, will win in New Jersey, 53–47.

McLAUGHLIN: Eleanor?

ELEANOR CLIFT, *Newsweek:* Florio wins substantially. Whitman's offer of a 30 percent tax cut, she lost all credibility. Last year's hustle doesn't work.

—*The McLaughlin Group,* October 15, 1993

DAN TODD'S NEW JERSEY ROOTS WERE DEEP. LIKE HIS SISTER, HE WAS raised on Republican politics. In addition to serving in the state assembly in the early 1970s, he had federal government experience as chairman of the National Transportation Safety Board under Richard Nixon. For Todd and Whitman, politics was the family business. Yet by 1993, he primarily focused on his 750-acre cattle ranch in the mountains of Montana. He had run just one recent campaign, successfully managing Lew Fleege's bid to become Winifred, Montana's, volunteer fire chief, and had no permanent Garden State home. State Republican leaders were dismayed when Whitman put him in charge of her gubernatorial bid. They wanted her campaign in the hands of a manager with a track record, such as Ed Rollins, who was working on media strategy.

For months, most GOP leaders held their tongues, beyond occasional behind-the-back snickers about Todd's trademark ascots and western outfits. After all, Todd was family. He was even living with the Whitmans in the attic at Pontefract. How could they possibly tell Whitman to fire her older brother? But now, with only weeks to go, the *New York Times* poll showed Florio with a seemingly insurmountable lead. While Whitman was never a staunch believer in newspaper polls, she knew that something had to change to halt the campaign's downward spiral.

"It got very difficult to maintain the upbeat sense, because [while] the twenty-one points was not what I was hearing from people in the street, I knew how much it affected our workers and how down everybody else was," Whitman conceded. "It became very difficult to be the cheerleader, which is what I had to be. I could never show I was discouraged by it or upset by it, and I had to pretend that I wasn't, though of course I was."[1]

Whitman went to Washington the night before the release of the *Times* poll for a tour of the U.S. Holocaust Museum and a birthday party for her older sister, Kate Beach. After a morning strategy meeting at Beach's home, Rollins drove the candidate and her husband to the museum, using the privacy of the twenty-minute ride to emphatically insist Todd had to go. His reasoning was simple: they needed a dramatic shift to jump-start the campaign again. Morale was too low to move forward without taking decisive action, he argued. Making a change would encourage potential contributors and convey the impression that she could still win in November.

"There's always the head game being played, the inside head game, (by) both the media and the inside political people. They

32

get a certain level of comfort. It changes the bias just slightly if they think somebody who they think is credible is in charge," Whitman said. "We went through it all summer. 'Your brother, how can your brother possibly be any good, what can he know?' "[2]

With her campaign in a meltdown, she faced two distasteful options. Politics was important, but family was sacred. Removing her brother from day-to-day control of the campaign would be painful for them both. Yet neither wanted her to lose. Too many people had worked too hard for too long, and much more was at stake than her brother's pride.

Reluctantly, she gave Rollins complete control. To Todd's credit, rather than argue or fight for his job, he put a strong public face on his new role as a campaign surrogate and sounding board for Whitman. To avoid sending signals of panic, the brother-sister duo insisted the shift was planned all along, though Todd conceded that "nobody believes that."[3]

"The switch of title was tough. It hurt Danny. I was very, very sorry to do that," Whitman reflected.[4]

Her poise and refusal to quit inspired her staffers. They remembered her resolve to survive the illegal-alien mess and now saw the same determination.

"She looked into the abyss and she moved forward. She never looked back, she knew what she had to do. She went out and campaigned her heart out. She never gave up," said Hazel Gluck, campaign cochairwoman.[5]

Rollins's promotion worried few outsiders. Florio's staff, which continued to run a nearly textbook-perfect campaign, knew that the *Times* poll figures were artificially high, based on their own polls. Still, they doubted that Rollins—or anyone else—could close the gap in four weeks. Democratic legislative candidates, buoyed by the governor's lead, began to talk about potential coattails for the first time. Cary Edwards, her opponent in the primary, even accepted a Florio invitation to head a state commission studying legalized gambling. Whitman could forgive Democrats, but she was incensed at Edwards's collaboration with Florio. Republicans, she had been taught, didn't turn their backs on other Republicans.

"There were some people who took for the hills in the Republican party," said Chuck Haytaian, one of the few outspoken advocates of Whitman's tax-cut plan. "There were a whole lot of people who said they were with her that weren't to be found. In fact, they were under the beds and under the covers and under everything else."[6]

While political pros, in New Jersey and around the country, recognized Rollins's political savvy, they also knew he was sometimes undependable. He had angered many Republicans during the last decade: openly criticizing George Bush for selecting Dan Quayle as his running mate; calling for the resignation of John Sununu, Bush's chief of staff; ridiculing Maureen Reagan's Senate bid; advising GOP candidates in 1990 to distance themselves from Bush's tax increases; and abandoning Bush to work for Ross Perot in 1992. Whitman's team, though, found him fatherly and friendly. With his gray beard and round glasses, he looked like someone's jovial uncle. The campaign's younger staffers appreciated his counsel; the few older aides respected his political wisdom.

He made changes immediately, shifting responsibilities and reenergizing disheartened staffers. Clearly, Rollins's style was more gregarious and open than Todd's. He had only a few basic rules. More people would be involved in planning the campaign's final weeks, and everyone would have to believe that Whitman would win. The people of New Jersey had to quickly discover Whitman as a person—and the campaign's best asset—to counter Florio's depiction of her as a stuck-up, rich Republican heiress who couldn't find her way around a supermarket. The campaign's only theme would be the tax cut—and it would be open season on Florio's record as a "tax-and-spend liberal."

"Negative campaigns work; it's one of the tragedies of American politics," Rollins said. "Obviously Florio has been running a very negative campaign and we have to do something about it. I think it is safe to say that if New Jersey voters have forgotten what Jim Florio did to them over the last four years, we are going to remind them."[7]

The first negative blows on television came from Florio. Soon after Labor Day, New York and Philadelphia stations began airing spots tying Whitman to the controversial National Rifle Association (NRA) and its efforts to repeal Florio's popular ban on semiautomatic assault weapons. Viewers heard that Whitman was soft on drunk driving and against stiff sentences for carjackers. The ads had a harsh, taunting tone, but as of late September there had been no return punch from Whitman.

The strategy, as outlined in the 147-page campaign plan Todd kept in a black loose-leaf notebook, was to hold back from commercials for as long as possible, to maximize their impact in late October. Mike Murphy, the media adviser who designed her spots, conceded that enduring Florio attack ads in September without launching a response was "a freak-out" period.[8] Republican leaders kept imploring Whitman to fight back, knowing that her nature was to reject negative ads.

"I hated it. And I really hated the, quote/unquote, going negative. I don't mind being tough, but I felt so strongly about sending a positive message of what I wanted to do in giving people a positive reason to vote," she said.[9]

Her first commercials, which started soon after she unveiled the tax cut, were boring, low-budget efforts featuring Whitman talking about her economic plan and complaining about Florio's accusations. Still, Rollins kept his word. By Saturday, October 2, five days after the *Times* poll, he was ready to launch the retaliation.

"To paraphrase James Carville's great quote 'It's the economy, stupid'—we feel this race is 'It's Florio, stupid.' My colleague is a first-rate professional. But they've got a very tough product to sell," Rollins said.[10]

The mostly black-and-white commercial was blunt, starting with a brief clip of Florio in 1989 vowing not to raise taxes and blaming him for the loss of 8,000 businesses and 280,000 jobs. The ad never mentioned Whitman, except for a legally required financial disclosure graphic, and ended on a strong note: "Now Florio refuses to rule out raising taxes again. Jim Florio. He may be the worst governor New Jersey's ever had."[11]

She stayed focused on the message of taxes and jobs. Everywhere she went, people talked about their fears of losing their job or their health care, or not earning enough to pay the monthly bills. The state's unemployment rate climbed sharply during the summer, giving credibility to her calls for change.

In a televised debate, she told viewers about someone she had just met "who was sitting on his porch outside in the rain, because he couldn't go inside, it was too hot and he couldn't afford an air conditioner, because he'd lost his job just a week before and they're trying to adopt a child. And he was scared to death for his future. This is what it's all about."[12]

Week by week, the economic climate—or at least Whitman's version of it—grew bleaker. In her first attack ad, the number of jobs lost under Florio was 280,000. By the second ad, the number had jumped to 300,000, and climbing.

Florio kept attacking, aided by critics in the media who seized on each Whitman mistake. During the first debate, she implied that part of her tax cut could be paid for by halting the practice of giving Adidas sneakers to state-prison convicts. Florio, whose sharp campaign skills were long underestimated by much of the media and many Whitman supporters, immediately seized the opening. Whitman's goof had two components: convicts wore generic, brandless sneakers—and their total cost was about eight dollars per pair.

"Adidas sneakers are going to be taken away from inmates, apparently. . . . Weathervane politicians really just won't cut it anymore. You can't tell people just what they want to hear by promising them anything," Florio said.

"Well, I would expect the governor to be in deep denial over tax cuts, because he's never met a tax hike he didn't like," Whitman retorted.

She stayed cool during Florio's attacks, remaining focused on the economy and emphasizing areas of government waste—besides the sneakers—such as the $4 million helicopter that Tom Kean had purchased and that now ferried Florio around the state. She also landed several well-placed and well-planned jabs.

"I do owe the Governor an apology. He's probably not the

worst governor. I give that honor to Benjamin Franklin's son, who was taken out of the state in handcuffs for supporting King George's tax increases," she said.[13]

On many social issues, they had little to argue about, agreeing in more areas than either wanted voters to believe. They both supported a woman's right to have an abortion, guaranteed rights for homosexuals, better crime-deterrent programs, and more. No one even hinted that either candidate exhibited racial intolerance or would tolerate displays of bigotry or prejudice. Indeed, Whitman's Rockefeller Republican convictions were probably closer to Florio's liberal Democratic beliefs than to the ideas of many conservatives in her own party.

They differed sharply, however, on their basic views of government's role. Florio believed government could—and should—be proactive, helping those it could. He echoed many of Bill Clinton's positions on welfare and health-care reform, and Clinton let it be known that he modeled his proposed gun-control bill after New Jersey's. The president also insisted he could move forward on gun control only if Garden State voters reelected Florio and sent a message to the nation that they supported his ban on assault weapons.

"By electing Jim Florio, you strengthen the hand of the first president who's had the guts to take on the gun lobby," Hillary Clinton told voters at a Florio rally. For years, the NRA and other gun groups had quietly supported many anti-Florio efforts, including the taxpayer revolt. "If there is any wavering from the support Jim Florio deserves to have, you know how politicians are. They'll say to themselves, 'Well, the people in New Jersey didn't really support that gun ban. The people of New Jersey weren't willing to stand with the only governor in the country willing to take on the NRA when he did. So why should we?' "[14]

By contrast, Whitman wanted government to be less involved in people's lives. She supported the concept of gun control but strongly opposed Clinton's plans for a federal overhaul of the health-care system. Government, she felt, should "problem-solve at the level closest to the problem rather than starting with the highest level of government and imposing solutions down. . . . Government cannot do everything for everyone."[15]

Whitman and Florio also differed sharply on their financial and budgetary beliefs, most notably on the usefulness of tax cuts as an economic stimulus. Yet to many voters—and to the strategists designing the candidates' ads—the only important issue was character.

For much of the year, the media focused on Whitman's blunders and gaffes, providing Florio with material for commercials about the illegal-alien problem, her farmland tax assessment break on Pontefract, and her alleged softness on crime, guns, and drunk drivers. Adding to Whitman's frustration was the skill of the Florio research team. While the governor's commercials might be misleading and often used information out of context, they quoted her carefully. She issued an ill-advised position paper in the spring suggesting that convicted drunk drivers who needed their cars for work might be issued special license plates, sort of a scarlet letter. She also once called Florio's assault-weapons ban a "lousy" law, giving Democrats the opening to portray her as an ally of the NRA. A Florio ad with a picture of Whitman, wearing goggles and ear protectors, shooting a rifle helped bolster the Democratic claim that the gun lobby desperately wanted Whitman to win.

The unflattering picture being painted by Carville, Florio, and their television ads took their toll. Whitman had worked the state for nearly a year, getting tendonitis by shaking thousands of hands and visiting nearly every corner of New Jersey, putting more than 70,000 miles on her green Mercury Sable. Still, most voters' image of Whitman came from Florio's commercials.

"If all you knew of me is what you got from the ads, I drive drunk at night with my Uzi hanging out the window shooting women who have their cars stolen. . . . That is the image he is portraying," she told *Asbury Park Press* editors.[16]

That was the problem Rollins identified when he replaced Todd: nobody in New Jersey really knew Christie Whitman. There were a handful of early efforts to humanize her, such as inviting reporters to visit Pontefract to rebut Florio's allegations that she unfairly received a tax break for land that produced no farm products. Whitman played the country farmer to the hilt, producing wonderfully homey stories and photos of her with the farm's sheep, calves, and pigs.

Rollins realized, though, that inviting reporters to the farm could work only once. They needed a way to reintroduce Whitman to the voters, to show them the woman who raised two kids and worried about their futures, rode a mountain bike, and could recite the starting lineups of most of New Jersey's professional sports teams, the woman who was torn about firing her brother as manager and who, despite her wealth, didn't have cable television but knew how to milk a cow.

The solution was a bus. Not just any bus, but a specific bus: a custom-built cruiser housed in Alabama that came complete with a driver named Johnny Williams, who loved campaigns. Williams drove Bush in 1988, Quayle in 1992, and a host of GOP state candidates in between. Campaign aide and former Quayle adviser Keith Nahigian wanted to bring Williams and his bus to New Jersey. It was far more visible than the anonymous Sable and could prompt great video footage, he argued. Rollins strongly supported the idea and presented it to Whitman, who insisted on one change: she would not ride in a bus with Alabama license plates. It had to be registered in New Jersey.

Nahigian also knew that bus tours worked well, at least in New Jersey. The year before, Clinton and Al Gore had launched their fall campaign with a six-day, multistate bus caravan that had begun in Camden. Voters responded warmly to the idea of a candidate arriving in a bus rather than a limousine, and to speaking to them one-on-one rather than at a huge, impersonal rally. Many analysts believed that the Clinton bus tour, repeated later in the Midwest, gave the Democratic ticket the edge it needed for victory.

"Wheels of Change," as the Whitman bus tour was dubbed, stopped everywhere, at strip malls, at diners, and at lodge halls. Supermarkets were a favorite target, along with high schools. She chatted with small groups of voters, compared products with them in markets, and read from *The Little Engine That Could*—an admittedly appropriate selection—sitting on the floor of a child care center with two dozen toddlers. She also grew more relaxed, spending time between stops with her friends and family in the bus's spacious front cabin rather than being trapped in the Sable's cramped front seat.

"Ever since she got on the bus, she has been more like Christie," said Gluck. "She was less stilted in her stump speeches, she could be more herself."[17] She exuded a sense of being comfortable with herself and others, in contrast to the always proper Florio. Whitman, wearing a sweater and jeans, would "high-five" teenagers or hug a child without a second thought. For Florio, in his dark blue suit, that would be unthinkable. She was beginning to emerge as a down-to-earth, approachable "mom," while Florio remained formal and aloof.

To many voters, that side of Whitman was new. They knew Florio could be somewhat cold, and his many months of labeling Whitman as a wealthy aristocrat generated a similar image of her. They hadn't seen her sense of humor or known that she didn't flaunt her wealth. Now, if they couldn't see for themselves, they could watch or read one of the endless interviews she gave to reporters in the bus's front cabin between stops.

"For every 100 people Whitman met, 100,000 people saw she was out there meeting people," wrote Ralph Siegel of the *Burlington County Times*.[18]

It was a largely informal journey—far more so than most Florio appearances—with Williams playing music from loudspeakers at each stop. Most appearances started to "Rock and Roll Music" (performed by Bob Seeger), as Williams introduced Whitman between stanzas. When it was time to leave, he would blast Willie Nelson's "On the Road Again" as a signal that Whitman should start saying good-bye. The bus was also a constant commercial for Whitman on the state's highways, the equivalent of a roaming billboard.

"The toll collectors loved it," Nahigian said. "At every one, they'd call over, 'Go get him, Christie.' She'd look up and say, 'Hey, we're coming to a toll booth, crank the music.' "[19]

"What the bus did was allow you to kind of advertise your presence every single moment you were on the road, while the rest of the time nobody saw you except in the individual events. They didn't see you in the traveling," said Whitman.[20]

While much of the informality came from Whitman's natural style, it also fit the propensity of her twenty-something campaign aides. Whitman, for example, never listened to the radio rantings of Howard Stern, the crude, often vulgar shock-jock who was a drive-time favorite of a younger generation. Nahigian and Rollins, at a campaign stop in Bergen County, heard his on-air offer to endorse the first candidate to call. They quickly convinced Whitman to phone his studio from her Sable. Soon she was on the air, with a larger audience of young voters than she could ever hope to reach on the campaign trail.

"By the way, may I say that I find you somewhat attractive," Stern said to Whitman. "Seriously, you keep yourself in good shape. You're good looking, you've got our endorsement."

"I'll take it any way I can get it," Whitman replied.[21]

In addition to Stern's bizarre endorsement, Whitman received enthusiastic backing from conservative commentator Rush Limbaugh. On his nationally broadcast daily program, Limbaugh regularly attacked Florio, telling listeners that only people who were "foolish enough to bend over, grab their ankles, and beg for new taxes" should vote Democratic.[22]

Polls showed she was closing the gap slightly. An Eagleton survey in mid-October gave Florio a twelve-point lead, while an *Asbury Park Press* poll the following week estimated Florio's margin at 45 to 40 percent. But too many people—particularly women—still harbored doubts, particularly about her character.

Whitman knew that women were traditionally hard on women candidates, believing that their standards were higher for females trying to break barriers. If they failed, women felt, it hurt them all. She was losing badly with them: the *Times* poll showed that the state's female population preferred Florio by nearly two to one, and the in-state newspaper polls showed her trailing among women by about twenty points.

"If it were up to the women of New Jersey, Jim Florio would be governor," noted Steven Salmore, an Eagleton veteran who worked with Edwards during the primary. Perhaps the senior member of the corps of pundits that reporters regularly consulted, Salmore believed Whitman's nearly exclusive focus on cutting the income tax and creating jobs alienated many women. "You tell a widow on Social Security that she'll cut the income tax, why should they care?" he asked.[23]

The state chapter of the National Organization for Women (NOW) backed Whitman, though narrowly and unenthusiastically, in a vote by its political action committee. Anna Quindlen, the Hoboken resident and Pulitzer Prize–winning writer for the *New York Times*, ridiculed both that endorsement and Whitman in a harsh column on the paper's editorial pages.

"Gender matters. But when it's the only thing that matters, we are back to square one. All things being equal, I would choose a woman over a man in order to even the balance of power, to insinuate a different perspective in the process, to give young women something to shoot for and someone to look up to. But all things are rarely equal. And certainly not in the New Jersey gubernatorial race."[24]

In a letter to the *Times* a week later, four NOW members from Teaneck, New Jersey, praised Quindlen, stressing that "our organization is a democratic one, and members have the right to disagree. Many look forward to the day when New Jersey has a female governor—but we want the right woman for the job."[25]

The campaign held women-only focus groups. "When we sat these women down and got them to go into the absolute specifics, it was the warm and fuzzy stuff that was missing," said Lonna Hooks, a campaign cochairwoman.[26]

"Women vote, yes, on jobs, the economy and taxes. But there's something else there, the soul," said Gluck, whose aggressive demeanor prompted most people to listen to what she had to say. "I don't think we've spoken to that piece, the soul."[27]

Gluck also believed that Republican women candidates faced different problems than did their Democratic counterparts. The perception, she believed, was that GOP women did not understand the needs of working families, or day care problems, or the plight of minority women.

The solution to repairing Whitman's image, media adviser Murphy believed, was new commercials showing a warmer, more personable candidate, coupled with a last-minute spending spree for television airtime. That was part of Dan Todd's original strategy: Murphy claimed he would outspend the Florio camp by more than $300,000 in media buys during the campaign's last ten days. Under New Jersey's campaign finance laws, candidates were limited in how much they could spend, making the timing of commercials crucial.

In one new spot, Whitman appeared on a windswept seaside boardwalk with Kate and Taylor, both smiling, insisting "I'm in this campaign because I'm a mother, and I worry about my kids, and about yours. . . . I don't have all the answers, but I know this: our families are hurting and we need a change."[28] The ad finished with Whitman talking to, and then hugging, a young blond girl on the boardwalk, adding another motherly touch.

A second spot, with Whitman standing in front of a flower bed, dealt with Florio's charges directly. "Jim Florio is trying to mislead you with negative ads about criminals and drunk drivers. It's a cheap shot and he knows it. I'm the mother of two teenagers. I know what it's like on a Friday night to worry about drunk drivers while my kids are out of the house. As governor, nobody will be tougher than me on drunk drivers and criminals, especially those who prey on women and children. And I'll continue to support the ban on assault weapons. So the next time Jim Florio tells you I'm soft on crime, remember: if he can't tell the truth about raising taxes, how can you trust him to tell the truth about me?"[29]

Putting the children in the ads was not easy for Whitman, who tried to ensure that they led normal teenage lives. Kate was angry about the attacks on her mother, though, and agreed to Murphy's suggestion that she cut a radio commercial in her defense. Although her parents would not permit a solo television ad, "a radio spot doesn't bother me because it doesn't identify you. . . .

There are very few people who will identify people by their voice print," noted John Whitman.[30]

Kate, attending school at Deerfield Academy in Massachusetts, rewrote the script to make it reflect her thinking and speaking style. In the final version, taped at the Deerfield school radio station, Kate talked about how her mother "taught me about honesty and integrity and about the challenges facing working mothers. . . . Jim Florio has said a lot of nasty things about her. He says she doesn't care about people, but I know that's not true. . . . I know Christie Whitman cares. She's not running for governor because she wants to be a politician. She wants to see New Jersey working again. I know, because Christie Whitman is my mom."[31]

No one expected a great impact, since radio spots seldom attract much attention, but the ad became an instant hit. Around the state, voters asked each other if they had heard it, and they mentioned it to Whitman at every stop.

"I don't know if I'd call it a turning point, but it was certainly a major component," said Carl Golden, Whitman's press secretary. "Her whole campaign was built around economic recovery, and male voters reacted to that. The ad by Kate Whitman was largely directed towards female voters. There's no question about that. And it worked."[32]

The ads—especially Kate's commercial—worried women aides in the Florio camp. They understood the ads' impact and relayed their concern to the campaign's top strategists. However, the men around Florio, unfazed by a potential threat from a sixteen-year-old on a radio commercial, never realized that women were starting to reassess his opponent.

"I don't think we had any idea it would have that kind of effect. But we'd been beaten to death in South Jersey on the fact that most women didn't think Christie had a family or could understand any kind of a family problem, so this was aimed directly at trying to convince people that she just wasn't somebody who got up in the morning and got out on her horse and rode after the hounds," said John Whitman.[33]

The candidate rejected just one commercial, an ominous ad

hinting at corruption in the Florio administration and alluding to two grand juries that were investigating his former chief of staff and other longtime allies. She just wasn't comfortable making that charge, she said. "I was comfortable going after records, after accomplishments, after actual things that had been done. Character is always something that I've been leery of going after because so much of it is personal and subjective in deciding what's morally correct or not."[34] Besides, it could backfire, and as Election Day approached, she was closing daily on Florio.

Her daily tracking polls showed that the movement among voters was largely from Florio to undecided, and then from undecided to Whitman. In their data, Florio never cracked 50 percent, and the two lines tracking the candidates had finally crossed on Whitman's chart on the campaign's final weekend. Most voters, though, still thought Florio would win: the final Eagleton/*Star-Ledger* poll gave him a nine-point lead, and the last *Record* poll predicted a ten-point margin. The newspapers released the polls on Sunday, October 31, two days before the election.

Whitman heard the poll results late Saturday afternoon, while touring an indoor mall after earlier bus stops were canceled by a cold, driving rain. She was not particularly alarmed, knowing that her own figures showed the race was much closer and that an *Asbury Park Press* poll, also set for release Sunday, showed her tied with Florio at 38 percent each. Unlike the Eagleton and *Record* polls, which stopped surveying voters before the weekend, the *Press* poll talked to voters through Saturday afternoon and found that a huge group—22 percent—had not definitely made up their minds.

Most pundits, looking over months of polls, chose to believe the Eagleton and *Record* surveys. Even *Press* editors expressed doubts; they moved their poll story to a less prominent spot on Sunday's front page, hoping their numbers were right but realizing that their survey stood alone in predicting a close finish.

None of the newspaper pollsters knew that the tracking surveys of both campaigns also showed the race too close to call. Basking in the late upsurge, Rollins told anyone who would listen that

Florio peaked too early, that "he had spiked the ball on the two-yard line."[35] Whitman's final internal poll gave her a two-point lead. An election-day television exit poll put Florio ahead by less than a percentage point, essentially confirming that the race was tied.

Whitman, her family, and hundreds of supporters gathered in the late afternoon to wait for results at the Princeton Forrestal Marriott in Plainsboro. It would be a long wait. By 10:00 P.M., with just over half the districts reporting, she led by about 27,000 votes, a 51 to 49 percent margin. Cautiously optimistic, Rollins disappeared to watch *NYPD Blue*, a favorite Tuesday-night television show, in his hotel room. When he returned, with all but a small percentage of districts in, Florio had cut the lead in half.

For the Whitman team, it was time to decide whether she should claim victory or wait until every vote was counted. They didn't know where the missing districts were, feared that Florio knew their exact location, and fretted that Democratic leaders had withheld districts in heavily urban Essex and Hudson counties. They also realized that Florio's knowledge of election-night mechanics was solid; he had endured a recount in the 1981 gubernatorial campaign that he lost to Kean by 1,797 votes. The bustling suite, with its blaring TVs and half-drained, half-giddy Whitman enthusiasts, was no place for debate, so the candidate and the team that brought her to the brink—including John Whitman, Rollins, Todd, Murphy, Golden, Kean, and attorneys Peter Verniero and John Sheridan—crammed into a bathroom, struggling to reach a consensus. They talked of impounding voting machines in the cities and a genuine fear that the election could be stolen.

"We decided that the way to do this was for her to go downstairs and claim victory, and let the loser file for recount. People who file recounts are losers. We claim victory, that makes Jim Florio, at least in the public perception, the loser," Golden said."[36]

Finally, Whitman signed papers formally challenging the election results in case they were needed. She got ready to tell her supporters in the ballroom downstairs that they still faced a long night and possibly several long weeks, in case a recount was needed. There was a brief delay, while aides searched for Kate and Taylor and for Kate Beach. Then the telephone rang: Florio was calling from his own headquarters in East Brunswick.

Shortly before midnight, Jamie Fox, Florio's deputy chief of staff, received the final disappointing results from Camden, the heart of the governor's former congressional district. Fox briefed longtime Florio intimate Doug Berman, who went to the gubernatorial suite to tell Florio he had once again lost one of the closest elections in New Jersey history. Florio didn't hesitate in calling Whitman at the Marriott. The conversation was brief. "We've looked at the numbers and there's nothing more we can do. Congratulations," the state's forty-ninth governor told its fiftieth.[37]

"I've won elections, I've lost elections. Winning is infinitely better," Florio said moments later in a brief, dignified concession speech. Many of his supporters were crying. Carville, looking stricken, said, "I feel like I've let the governor down."[38]

At the Marriott, Whitman listened to Florio and gave a quick thumbs-up, producing instant pandemonium in the suite. She reached center stage in the ballroom moments later, shortly after Florio started his address. Surrounded by family, campaign staff, and well-wishers, including the state's GOP congressional delegation, Whitman told more than five hundred supporters—and the television audience that had just been watching Florio— "First, I just want to tell you, I just got a telephone call from the governor."[39]

The final margin was 26,620 votes, or about 1 percent of the 2.4 million votes cast, making Whitman the first person since New Jersey adopted its latest state constitution in 1947 to topple a sitting governor in a general election. The dramatic upset in New Jersey, combined with Republican wins in the Virginia gubernatorial election and the New York City mayoral contest, gave the GOP a clean sweep in the off-year election.

"I think, clearly, there was a mood for change last year, and it was not fulfilled, and I think one of the reasons is Bill Clinton didn't turn out to be the new kind of Democrat that a lot of people thought they were voting for last year," said Haley Barbour, the Republican National Committee chairman.[40]

Bob Dole predicted that "it's certainly going to be analyzed, I assume, by people at the White House. It's not good news. You can't find much good news in it. It's good news for us."[41]

Clinton tried to insist that the GOP sweep did not reflect on his policies, claiming that local issues dominated most contests. Few political experts accepted his rationale. "This is terrible news for Bill Clinton. It's a real kick in his pants, also for his campaign manager, James Carville," said CNN political analyst William Schneider. Wolf Blitzer, CNN's White House correspondent, said that "the president and his staff got a nasty wake-up call this morning, one they were not expecting."[42]

While the other GOP victories were important, David Broder, the *Washington Post* political columnist, said the New Jersey race "was the biggest election that Republicans had won since their big defeat in '92. They elected a governor in Virginia, but Virginia is not New Jersey."[43]

The state's reporters and pundits who had confidently forecast a Florio victory groped for answers. Whitman won because of the residual disdain for Florio, many speculated: thousands of people had apparently walked into the voting booth and been unable to pull the lever for the incumbent after hoping to be "Florio Free in '93."

"One friend said he reached for the Florio lever in the voting booth and his hand began to tremble. Another said he intended to vote for Florio, but his hand jerked over to the Whitman column as if by electrical reflex. A third ran from the voting booth and threw up in the bushes, a broken shell of a man," Ralph Siegel wrote.[44]

Maybe it was the promise of Whitman's tax cuts, they said. Even if voters doubted she could slash rates by 30 percent, any reduction would be better than the economic future offered by Florio. Or maybe voters preferred Whitman's focus on pocketbook issues to Florio's emphasis on banning Uzis and AK-47s, or liked her informal style more than the governor's intensely formal demeanor. Or they might have been put off by Florio's constant attacks on her character.

"Negative campaigns backfire. Voters get tired of them and they punish the people who do it," said Thomas Hartmann, a Rutgers media professor and longtime adviser to Bill Bradley. Or perhaps, Hartmann said, Whitman won because "Jim Florio has never been a popular man. If she had run a good campaign, she would have beaten him easily."[45]

"It's a question of momentum," former governor Tom Kean said. "If the election had been held two days ago, Florio would still be governor. If it was two days from now, the margin of victory would have been even greater."[46]

There was only one broad area of agreement. The forecasters—with the exception of the relieved *Asbury Park Press* pollsters—had been very wrong. Sheepishly, they admitted it, even before Whitman reminded them of it at her first statehouse press conference after the election.

"The voters of New Jersey did a couple of things yesterday, one of which was to prove the pollsters and political pundits wrong," Whitman said.[47]

"I think a lot of people have egg on their face, and some of them are named Eagleton," quipped Kean.[48]

At both Eagleton and the *Record*, pollsters reviewed their numbers and reinterviewed the people they had talked to. Clifford Zukin, an Eagleton professor, said 9 percent of those polled made their choice in the voting booth, with most picking Whitman. He also noted that "one thing I found interesting was how hostile the Statehouse press was to Christie Whitman."[49]

Jim Ahearn, the political columnist, admitted he had goofed. "It wasn't the first time, it won't be the last. She might have been talking directly to me when, the day after the election, she joshed pollsters and pundits. When the crow is served, I'll take a portion."[50]

Reporters had counted Whitman out against Bradley in 1990, and then again in the winter of 1993 following the illegal-alien episode. After she survived the primary, they initially expected an easy win against the unpopular Florio, then confidently forecast her demise when the campaign stumbled. She found the low expectations were degrading and frustrating, as well as occasionally beneficial. "In fairness, I've used it to my advantage on occasion ever since I first ran for office. I think that it very much has been part of being a female in politics. Expectations were so low that if I could string two or three sentences together, people thought I was brilliant," she said.[51]

Yet for Whitman, it was also a sore subject. The new governor-elect and many of the people closest to her felt that some of the press—notably the so-called statehouse regulars who covered the governor on a daily basis—favored Florio. Most newspapers endorsed him, and the stories featuring the governor easily outnumbered those focusing on his challenger. The *New York Times*, which published few favorable pictures or portrayals of Whitman, even produced a lengthy and often flattering profile of Florio in its influential Sunday magazine two weeks before the election.

Steve Giegerich, an *Asbury Park Press* writer noted for a tongue-in-cheek style, went further than most in his mea culpa, boldly starting his post-election column with a repeat of his pre-election forecast. "Unfortunately for the Republican, it looks like that old bus is going to deposit Whitman at the same place it took Bush and Quayle. Back home.—Oct. 29.

"Gulp. The sound you just heard was that of a pundit swallowing crow. In my own defense, I'd like to point out that I never have been much good at siding with winners. Witness my lifelong allegiance to the Chicago Cubs," Giegerich wrote.

At a supermarket where Whitman stopped on her final "Wheels of Change" trip—this time, in a post-election victory tour to thank supporters two days after the election—Giegerich got some advice from Republican assemblyman Joseph Azzolina, a conservative with little affection for reporters.

"There are certain members of the press who think they are God's gift to the world," Azzolina told Giegerich, as reported in the column. "They think they know it all and they really don't. They should do their homework. The press is too caught up with itself, they don't know what's really going on."

"That, in light of what transpired Tuesday," Giegerich concluded, "is pretty obvious."[52]

4

Ed Rollins

Rollins has embarrassed Mrs. Whitman and put her election into a sordid purgatory.

—Carl Rowan, nationally syndicated columnist,
November 21, 1993

THE FUROR CAME WITHOUT WARNING AND AFFECTED EVERYONE IN the campaign. Whitman was "totally stunned."[1] Keith Nahigian felt like he had taken a blow to the stomach. Peter Verniero, Whitman's newly appointed chief counsel, stood "totally shocked"[2] on his driveway well before dawn reading the *Star-Ledger* headline—and looking at a picture of himself on the front page. Lonna Hooks considered it a bad joke. Hazel Gluck thought, "That's bullshit."[3]

No one could have foreseen it, especially only a week after the election. Ed Rollins, openly relishing his national acclaim for rescuing Whitman from the brink of political oblivion, starred at an early morning breakfast hosted by Godfrey Sperling of the *Christian Science Monitor*. Everyone knew the drill of these Washington breakfasts. Senior reporters picked a political bigwig, invited him for runny eggs and Danish, and tossed him on-the-record softball questions for an hour. The weekly breakfasts had been around for nearly thirty years and seldom produced headlines. It was all very insider, very chummy, very Capitol Hill.

It was also supposedly very routine. Several reporters were half asleep, as always, and initially paid scant attention to whatever Rollins was jabbering about the Whitman campaign. He was talking about "street money" in New Jersey politics—funds that can be used to promote voter turnout on Election Day—and claiming that the campaign spent "somewhere in the neighborhood of half a million dollars."

> We went into black churches, and we basically said to ministers who had endorsed Florio, "Do you have a special project?" And they said, "We've already endorsed Florio."
>
> We said, "That's fine, don't get up on the Sunday pulpit and preach. We know you've endorsed him, but don't get up there and say it's your moral obligation that you go on Tuesday to vote for Jim Florio."
>
> Equally as important in some places, obviously we have a [Republican] mayor now in Jersey City, and we had some unhappy black mayors in other cities. We said to some of their key workers, "How much have they paid you to do your normal duty? Well, we'll match it; go home, sit and watch television," and I think to a certain extent we suppressed their vote.[4]

Suddenly, the reporters were awake. Stunned and awake. A major political consultant, an adviser to presidents, was claiming he had bribed clergy to keep people away from the voting booths. They had to be sure. "You paid ministers not to say something?" one asked.[5]

"We made contributions to their favorite charity, which usually is some special project. What we did, I think for the first time, is we played the game the way the game is played in New Jersey or elsewhere."[6]

Rollins's tale, the reporters concluded, could be plausible. Or the general theme of voter suppression might be accurate, even if the details were off. They knew Rollins often spoke more freely than most consultants—and got himself in trouble for it occasionally—but they had never caught him fabricating a story. The reporters had also believed the predictions of the New Jersey pollsters and were just as stunned as the Trenton press corps about Whitman's win. Quick checks revealed that turnout in New Jersey's urban areas was light and that Florio's support in African-American communities dropped from his 1989 levels.

And New Jersey, they recalled, had a reputation for election-day shenanigans. In 1981, Republicans paid for a "Ballot Security Task Force" that hired off-duty cops, some wearing guns and armbands, to hang around inner-city polling places, supposedly to guard against voter fraud. A federal judge denounced the task force as an effort to intimidate voters and issued a restraining order—still in effect twelve years later—to prevent the GOP from trying it again.

For a few hours, Rollins's tale of payoffs remained a relative secret. "Not all of them got the import of the story right away," admitted Sperling.[7] The reporters at his breakfasts were primarily Washington political writers unacquainted with New Jersey insiders or African-American ministers. "The ramifications of what he was saying took all day to really go in. I tell you, back at work, I was writing this on my computer, and the editor sort of saw this story coming, and it moved, literally from about page five, to page two, onto page one by the end of the day," said Tom Edsall, a *Washington Post* reporter who was at the breakfast.[8]

By nightfall, many reporters reached Carl Golden, Whitman's chief spokesman, who initially assumed Rollins was being badly misquoted or being quoted out of context. Within a few hours, though, he changed his mind. Too many news organizations called with the same question. Besides, reporters at the breakfast had Rollins's tale on tape.

Rollins quickly backed off, telling reporters who called that night he had no "direct knowledge" that the Whitman campaign paid churches, ministers, or Democratic workers. His comments, Rollins explained, meant only that Republicans fared better than usual in urban areas traditionally dominated by Democrats. In two phone calls to Trenton, he assured Golden, with whom he had become friendly during the campaign—perhaps because there were few fifty-plus veterans working for Whitman—that the story was being misinterpreted and that Whitman need not worry.

No reporter reached Whitman that night. She heard about the breakfast discussion late Tuesday from Golden, who passed along Rollins's assurances that it would produce only minor stories. "We didn't anticipate anything, nothing. You know, he knows what's a big deal and what isn't. He handles the press all the time," Whitman said.[9]

Early the next morning, they painfully discovered their mistake. Most broadcasts led with the story, which was plastered on the front page of the *New York Times* beneath a headline that said WHITMAN TEAM PAID TO CURTAIL BLACK TURNOUT.[10] The *Washington Post*'s headline read ROLLINS: GOP CASH SUPPRESSED BLACK VOTE,[11] while the *Record* stated baldly that GOP PAID OFF DEMOCRATS.[12] Even publications that attempted caution, such as the *Asbury Park Press,* couldn't avoid the furor altogether. BLACK VOTES BOUGHT OFF? asked the *Press* headline, with a subheadline calling Rollins's allegation a "boast."[13]

Reading the headlines at Pontefract, Whitman—an early riser—first called her brother, then Verniero, at about 6:30 A.M. and Golden shortly after. She asked each of them two questions: What was Rollins talking about? Did they know of anything the campaign had done that could remotely match what he said at the Sperling breakfast? Whitman's top staffers all went to their own sources, asking whether there was any possibility that Rollins might be telling the truth. The answer, all around, was no.

"It couldn't have happened," said Verniero, who oversaw the

campaign's accounting team. "I was there every day. . . . I maintained the books and records of the campaign, in terms of the compliance aspects of it. There was no trace of this anywhere."[14]

Verniero's insistence that he could account for every dollar spent in the campaign reassured Whitman. He was her personal attorney, and few people could match his reputation in Republican circles for being methodical and by-the-book. At age thirty-four, Verniero behaved differently from the other twenty- and thirty-something aides working for Whitman, like Nahigian and Jason Volk, her young aide-de-camp who went with her everywhere. It wasn't that he seemed older, his supporters contended, even if he was unfailingly courteous. Verniero just fit the perfect image of how an on-the-rise young, cautious, Republican lawyer should look and act. His shirts were always crisp and white, his gray business suits perfectly pressed. He always appeared to be working too hard. While Whitman carried the ruddy look of an athlete, Verniero was pale and scholarly. Reporters couldn't imagine him in the touch-football games they occasionally played against Whitman's staff. He never refused to answer their questions, though he invariably thought carefully before responding, whether about the law or about politics.

Verniero first entered Republican circles as a volunteer doing menial tasks, including serving as Tom Kean's driver, and rose to become executive director of the GOP state committee in 1989. His trademark was a refusal to leave even the smallest detail to chance. During the campaign, he personally delivered 1,500 pages of campaign forms to the state Election Law Enforcement Commission in boxes that he loaded onto a handtruck and pushed through the downtown streets of Trenton. He couldn't rest, he explained, until the forms were filed and stamped.

As the new chief counsel, Verniero knew he would oversee any formal response to the allegations. The problem he faced, Verniero quickly realized, was not handling Rollins. Clinton might have leaned on James Carville for political advice after reaching the White House, but there was no such role planned for Rollins in a Whitman administration. No, the problem was how to confront

Rollins's allegations—and whether they could damage Whitman's credibility, or even her prospects for being sworn in as governor.

Each of Whitman's top aides offered a different idea about how to respond. Several people suggested creating an independent commission, while others wanted established agencies to launch an investigation. Much of the discussion at an early-morning strategy session in the cramped, dreary transition office two blocks from the statehouse centered on issuing a simple, flat denial from the governor-elect. It never happened, she should say. She was adamant on that point, even pounding her fist on a table. Yet that plan posed hazards. If even one or more campaign workers acting on their own had paid anyone to keep turnout low, Whitman's denials would appear false.

"You're always concerned about that. Things like that can happen, but . . . he was talking about hundreds of thousands of dollars. That just couldn't happen in the way we had the finances structured," Whitman said. "It really would have to have been somebody completely outside the campaign organization. And that's fine. Then you just face that."[15]

Lonna Hooks, Whitman's chief of staff at the Board of Public Utilities and the campaign's contact with the African-American community, was more adamant than most that Rollins had to be lying. "Ed Rollins never had any contact in the field with any of the black ministers he was supposed to have bribed, especially all of the ministers in Newark. Ed never stepped forward, never, in one community center or church in Newark during that whole campaign. It's literally incredible to me how he would translate a war story," she said.[16]

None of the top staff doubted that Rollins had lied, though many preferred to believe he was trying to make himself look good rather than to hurt Whitman. Through the summer and much of the fall, the campaign he was running had endured ridicule while the media praised the Florio camp—led by Carville, Rollins's close friend and political rival—for textbook precision. Perhaps Rollins had only been trying to reverse that impression at the breakfast. "We were street smart. This was not the stupidest campaign ever run, as some people wanted to write. In the end, it was a fairly smart campaign, we knew what we had to do," he said.[17]

For years, Rollins and Carville had enjoyed a competitive friendship. He would exchange hugs with Carville after a campaign debate, then lampoon him moments later. On Election Night, he stood in a Marriott hotel hallway, right arm and middle finger extended in an obscene gesture of disdain. Mike Murphy, realizing that a camera crew was filming the scene for a documentary, urged him to stop, but Rollins told him not to worry. "I'm sending my sentiments to James," Rollins said.[18] Rollins was two years older, but Carville became a national celebrity by propelling Bill Clinton into the White House. Carville had a book contract, an open door to the Oval Office and a major role in the president's health-care reform proposals, and he commanded thousands of dollars for speaking appearances. The highlight of Rollins's immediate future was a potential return to New Jersey in 1994 to run Chuck Haytaian's Senate campaign and occasional stints as a political expert on NBC's *Today Show*.

In the week after the election, he had basked in the well-deserved glow of Whitman's win, with political writers predicting a prominent place once again for him high on the GOP heap. Beating Carville had more than made up for his defection from Bush to Perot; for many GOP leaders, the victory had resurrected Rollins's reputation.

"He was on top. He didn't need to say any more. He didn't need to puff it up. He didn't need to do anything more to James Carville than what he'd done, which was to win," said Whitman.[19]

After Rollins's breakfast allegations, Whitman's former good feelings for her manager rapidly evaporated. This was no minor faux pas. It was insulting and inexcusable. Several aides had never seen her so incensed.

"Here we'd gone through all this and we'd finally gotten elected. This is sort of our moment. At your absolute moment of exaltation to have that taken away from you, it was just devastating," John Whitman said.[20]

The one call between Whitman and Rollins, quick and to the point, came in late morning, the day after the breakfast.

"What are you talking about?" she asked bluntly.

"Oh, I'm really sorry, and what do you want me to do?" Rollins replied.

"Well, you've got to deny it. You've got to tell the truth. . . . You've got to make this right. I mean, it didn't happen."[21]

Rollins faxed a statement of apology to Whitman, but it contained no direct admission that he had lied. It was rejected as too soft and ambiguous. He could not be allowed to dance around the issue, leaving Whitman's integrity—or her election victory—in doubt, staffers warned. He had lied, and he had to admit it. The revised statement was ready by early afternoon.

"This is the first time that my desire to put a spin on events has crossed the line from an honest discussion of my views to an exaggeration that turned out to be inaccurate. I went too far. My remarks left the impression of something that was not true and did not occur." He refused to talk to reporters, apologizing in the statement to Whitman and to New Jersey's African-American community. "I know that the Whitman campaign, which I managed, itself in no way sponsored, funded, or sanctioned improper voter turnout activities. I have no knowledge that the party or any other entity connected to the campaign did so."[22]

Armed with the statement, Whitman walked out to face an openly skeptical mob of reporters and camera crews jammed into a small conference room at her transition headquarters. They perched on ledges and spilled out into other offices and a hallway next to a bank of ancient elevators, shouting at each other to be quiet or to stay out of a camera shot. A few reporters even crawled under the conference room table, extending arms that gripped small tape recorders. For many, trying to write down Whitman's words without elbowing someone or losing balance was impossible. Verniero, Golden, and Judy Berry Shaw, Whitman's choice for chief of staff, squeezed along the front wall, straining to hear, while other aides tried to listen from the hallway. Hooks stood in a row of African-American ministers who came to support Whitman.

In a room packed beyond capacity, Whitman appeared very alone against the avalanche of questions and doubts. Many of the state's top African-American clergymen were by her side, but all of the doubts were aimed at Whitman. What would motivate Rollins to lie? reporters asked; Whitman had no sure answer. Can you prove it didn't happen? they asked; how can anyone prove a negative, she retorted. Rollins obviously lied either on Tuesday at the breakfast or in this new statement, so why should we believe the statement, they insisted; because "it did not happen," Whitman said.[23]

"It is inconceivable to me that someone could make these kinds of statements. I've spent some time in Washington and the air is a little rarefied and I understand about egos and I understand about wanting to put a spin on things. . . . That's the only way that I can possibly conceive that this kind of thing could have happened." The easiest question was about how she felt: "Of course I'm mad."[24]

Many African-American ministers were also outraged and backed Whitman's version. A Florio supporter, the Rev. Reginald Jackson of Orange, stressed that "even the idea that the black clergy and the black churches are for sale is repugnant and an affront to us."[25]

"My father always told me you never go to bed and leave a fox in your hen house. So we will be watching him [Rollins] very carefully from now on," said the Rev. Percy Simmons of Newark, who voted for Whitman.[26]

"I find this whole thing, everything that was alleged . . . degrading to the voters of New Jersey, degrading to the African-American community, the African-American churches and frankly to me," Whitman said.[27]

To Whitman, that should have been the end of the issue. Rollins had lied, he admitted he lied, and he withdrew his allegations. In her mind, there was nothing more to talk about, and certainly nothing more for reporters to write about. Democrats, enjoying the taste of their reversal of fortune, had no intention of letting the matter end with a Whitman denial and a Rollins apology. For a week, party leaders had been reeling from Whitman's come-from-behind victory, the loss in the Virginia gubernatorial race, and Rudolph Giuliani's upset win over New York City mayor David Dinkins. Now, at least they could explain their New Jersey defeat by embracing Rollins's story that GOP workers had bribed African-American ministers and Democratic poll workers.

"I think we need to get their left hands on the Bibles and their right hands in the air," said Carville, among Democrats pushing for a federal investigation. Florio's defeat was Carville's first major loss since becoming a national celebrity, and he suffered much of the public blame. The hint of scandal gave him an out. It might even involve a federal crime. Although it was a state election, suppression of minority-community turnout could violate the 1965 Federal Voting Rights Act and potentially involve the FBI in any inquiry. "No one in Washington is buying this [denial] at all. I have no doubt that it happened."[28]

President Clinton soon joined the growing Democratic chorus. "If it is true, then it was terribly wrong for anyone to give money to anyone else not to vote or to depress voter turnout. . . . And it was terribly wrong for anyone to accept that money to render that nonservice to this country."[29]

Democrats planned to monitor the controversy, to keep Whitman and the Republicans uncomfortable and off balance—and to ensure that the media stayed intently focused on the story. Like many of the reporters, Florio and other top New Jersey Democrats did not believe $500,000 reached African-American ministers or traitorous Democratic street workers. The sum, especially in a small state like New Jersey, seemed incredible. How could that much money be on the street without a whisper reaching reporters or Democratic officials? Still, smaller sums could certainly have been paid to someone, somewhere, to keep urban turnout low. At the statehouse, Florio quietly urged demoralized aides—who were starting work on their resumés—to keep the pressure on the press. He made his own contribution in a statehouse news conference about the controversy involving his successor, whom he always called Mrs. Whitman. "The idea of paying money in any way to inhibit any group from voting or participating in a democracy is very, very troubling. Mrs. Whitman's campaign manager describes his activity as the way the game is played in New Jersey. Wrong. That's not correct, and it's obscene to say it is."[30]

Democrats also plotted legal maneuvers to keep Whitman off balance. Few party leaders believed they could force a new election or disqualify enough votes to declare Florio the winner. Proving that tens of thousands of voters had been discouraged to vote would be nearly impossible without substantial evidence, and Rollins's story and subsequent apology were insufficient. Yet the Democrats' public statements boasted about their plans to overturn the election, forcing reporters to find neutral legal experts who could evaluate the prospects. The verdict was nearly unanimous: even if a minister admitted accepting money, there would be no simple procedure for counting the votes that might have been affected. "You'd have to do a detailed analysis of the congregation, and how the hell do you do that?" asked Professor Roy Schotland of Georgetown Law School.[31]

Democrats had ample legal avenues to annoy the Republicans. By Wednesday afternoon, less than thirty-six hours after the Sperling breakfast, the Democratic State Committee filed complaints with U.S. Attorney Michael Chertoff and with the Justice Department's Civil Rights Division and asked a U.S. district judge for permission to interrogate Rollins and Dan Todd as part of the party's own investigation. The same judge had presided over the 1981 voter GOP intimidation case, in which the Republicans promised they would not carry out any more of their "ballot security activities" in racially mixed areas. Ignoring any internal doubts about the prospects for success, the Democratic national and state committees also filed a lawsuit trying to overturn the election. Why not? asked Democratic leaders, calculating they had nothing more to lose.

"To bribe people in order to discourage people from voting, it's got to be one of the most reprehensible acts in the entire history of United States politics," said State Senator Raymond Lesniak, the Democratic state chairman—and the leader of the attack.

"If this is widespread and extensive, it can be grounds to overturn the election. We would have to determine how pervasive it is."[32]

Investigators needed no prompting from the Democrats. Chertoff, a Republican appointee, promised a dispassionate FBI inquiry, explaining, "When allegations are made concerning federal criminal activity, it's our responsibility to investigate."[33] New Jersey's Election Law Enforcement Commission, which oversees campaign finance regulations, launched its own probe into how the campaign spent its publicly matched funds. Florio's acting attorney general picked two former state attorneys general—one Republican and one Democrat—to direct an investigation by the state police and the Division of Criminal Justice.

The growing number of investigations initially angered Whitman. She changed her mind quickly, realizing that vindication by government inquiries might be the only way to really convince anyone that Rollins had lied. Many Republicans, however, still felt a half dozen investigations were too many: they could easily overlap and probably confuse the message Whitman hoped that they would send.

Yet Whitman's pique over the investigations paled next to her furor at the media's obsession with Rollins's allegations. The story grew bigger each day, expanding from allegations raised at an insiders' political breakfast into a scandal broadcast around the world. Verniero's brother watched the story unfold on television in Tokyo; Herb Jackson, then of the Associated Press, on vacation in Bermuda, found he couldn't escape the story even there.

"It was very frustrating to read the front page of the paper every single day on this thing for a week, and it led off on the evening news," Whitman said later. After the months of being ridiculed by the press—and then winning, despite their predictions—she believed that many reporters were trying to prove Republicans stole the election. "There were a lot of people out there the weekend before saying, 'This ain't going to happen, you know, Florio's in,' and [they] were taking bets on that around the statehouse and other places, and they were wrong. So there would be a nice satisfaction thing. And there was some of 'This is a nice kind of dirty scandal that we love and particularly because the Republicans [were] trying to deal with the minority community, which they're not very good at anyway.' . . . The feeling I got was they really wanted to see that something had happened, and they were . . . disappointed and frustrated that there wasn't something there."[34]

Whitman's top aides didn't hide their annoyance, either. Golden blasted reporters for pursuing ministers in every corner of the state. Verniero fumed that "there was a presumption in the media . . . that if this was said, it must be true."[35]

No one was madder than John Whitman. For months—some said, even years—he had been angered by the state's political reporters, criticizing their coverage as often shallow, sloppy, and uneven. He openly admitted he was not cut out to be a politician: he was too quick to anger, too tempted to say what he really thought. Usually he kept his anger at the media to himself, though he occasionally complained to reporters who he thought wronged or underestimated his wife—or wrote that he was making decisions for her. Shortly after the primary, he had threatened to cut off the access of a New Jersey Network reporter to the campaign if NJN continued to run negative stories. His wrath could be formidable. Reporters who ran critical pieces knew to avoid John, unless they wanted an argument.

"I try not to do it except when there's a purpose behind doing it. Everybody likes to view me as an unguided missile, and at times I get mad. But you try not to get mad until one, you have a reason to, and two, you're trying to accomplish something. Getting mad for just getting mad's sake doesn't do anything."[36]

Several times staffers had to discourage him from angrily approaching reporters. "But we understood it," Hazel Gluck said. "She was his wife, he loves her."[37]

No one believed that the governor-elect fully shared the depth of her husband's anger, though there was no doubt that she respected his perspective. He didn't speak for her, but they clearly shared their frustrations. As each day passed, and the doubts lingered about whether Rollins had lied, John's anger grew. After two weeks, with no evidence emerging to support the original allegations, he had had enough. Although the governor-elect had just appointed 308 people to more than a dozen task forces that would guide the transition, reporters asked only about Rollins.

"I think any sensible person feels, we've created a publicity firestorm. If there were to be any substantiation, we would have certainly have heard about it by now, I would think, and any substantiation we hear from now on is probably pretty suspect. . . . You tell me," he said to reporters. "What are the only questions people have asked?"[38]

Reporters from New Jersey and from around the country defended their efforts to prove—or disprove—Rollins's allegations. The Rollins story offered a long list of intriguing elements, including race relations, potential criminal activity by political leaders, prominent personalities ranging from President Clinton to the Rev. Jesse Jackson and the psychological factors that had prompted Rollins either to reveal such dark secrets or fabricate the entire episode. Kean put it succinctly: "There was race, there was politics, there was money. . . . It smelled like a very good story."[39]

News organizations from around the country sent reporters to Trenton, with firm orders from the boss: find the ministers involved. No editor wanted to learn the truth—one way or another—by reading or watching the competition. Several regional newspapers spread nearly a dozen reporters each throughout the state, searching for Republicans, Democrats, ministers—anyone who might confirm Rollins's original claim.

"We're all working like dogs to find out exactly what did go on in New Jersey. Political consultants are kind of a notorious crowd. Rollins, however, has a reputation and a history of having been a pretty straight-on guy. In fact, exceptionally so in the past," said Edsall, the *Washington Post* reporter. "And he may have exaggerated, but if I were to have an inclination, it would be to at least believe him somewhat. I don't think he's the kind of guy who makes up things out of whole cloth."[40]

Reporters were determined to pursue the story on their own

rather than to wait for official developments, whether or not Whitman was annoyed at the intense focus.

"We needed some explanation for the relatively low turnout in the black community," noted Dan Weissman, who covered governors for the *Star-Ledger* for two decades. There were no thoughts about dropping the story, despite the repeated denials by Rollins and Whitman. "How could we? The investigations kept broadening . . . and things kept coming up over and over again."[41]

It was a difficult—and racially sensitive—story to cover, especially with Whitman contending that reporters were too accepting of Rollins's original premise. Like most reporters, Herb Jackson did not think he would find any minister openly admitting that he had accepted a bribe and planned to mislead his congregants. "But that doesn't mean you don't ask the questions. You don't know what the answer is going to be until you ask the question. There might have been someone who would say, 'They approached me,' " Jackson said.[42]

Many in the media didn't know whom to believe, or what to think, other than that Rollins had been a fool. "Once someone admits to having made up a story, how can anyone tell if he isn't lying about having lied?" asked an *Asbury Park Press* editorial.[43] The *New York Daily News* noted, "One thing is clear: Rollins is at least a liar. [The] question is, when?"[44]

The *Wall Street Journal,* which had endorsed Whitman a few weeks before, came to her defense: "We suppose it's too much to expect that the Democrats would pass up an opportunity to delegitimize Mrs. Whitman's victories."[45] Jim Ahearn was among the political columnists to praise Whitman, calling Rollins a "fatuous oaf " and noting that she "will never have a tougher week. She did well, considering. Actually, she did very well. . . . While pundits and politicians and sidewalk philosophers debated, she acted. . . . Throughout, she has projected indignation, seemingly genuinely distressed at the controversy. No minister has surfaced claiming to have been contracted by Rollins's agents. And so far at least, no evidence has emerged of Republican hanky-panky with Democratic get-out-the-vote workers."[46]

Others refused to give Whitman any leeway. Carl Rowan, a nationally syndicated African-American columnist, said twelve days after the Sperling breakfast that "almost nobody believes that Rollins was on an ego trip, or flat-out lying when he boasted of the dirty trick. . . . I just know that just as there are journalists, black and white, who can be bought, there are many preachers who will take a political payoff."[47]

Arguments about the potential harm to Whitman even reached the set of ABC's *This Week With David Brinkley*. Commentator George Will asserted, "One person has come out of this looking, I think, just tremendously, and that is Governor-elect Whitman, whose cold fury in this disproves the old hypothesis that an absence of honest emotion is a sign of professional wrestling and American politics."

"Well, she ought to be angry," retorted Sam Donaldson, "because if Ed, Ed Rollins has ruined himself, he has ruined her completely."[48]

Each day, reporters found new developments to follow or new clues to pursue. A Camden minister, for example, claimed to have heard stories of African-American clergy being approached by Republican officials. Reporters also recalled that Golden and Todd both hinted within a few days of the election that the campaign had tried to keep voter turnout light in urban areas. In Washington, two of Rollins's acquaintances, retired columnist Rowland Evans Jr. and GOP strategist Mary Matalin—Carville's wife—claimed he had told each of them days before the Sperling breakfast about payoffs to African-American ministers. And the Rev. Jesse Jackson's national Rainbow Coalition threatened to file a $500 million slander lawsuit against Rollins.

Jackson and the Rev. Al Sharpton—a duo that would have attracted a media crowd even without the allure of Rollins's allegations—met with Whitman behind closed doors four days after the Sperling breakfast. Jackson, initially skeptical of Whitman's denials and her vow to support the investigations, was gradually convinced by Sharpton to drop her from the Rainbow Coalition's lawsuit. "I was impressed with Governor-elect Whitman's forthrightness, her willingness to call for a complete, thorough investigation [and to] leave no stone unturned, including Ed Rollins, who she called a liar, [and] including her brother, who she said was misunderstood," Jackson said hours later on CNN's *Inside Politics*.[49]

Though the demands of the transition were considerable—Whitman had just ten weeks to pick a staff and cabinet, formulate a program, and move into the governor's office—repudiating Rollins quickly became a full-time job. The national press corps wanted private interviews, statehouse political reporters were still hunting for the elusive ministers who might have taken money, each investigation carried its own demands for time and information, and Jackson's understanding did not convince all of the nation's African-American leaders that Whitman could be trusted. She grew tired of making the ritual daily denial, though there was no choice except to refute every allegation. She also tried to regain credibility in the African-American community by attending services at two African-American churches, where the state's new First Couple clearly stood out among the largely African-American congregation. For Whitman, that was intentional.

"Do you see what the devil is doing to our church?" the Rev. DeForest B. "Buster" Soaries Jr. asked in his sermon. "The integrity, legacy, and authenticity of black churches has been disrespected and denigrated. I am here to tell you that with one stroke of the pen and one word out of his mouth, Ed Rollins has wreaked havoc in the black community. And I want to assure you there was no money, there were no meetings, there were no offers. Don't you know that if Ed Rollins had offered me money . . . I would have reported him to God, the FBI, CIA, Christie, Florio, and everybody else."[50]

Rollins, stripped of his job on NBC's *Today* program and his posts with Haytaian's Senate campaign and a Pennsylvania gubernatorial bid, resurfaced from ten days in seclusion to repeat his recantation in a five-hour session before a federal grand jury. His deposition with Democratic attorneys took another entire day, producing a transcript that ran nearly three hundred pages. "I should have had breakfast at home that morning," Rollins told journalists who thrust microphones and cameras in his face as he entered Newark's federal courthouse.[51]

In a mea-culpa *Washington Post* column, Rollins said that "I weaved together some old war stories and a couple of rumors and before I knew it, my words took on a life of their own. . . . There have been many times in my career when I got into trouble for talking to reporters, but I always slept well at night, content that my integrity was intact because at least I'd told the truth. A lot of things have been disturbing my sleep lately, but the main source of disturbance is . . . that I have mistakenly impugned the integrity of others."[52]

Golden, Todd, Hooks, and other campaign aides also testified before the grand jury, and Whitman answered questions from U.S. Attorney Chertoff in an informal meeting after Thanksgiving. Chertoff stressed that credible leads from various sources, including media reports, were pursued by investigators through interviews and, in some instances, through testimony before the grand jury. Dozens of FBI accountants combed through more than 5,500 pages of financial documents subpoenaed from the campaign and the Republican State Committee, and investigators questioned more than sixty people. To gather as much information as possible, the FBI even publicized a twenty-four-hour telephone tip hotline.

"Anybody could call up and make any kind of allegations, so you're sitting there on pins and needles not knowing what you're going to have to deal with, because it's a wonderful opportunity for some wacko or somebody who had a grudge to get out there and accuse you of all sorts of things, and even that didn't happen," Whitman said. "And then the press still wouldn't give us the benefit of the doubt."[53]

"Yes, you can't prove a negative," Verniero conceded. "But at the same time, if Rollins's allegations were true, there would have been some trace of evidence, something for the federal regulators to hang their hat on. And there was nothing."[54]

Whitman hoped she could escape the white-hot media spotlight in the Arizona desert at the annual fall meeting of the Republican Governors Association in Phoenix. Her debut on the RGA stage, at the swank Arizona Biltmore, was designed as a celebration: her victory three weeks before, along with the win by Republican George Allen of Virginia, enabled the GOP to regain a majority of the nation's statehouses. The Republican governors wanted to talk about the recent elections, tax-cutting programs like those being pursued by John Engler in Michigan and Bill Weld in Massachusetts, or the welfare reforms initiated by Tommy Thompson of Michigan.

At the opening press conference, the assembled national political reporters made clear they had little interest in Allen or the issues being pushed by the governors. Only Whitman had to hold an individual press conference to handle a siege of questions. Only Whitman was bombarded by interview requests from the local Phoenix media. And only Whitman faced repeated questions about holding onto constituents' trust, about grand juries and federal probes.

"I would hope that somehow the Democrats in the state finally begin to recognize the damage that they're doing to the state as a whole by keeping this issue alive. . . . There has been no substantiation, and it has been ten days now," Whitman told the crowd of reporters. "I question now, ten days or twelve days later, that it's still front page news."[55]

For Whitman, "it was very awkward. I didn't feel it was a terribly good way to get started with my brethren. . . . I think some of them, when they saw all that press attention, resented it just a little. . . . I would have been happy to have avoided that amount of press attention. As the new kid on the block, I tend to go to things like that thinking, I'm here to learn, . . . and I'm just going to be quiet and see how things happen, and get the lay of the land and feel my way around, and I certainly was not allowed to do that with much anonymity."[56]

She could escape at times, such as when she went horseback riding while Larry Kudlow—still an informal economic adviser—briefed the other governors on reducing taxes and government spending. Haley Barbour, the Republican national chairman, came to her defense at the conference, complaining that "every newspaper reporter in the country has been strutting around New Jersey for two weeks trying to find one scintilla of evidence, and there is no evidence. . . . Some people want to continue to stir it up. The Democrats in New Jersey certainly have nothing else to do."[57]

A few governors tried to be encouraging. At a group meeting, Whitman recalled, Ed Schafer of North Dakota passed her a note urging, "Hang in there, you're doing a great job." Eventually, most governors "understood that it wasn't pleasant press attention, that it wasn't what I wanted particularly," Whitman said.[58]

Finally, after Whitman's return from Arizona, the weeks of hard work and denials began to yield results. The Democratic team handling the depositions—led by attorney Gerald Krovatin, husband of Anna Quindlen, the *New York Times* columnist who had encouraged readers to vote for Florio—publicly conceded they had found nothing they could use to overturn Whitman's election. With the caveat that their motions would be refiled if major new information were uncovered, the Democratic state and national committees dropped their lawsuit just after Thanksgiving.

"We are the first to admit the Rollins and Todd depositions did not provide evidence of . . . a systematic effort on the part of the Whitman campaign to prevent African-Americans from voting," Krovatin said. "We didn't want to drag this one out one day longer than absolutely necessary."[59]

For Whitman, it was one lawsuit down, and three state and federal investigations to go, though the Democrats' decision removed the last legal obstacle to her inauguration. It also largely ended the media's obsession with what Rollins might or might not have done. The deluge of daily stories slowed to a trickle, with national reporters returning home and New Jersey writers focusing on the less glamorous task of covering a gubernatorial transition. Whitman said that "it will finally be over when all the final depositions are taken and when the federal probe is ended, but it's over."[60]

Michael Chertoff and the two former state attorneys general overseeing the New Jersey probe reached the same conclusion six weeks later. Whitman and the members of the new administration called their report—and the subsequent decision in February by the state Election Law Enforcement Commission to drop its own civil investigation—final proof that Rollins had lied at the Sperling breakfast. "Suffice to say that no campaign in the history of New Jersey had ever been so thoroughly reviewed as that one, and we came through it with flying colors. Just total vindication by federal [and] state prosecutors," Verniero said.[61]

Yet a handful of African-American leaders and some statehouse reporters insisted the lack of evidence did not prove Rollins had lied. There were distinct differences of opinion, too, about whether the episode was a boost to Whitman's standing in the state or a hindrance that smeared the African-American community and delayed her transition efforts. Most political leaders contended that the distasteful episode gave her a new image as a commanding, confident chief executive with stronger ties in the African-American community. "Out of a crisis, you can forge trust. And out of trust comes friendships and relationships," Kean said.[62]

To Assembly Speaker Chuck Haytaian, Whitman's performance displayed "a character that I always knew she had, and that is a character of toughness and grace under fire. And when you have that, you will do pretty well."[63] The *Asbury Park Press*, in an editorial after the Democrats dropped their lawsuit, praised Whitman for displaying a "rare blend of sensitivity and decisiveness under intense fire the past few weeks. If this is a sign of how she will conduct her administration, New Jersey will be much better off."[64]

The new "first couple" were among the few who believed that any upside from the hectic, infuriating weeks was minimal. Whitman rapidly grew weary of performance reviews that suddenly discovered she was tough, or determined, or capable. "If I were a man, would I have had to have gone through that to have proven that I was worthy of the office, or would we just let the record prove itself?" Whitman said. "Did I feel I wasn't taken particularly seriously, yes. Do I think another type of candidate might not have gotten the same reaction to the 30 percent tax [cut plan]? Yes."[65]

In John Whitman's view, the damage was permanent. "She is the woman that bribed the black ministers. Totally untrue, but it will be reported by the papers every time somebody says it. And it makes it more difficult for her to deal with the black community as well," he said. "I think we'll have that Rollins to the grave. In her obituary, the Ed Rollins incident will be mentioned."[66]

5

Transition

For Christine Todd Whitman, the hard part is about to begin. . . . Mrs. Whitman will have to pour money out of a bag that already has a hole in the bottom.
—*New York Times,* January 16, 1994

COMBATING THE DAMAGE DONE BY ED ROLLINS DRAINED MUCH OF Whitman's time and mental energy, but it was just one of many problems she faced after her election. Peter Verniero, still coordinating the legal response to Rollins, noted that the transfer of power would be difficult because "this was the first time in modern [New Jersey] history where we defeated an incumbent, so we were making a transition with our previous political adversary."[1] Rollins's outrageous story about paying off African-American ministers detracted from Whitman's efforts to form a new administration and to build her credibility among voters who backed Jim Florio. While the come-from-behind victory may have temporarily quieted the pundits who had confidently forecast Florio's reelection, it did little to convince them—or anyone else—that her ambitious income tax cuts would become a reality.

She also had nothing new to say on the subject, primarily because there had been no time to concentrate on anything except the Rollins mess. With Florio's budget figures slated to remain a secret from Whitman until after her inauguration on January 18, and the hunt for a new state treasurer still in its infancy, she could only stick to her standard responses about the tax cut. The three New Jersey reporters who followed Whitman to the Republican Governors Association conference in Arizona could almost recite the lines by heart. For journalists from major national publications such as the *Washington Post* and *Los Angeles Times,* it was the first shot at the governor-elect. After they exhausted their questions about Rollins, they started with more, this time about the tax-cut proposal.

Even if the Rollins incident had never happened, Whitman would have been on display as a rookie Republican star. She was the party's only woman governor and had ousted a nationally known incumbent who was close to President Clinton. Her tax-cut plans, if implemented successfully, could become a showcase of Republican fiscal prudence for the upcoming 1994 congressional elections and the 1996 presidential battle. So, on the conference's first full day, party bigwigs put Whitman and Larry Kudlow center stage to talk about their plans to cut spending and sharply reduce New Jersey's income tax rates.

"We saw this year that in New Jersey, the Clintons had hoped for Jim Florio to be their poster boy for their high tax campaign in 1996. . . . The people of New Jersey saw through that, and they realized that Christie's idea of cutting taxes would help the economy in New Jersey," Haley Barbour said.[2]

In a morning address to the governors, their aides, and high-powered corporate guests, Whitman explained her sense of urgency about the tax cuts. "For all the negative campaigning that was done in the course of the election, what came through from the public was that they wanted to see cuts in taxes and cuts in government spending. . . . It's another reflection perhaps of the cynicism that is out there among some, that the day after the election . . . when I reiterated my promise to cut taxes and to cut government spending, it made banner headlines. I couldn't understand why; it was what I was saying all along."[3]

To the assembled Republicans, Kudlow's economic word was close to gospel. He had accurately forecast the 1990–91 recession and the subsequent weak recovery and was David Stockman's chief economist during the early, heady days of Ronald Reagan's economic boom. He had studied at Princeton and regularly hobnobbed with Jack Kemp, Dan Quayle, and Bob Dole. He also staunchly believed in cutting taxes to bolster the economy and stressed that "Mrs. Whitman should ignore any advice to postpone" her proposed cuts. "Color me fairly optimistic. . . . The advice an economist would give is to go forward as quickly as possible,"[4] said Kudlow.

Whitman knew the pitch well, justifying her decision to skip Kudlow's economic forum by telling reporters that "I've spent a lot of time with Larry and I've heard it all before."[5] She also heard conflicting voices that recommended postponing tax cuts until the economy strengthened or that still scoffed that the cuts were possible at all.

Florio, who still harbored private doubts, refused to publicly second-guess his successor and insisted, "I'm going to be as constructive as possible. . . . The most significant thing is that the state grows and prospers."[6] Most others were not as generous. Within days of the election, columnist Richard Reeves, who would soon publish a widely acclaimed narrative of John Kennedy's administration, wrote that Whitman "is a demagogue who promised to cut state income taxes 30 percent over the next three years. Good luck, lady!"[7]

Don DiFrancesco joined the chorus of public skeptics, warning that his senate Republican caucus would not be a rubber stamp for Whitman's proposals. As fiercely partisan as Chuck Haytaian, DiFrancesco lacked the assembly speaker's unwavering faith in the power of tax cuts and was not afraid to let Whitman know that her proposals would face severe senate scrutiny. "It's a starting point, and we're going to talk about what's doable . . . It may not be what she wants," DiFrancesco said.[8] As an alternative to rate reductions, he proposed reinstating a property tax deduction on the state's income tax form.

Many doubters cited an expected revenue shortfall that could exceed $1 billion—largely caused by Florio's heavy use of one-time revenues that would not be available to Whitman—as another reason to postpone cuts. "Despite repeated assurances from him that Whitman will inherit a truly balanced budget when she assumes office January 18, Florio's ledgers, in reality, resemble Swiss cheese," wrote Lee Seglem, managing editor of the *New Jersey Reporter*.[9]

Doubts also came from business leaders who many assumed would automatically support a tax cut. Bruce Coe, president of the powerful New Jersey Business and Industry Association, suggested Whitman reconsider her first round of cuts, just as the governor-elect was telling the governors in Phoenix about her determination to move forward. Coe, a member of her transition team, believed in what Whitman was trying to do. He warned, though, that lower-than-expected income and sales tax collections could wipe out any surplus that might have bailed out Whitman's first budget, and he unveiled a survey that found only 25 percent of business leaders expected economic conditions to improve in the following year.

The state's small-business owners were "kind of like a football team that has been getting battered. They're going into the fourth quarter, and they are a little tired and a little discouraged," Coe said in Trenton. Whitman, more than two thousand miles away, heard about his warning from reporters. "I'm going to do what I said I'm going to do," she insisted. "It's too early to say this is going to put a huge strain on the tax package."[10]

Much of the skepticism came from the sheer magnitude of Whitman's plan. Other recently elected Republican governors, such as Massachusetts's Bill Weld and Michigan's John Engler, won praise for sharply reducing spending in their states without radical tax cuts like those promised by Whitman. Weld, during his first months in office, slashed spending by $2.6 billion in a $12 billion budget—an amazing 22 percent reduction—without cutting the income tax. The Michigan legislature approved Engler's bid for a major reduction in property taxes, partially financed through a sales tax increase. Wisconsin's Tommy Thompson used his line-item veto to cut spending and taxes more than 600 times and eliminated the state's gift and inheritance taxes. He also lowered income tax rates, though his state's brackets still rivaled—and for some people exceeded—New Jersey's rates. Whitman, who cited her Republican colleagues as proof that substantial tax cuts were feasible, vowed to outdo all of them.

At the state level, "there was no experiment . . . to show that if you cut taxes you'll boost revenues and increase the number of jobs. We had the opposite. We had the result of what happens if you raise taxes: you reduce revenues and drive jobs out. But there was no proof. So people like Jim [Florio] or anyone else could yell, it won't work," John Whitman said. Though he might argue with reporters when they made what he considered personal attacks on his wife, he largely kept quiet about the skepticism over the tax cut. That didn't mean he was happy about it. "She sat there and took all this stuff from everybody and said, basically, in a way, 'You have to take it on faith.' And what she was really saying is, 'You know what's going to happen if we go on with what we're doing. We've lost 400,000 jobs. So what have you got to lose.' "[11]

While the number of lost jobs cited by the Whitman camp kept growing—her campaign commercials had originally put the number at 280,000, and then 300,000—the days left to form a new administration and concoct a tax cut were rapidly dwindling. There had been no time for a post-election letdown "because there was so much to do. It was such a huge responsibility that one thing just kept going right into the next," Whitman said.[12]

She had started quickly, naming Hazel Gluck and attorney John Sheridan to head the transition team within twelve hours of claiming victory. Both were well-connected lobbyists, and both had served along with Whitman as a member of Tom Kean's cabinet. She also immediately picked her top two staffers. Judy Shaw, who wrote speeches and worked on policy during the campaign, was named chief of staff, generally considered the second most powerful job in the executive branch. Peter Verniero would be chief counsel, handling legal and legislative matters. Neither had expected the job, and neither hesitated to say yes. "I instantly accepted, and then I called my wife. I probably should have reversed that, but I didn't," Verniero said.[13]

The staff appointments surprised many who were not close to Whitman. Verniero and Shaw had been far from public view during much of the campaign and outside the core group that thrashed out the income tax proposal during the hot summer debates at Pontefract. They carried qualifications that were overlooked by many critics, such as Shaw's master's degree in public administration from Rutgers University and seven years in top staff jobs during the Kean administration, and Verniero's two years as a clerk for state supreme court justice Robert Clifford and his summa cum laude law degree from Duke University. Still, statehouse insiders—notably Republicans who were outside of Whitman's inner circle—scoffed when they talked about dealing with a chief counsel they remembered as a youngster and with a chief of staff who had never held a high-level state government post. True, neither was flamboyant or well known to the press corps, but Whitman was not hiring people to fit the expectations of reporters or GOP critics. She needed people who could be trusted. Verniero was already handling her personal affairs, and Shaw had worked for Hazel Gluck twice before, as an aide when she was in the assembly and then as her chief of staff when she was transportation commissioner. She also owned a piece of Gluck's Trenton lobbying and public relations firm.

"She picked people who didn't have that much experience, but she picked people who were very loyal to her," said Harold Hodes, a prominent lobbyist who had been chief of staff in Governor Brendan Byrne's Democratic administration. He was also a close Florio confidant and understood the staffing needs of the governor's office better than most Trenton insiders. After being rejected and ridiculed by many party leaders during the campaign, Hodes realized, Whitman "wanted core people that she trusted, and that's natural."[14]

The obstacles ahead of the new team were formidable. More than 3,500 jobs had to be filled, and unlike most states, New Jersey had no lieutenant governor who could help out. Although Florio's staffers were cooperative, they were more focused on finding new jobs than on helping their successors. The frantic pace of the election, coupled with the uncertainty about whether she would win, left little time for planning a transition. There was no blueprint, no master plan, and the Florio staff could hardly be counted on for that type of advice. And Whitman, unlike Kean and Florio, had never worked on a regular basis in Trenton.

To many staffers, the transition resembled the campaign, a short intense period of activity working toward a specific date, but picking the cabinet was a slow, arduous process. New Jersey had nineteen executive departments and dozens of semi-independent agencies like the Sports and Exposition Authority, which operated the Meadowlands sports complex. A few of the cabinet posts, notably treasurer and attorney general, would be vital to the administration's success because of the tax cuts and Whitman's tough stance during the campaign on criminal justice. Her ambitious job-creation goals also required a strong commerce commissioner, and she wanted to strengthen the largely ceremonial job of secretary of state into an ombudsman for business.

Gluck, Sheridan, and Shaw supervised the selection process, shifting through recommendations and resumés that came from every crevice of state government and New Jersey's Republican party. "I'm back on a lot of Christmas card lists," quipped Golden, who was eventually named communications director.[15] Picking staffers was less difficult than selecting a cabinet. While Whitman personally asked Jason Volk and Keith Nahigian, the young campaign aides, to stay on, Gluck handled most of the major policy and cabinet positions.

Gluck's resumé was more impressive than the vast majority covering her desk. She was finishing her first term as a commissioner of the politically powerful Port Authority of New York and New Jersey, which manages the region's bridges, tunnels, and airports. Her career began in county government in the 1970s as a consumer affairs director and then freeholder director in Ocean County; she and Whitman were among the first women in the state to hold the latter post. Gluck then came to Trenton as an assemblywoman. After losing a Senate bid, she became Kean's jack-of-all-trades, serving as lottery director, then insurance commissioner—a thankless job in a state that routinely had steep liability and car insurance rates—and finally transportation commissioner. She got out of the statehouse just before Florio came in, starting a lucrative lobbying business that she had partially abandoned to help Whitman become governor. No one doubted she would make up the lost income and much more in the new administration, with clients seeking her easy access to Whitman, Shaw, and the staffers and commissioners she was helping to select. She knew she would have to be careful in running her lobbying business to avoid conflicts of interest and appearances of conflict. Reporters and a few competitors were already watching closely, in case her firm crossed the tenuous line between lobbying friends or former colleagues and exercising unfair influence. There was no question, though, that she had reached the top of the heap.

"There's always going to be a star, someone who's stuck with a candidate through thick and then," Hodes said. Hodes knew that game well, having enjoyed instant access to Florio during the past four years. "Hazel Gluck did that, and Hazel deserves to be where she is right now."[16]

Her priorities in the screening process were simple. She believed in Whitman's insistence that commissioners had to be willing to scale back or even shut down their departments in the grand effort to reduce the size of government. Applicants also had to be comfortable with the governor-elect, though Republican roots or New Jersey residency were not mandatory. Veterans of the Kean administration were clearly favored—and it helped to be a woman.

Gluck had spent more than two decades fighting Trenton's so-called old-boy network, the locker-room mentality, the view that women officials were tokens seldom to be taken seriously. There was just one woman in the state senate, and only two in the Florio cabinet. There had never been a female chief of staff, chief justice, senate president, or attorney general. Only three women had been elected to Congress from New Jersey since 1960. Just two women—Gluck and Marion West Higgins, a former assembly speaker—had been acting governor.

To many women, Gluck was the godmother of the effort to break through the male barriers. Anyone who worked with Gluck knew she had the grit and determination to make sure it would happen, especially in an administration run by a woman. "I don't think people can understand, personally, what this election means to a whole group of us. It's everything we worked for, to show people we had the ability to do what women had never done before. This is what it's all about," she said.[17]

Trenton's State Street regulars—lobbyists, legislators, and staffers who had become fixtures of state government over the decades—wondered just how far Gluck and Whitman would go. There were many backroom jokes about "PMS and the broads," Gluck knew.[18] Telling the jokes in public, though, could be politically hazardous, because Gluck was no pushover. Whitman might refrain from displays of anger, but Gluck would forcefully let her feelings out. A statehouse veteran once described her as "five feet two of pure determination."[19]

"You just don't stop Hazel," Kean said. "She has no hesitation. Whether it's a union leader or a legislator or whoever happens to be standing in the way, she comes right at them."[20]

The return of women who had worked for Kean, and Gluck's imprint on the burgeoning administration, were immediately clear in the cabinet and the governor's office. Jane M. Kenny, Whitman's choice to run her large policy and planning staff, had been Kean's cabinet secretary; she was on leave from her job as a vice-president of Beneficial Management Corporation, working on the transition staff, when Whitman noticed her talents and offered her the last of the top three staff jobs. Shaw, who sold her partnership in the lobbying firm to Gluck, would manage the entire gubernatorial staff.

In the cabinet, two of the top three slots also went to women. Deborah Poritz, named as the state's first female attorney general, had held several top legal posts for Kean before serving as his chief counsel. Lonna Hooks was picked to become the state's first African-American secretary of state. Whitman had unwavering confidence in Hooks and wanted her to do more than the mundane constitutional chores of overseeing elections and handling corporation registrations. The new job description included unraveling the endless maze of red tape that snared Garden State businesses when they tried to weave through the state bureaucracy and overseeing outreach efforts to New Jersey's minority communities. Several other women, mostly Kean administration veterans, were also picked for top staff jobs or cabinet posts.

" 'Oh my God, look at all these women,' " Gluck said, mimicking the worried men, who had to "get over it. . . . Everything is going to be fine. Maybe part of the problem is that they know now that we're capable of handling it, and they're worried about it," she added.[21]

Lobbying for many of the jobs was intense. Whitman owed few IOUs, partly because of the myriad of party leaders who essentially abandoned the campaign after the tax-cut proposal. A few advisers who could have claimed top posts, such as Larry Kudlow and Steve Forbes, were unwilling to take the pay cut that came with public service. Gluck turned down Whitman's offer to be the Port Authority's first woman chairman, preferring to concentrate on rebuilding her business as the latest lobbying star. Every other GOP legislator, Republican county chairman, and top contributor pushed candidates they claimed could contribute to the new administration. Only a few rules in the selection process were inviolate, most notably Whitman's determination that commissioners be open-minded about downsizing their departments and her insistence on interviewing three candidates for every cabinet position.

She trusted the transition team's judgment—to a point. "I did not want to be given one recommendation from this group because I wanted to be my person, I wanted some choice. So they went and narrowed it down to three in almost every instance," Whitman said. She talked little in these sessions. Instead, she listened "to what they thought they wanted to do, what they thought was important. And then after that it gets pretty easy to sort out who has the kind of vision that I shared."[22]

The search for a state treasurer was the most intensely monitored and the most important to the administration's success or failure. On the day after her election, Whitman cited the treasury post first when asked about her most important appointments. Potential candidates saw it as a thankless job, believing that a 30 percent income tax cut—and achieving the other promised reductions, such as ending the corporation tax surcharge—was just not feasible. If the administration somehow reached that goal, Whitman would get the credit. If the tax-cut program faltered, a new treasurer could conceivably be a convenient scapegoat. The trio of John Whitman, Forbes, and Kudlow—Whitman's personal economic advisers—could also be an intimidating force to any newcomer.

"It takes someone who's very bright, it takes someone with a certain amount of chutzpah, and someone very articulate," Gluck said. "That's not something you put an ad in the paper for."[23]

By mid-December, the transition team began focusing on Brian Clymer, a dark horse who was a stranger to statehouse reporters, virtually all legislators—and the governor-elect. Although Clymer was a certified public accountant, his resumé primarily listed transportation jobs, including four years as director of the Federal Transit Administration and nine years on the board that ran the mass transit system in the Philadelphia area. In an initial interview, Clymer impressed Whitman with his aggressiveness and cautious, conservative fiscal views, the qualities she wanted in a treasurer.

"He was very eager to accept the challenge, and that's really what I was looking for. It was going to be a tough job, and we were very frank about it. And I talked to him and I said, 'This is going to be a thankless job. I am committed to delivering on the tax cuts,' " Whitman said. "He had been transportation oriented, but he certainly had a financial background. But [what decided me] was his desire to do it and his aggressiveness."[24]

The treasury post appealed to Clymer, particularly the challenge of putting together a budget—complete with a tax cut—that would prove the doubters wrong. He had viewed Whitman's original proposal with the same skepticism as most voters, but his interviews with her convinced him that the cuts were indeed going to happen. The key ingredients were a new boss with a very clear agenda, who he said promised, "I will be behind you to make it happen."[25]

Reporters, Florio's staff, and lawmakers from both parties were stunned by the selection. Clymer had less than three months to produce a balanced budget of about $15 billion that retained services while giving voters the first income tax reduction in state history. He had never worked in New Jersey, knew virtually no one in state government, and had no political base, allies, or mentors to fall back on. The legislature's senior GOP budget officials, who would have to work closely with Clymer and sign off on his proposals, were not consulted by the incoming Republican governor. They never expected a veto over the selection, but it might have been nice to have some input, lawmakers said.

Clymer was not the only choice that raised eyebrows in the statehouse. While Florio had used his cabinet appointments to pick Democratic insiders who could help him solidify control and build ties to the party, Whitman brought in bureaucrats and strangers to Trenton. She also vowed that her cabinet officers would have freedom to develop programs and speak for their departments, a distinct change from Florio's habit of closely supervising his commissioners' work. Florio's love of policy development was well known—many, either affectionately or critically, called him a policy wonk.

The relationship between the outgoing governor and his successor deteriorated rapidly, despite the goodwill pledges at their initial meeting at Drumthwacket, the gubernatorial mansion. They might have set a precedent by working closely together, the vanquished incumbent and the inexperienced replacement. Instead, tensions grew as the inaugural drew closer.

"I don't think there's any love lost between the two," said Roger Bodman, a lobbyist and GOP analyst for New Jersey Network. He understood that Florio and Whitman were the first pair to endure a transition after battling each other through a campaign and that hard feelings could linger after those long, bruising months. "They're human beings, after all."[26]

For Whitman, there was little time to be nervous about the responsibilities that lay ahead or to worry about soothing Florio's feelings. "It got to be very frustrating because you got to the point, once I'd appointed the cabinet, I wanted to just get it done. I wanted to be governing. I was tired of always being introduced as governor-elect. We had everybody in place. I knew what I wanted to do. We knew what our initiatives were going to be, and we just wanted to get them done."[27]

A few days before the inaugural, Gluck said, Whitman "began to feel for the first time what was coming on her, which was pretty awesome stuff. I told her, 'You still put your pantyhose on one leg at a time like the rest of us.' "[28]

There were changes for everyone around her. Kate Whitman needed time to become used to the idea that state troopers constantly guarded her mother—and that their presence did not mean anyone was threatening her. At least two troopers, and often more, always stood watch over a New Jersey governor, partially for security and partially to expedite communications and gubernatorial travel. Still, Pontefract took on a new dimension, with around-the-clock protection. Drumthwacket was the gubernatorial mansion, but Pontefract was Whitman's home, and she planned to stay there on weekends and when her children were home from school. The troopers also underwent changes, bringing women into the state police Executive Protection Unit for the first time.

While there were always adjustments around the statehouse for a new chief executive, the first female governor presented new challenges for many people, including the largely male press corps. If they wrote about what Whitman wore to the inauguration or the inaugural ball, would it be considered sexist? How aggressive could they be in their criticisms of Whitman? And what would they call John Whitman? First Husband? First Spouse? First Mate?

John had decided long ago there would be no Office of the First Lady or the appropriate male equivalent. Too many people already assumed that he would be telling his wife how to run state government for him to be around the statehouse on a regular basis. They still didn't understand, he believed, that a woman could handle the job on her own. Besides, he'd be attending plenty of formal functions with the governor, and he had his own business to run.

There was much that the press—and many Republican insiders—didn't know about him. Few realized that he won his Bronze Stars in Vietnam as an army lieutenant or that he met the future governor while on a Harvard University fellowship. Nor did most people know he had a self-effacing, sarcastic sense of humor. "I said to her, if she divorces me, I get half of New Jersey," John quipped.[29]

He'd heard all the First Husband jokes through the years, especially when he tried to become the first male member of the Somerset County Freeholders Wives Club. The freeholders' wives, all older women, had not quite known how to respond. In Phoenix, at the RGA conference, he went shopping with thirteen women, all spouses of other Republican governors. Their tags all read FIRST LADY. His said simply JOHN WHITMAN.

Despite Whitman's claim that John would have no role in planning the new budget, few doubted that the governor-elect would seek his counsel. The distractions of cabinet selections and inaugural planning never lessened the widespread skepticism over the tax-cut plan or the media's push for explanations about potential spending cuts.

"We had some big problems. The budget without doing anything, if we just sat here and kept every program at current levels, it would grow. Spending would grow a billion dollars a year. So we had that gap that you had to make up at the same time you're talking about cutting taxes," the governor-elect said.[30]

Notifying the legislature of a planned month's delay in her first budget address—from February 15 to March 15—did not inspire confidence, even though Florio and Kean had needed similar delays after their inaugurals. She tried to downplay the request with a dig: "If Jim Florio can take an extra month to decide how to raise your taxes by $2.8 billion, I can certainly take an extra month to decide how to cut them."[31]

No one was laughing. If anything, they were shaking their heads in confusion at the messages Whitman sent each time she talked about the budget: we're going to cut state spending while enhancing efforts to care for the poor, the disabled, the infirm, the disadvantaged.

"She is more sure of herself, less reluctant to rely on boilerplate, ambiguous phrasing as she did during the campaign when she described her economic plan," wrote Michael Kelly, a columnist for the *Record*. He also noted that "in the same discussion of cutting back on state government, she talks of the need to prompt people to devote more attention to the homeless and the disadvantaged."[32]

At an AIDS awareness program in Newark, she promised not to cut research funding for the disease. At a budget forum in Piscataway, she complained that the state's community colleges needed more funding, vowed to maintain a Lyme disease prevention program, and repeated her belief that social programs—which were usually expensive—were the best way to prevent crime. Still, she offered no specifics on possible cuts, insisting that "we are in a learning process" and worrying many Republican lawmakers with her refusal to specify programs that were likely to be downsized or eliminated.[33]

Assembly Speaker Haytaian held onto his title as the tax cut's biggest cheerleader, telling lawmakers, "My friends, a tax cut of this magnitude can be done. . . . It must be done. Nothing less than New Jersey's economic future is at stake." He conceded that there would be differences with Whitman but promised that Republican assembly members "will not be obstructionists."[34]

Whitman didn't know if Senate president DiFrancesco would

make the same vow. Far more cautious than the aggressive Haytaian—the *New York Times* once described DiFrancesco as "Mr. Bland"—he had never been comfortable with the bold nature of the tax-cut proposal. Remembering vividly how Florio had rushed his economic programs through the legislature in his first months in office, he worried that similar haste by Whitman might produce the same disastrous consequences. He preferred a more cautious approach and suggested delaying the first cut until January 1995. Many top GOP legislators liked the idea of a delay, which allowed them to support Whitman while giving themselves flexibility in the upcoming budget debates. "I think it's more practical and reasonable," he said. "People should be aware we're not going to pass [Whitman's tax cuts] like Jim Florio did his tax increases."[35]

In his farewell speech, the annual State of the State message that he delivered a week before Whitman's inaugural, Florio, too, warned against rushing into a tax cut. In a rare display of public emotion, he choked back tears while thanking his wife, Lucinda, for her support "through thick and thin." Tears rolled down Lucinda's cheeks; twenty feet away, many of Florio's top aides were also quietly crying. "I feel a little bit the way coach Dan Reeves would feel if he took the [New York football] Giants into the locker room at halftime for a talk and then found out the game was over," Florio said. "I know that he'd too, undoubtedly, have had more plays to run, more things to get done."

At the top of Florio's list was a call for cuts in local property taxes, rather than the income tax reduction that Whitman wanted. His 1990 tax hikes had helped stabilize property taxes through boosts in state aid to towns and school systems. Now, with Whitman about to take over, Florio issued a veiled warning that risking the state's fiscal health to fulfill a campaign promise could lead to economic disaster.

"We had a spirited campaign with its share of differences, but this is the time for all of us to be together and I wish her well," he said. But he cautioned that "short-term expediency as a way of avoiding the long-term public interest is, in the ultimate reckoning, a sure-thing losing cause.

"The people of New Jersey are entitled to an honest debate," said the state's forty-ninth governor. "Not the empty rhetoric of false choices like 'Are you for or against taxes.' "[36]

6

Dogs and Taxes

Given her limited experience in government, the fumbling
that marked her election campaign and the tumult over her
campaign manager's braggadocio about playing dirty tricks
with "street money," her modified tax gambit was a sign
the new Governor is gaining a grasp of political reality.

—*New York Times* editorial, January 19, 1994

ON THE EVE OF CHRISTIE WHITMAN'S INAUGURATION AS NEW JERSEY'S
fiftieth chief executive—and the Republican party's only female
governor—she was keeping a very big secret.

Her top staff—the troika of Judy Shaw, Peter Verniero, and
Jane Kenny—knew what it was. So did a handful of other insiders,
such as Jason Volk and Carl Golden. John Whitman and Dan Todd
were in on it, of course.

Reporters covering the incoming governor, print and television
alike, had no clue about how much they didn't know, and Whit-

man wanted it that way. Tradition dictated that major announce-ments were leaked to the press in advance, to pique interest in positive developments or defuse the anger over bad news. Since the death of the beloved *Newark Evening News* two generations ear-lier, the *Star-Ledger* proudly served as the prime depository of gubernatorial leaks, and its large circulation and territory ensured they would be seen throughout much of the state. The newspaper would gladly put statehouse leaks on the front page. Stories leaked to other publications would often receive meager coverage from the *Star-Ledger,* sending a clear warning to the offending official.

Trenton insiders, ranging from lobbyists to legislators, auto-matically looked for the details of a governor's budget proposal on the front page of the Sunday *Star-Ledger,* two days before the delivery of the budget address. Its reporters bristled at the sugges-tion that they were routinely handed information, correctly con-tending that they often broke stories on their own. Still, they knew that each governor was expected to go along with the game. Golden, during his years with Tom Kean, had been a master at it, to the consternation of editors at other publications. He'd be run-ning the press operation again under Whitman, so most statehouse reporters assumed that nothing would change.

Whitman, however, had little interest in playing by someone else's rules and resolved that any leaks would be spread among the statehouse's largest news bureaus. But there would be no leaks about the inaugural address, for Whitman was determined to keep her secret out of the media until she delivered her speech. She wanted to announce this news herself.

"I wanted this to be mine. I wanted it to be something that focused attention on that speech," Whitman said. "The problem with leaking things, unless you're very careful about how you pres-ent it, the context in which you put it is very important to the ultimate success or failure of an idea very often. And so you want to be able to frame it the way you want it looked at, at least ini-tially. It will take on a life of its own after a period of time, but if it's something that's very important, I want to put it out there."[1]

No one who worked in the news bureaus along the dark second-floor statehouse hallway dubbed "Press Row" doubted Whitman would announce details about the tax cut or her economic program in her inaugural address. For weeks, she had been promising there would finally be some answers at her inaugural. Failing to deliver on her first day in office would be sheer folly, the Press Row regulars agreed. However, discovering the specifics in advance appeared impossible. Determined to keep their secret intact, Whitman's staff did not even confide in legislative leaders until twelve hours before the ceremony. Legislators tended to talk, they realized. Logically, the fewer people who knew, the better the prospects of keeping the secret.

Most reporters were also busy covering the record-breaking number of inaugural events that stretched from Atlantic City to Newark. Since the election, a sixteen-member team had worked around the clock to put together a week-long festival focusing on Whitman's theme of "New Jersey, one family." Besides the inauguration, the highlights would include an ethnic entertainment and food festival at the Atlantic City Convention Center, a charity concert by pop singer Barry Manilow, a parade through the streets of Trenton, and a $500 per person black-tie inaugural ball for about 3,700 Whitman well-wishers. Proceeds from the concert were slated to go to Children's Hospital of New Jersey in Newark and Respond Inc., a nonprofit agency in Camden.

Every detail was anticipated, the planners hoped. There were only two things they couldn't control, the weather and Manilow's temperament, and both put a damper on the festivities. The Atlantic City festival was well underway when Manilow's staff called with the message that he would not be appearing. They were sorry, the staff said, but there was nothing they could do.

"In the afternoon, he [Manilow] came in and we got a call that he was upset," said Keith Nahigian, part of the inaugural planning team. "He was upset that her name was above his name on the marquee, and that was it. . . . We went into negotiations. I'm sorry, I'm sorry, I'm sorry. We'll change this and we'll change that, and he was already gone."[2]

For a few hours, a public-relations disaster loomed. Thousands of tickets were already sold, and people with some distance to travel were already on the road. The embarrassment of Manilow's withdrawal was bad enough, without television footage of angry concertgoers mobbing the convention center, demanding refunds. Manilow, who had headlined at President Clinton's inaugural, issued a statement claiming that he had not known the concert was part of Whitman's inaugural and stressing that he would not have agreed to endorse her, since he had never met her, spoken to her, or read her political platform.

A few quick phone calls and the cooperation of casino mogul Donald Trump solved the dilemma. Entertainer Paul Anka, performing at the nearby Trump Plaza casino, stepped into the void when Trump offered to move the concert from the hotel to the far larger convention center. "Actually, I think we did even better at the end of the day," said Whitman, who was not a particular Manilow fan even before his withdrawal. "Hey, I was very happy."[3]

She was less happy about the weather. Frigid temperatures had gripped the state since early January, covering streets with a treacherous layer of ice. On the eve of the inauguration, a mixture of sleet and snow forced distraught aides to cancel the planned two-hour parade through Trenton.

Indeed, the slick streets wreaked havoc with the entire inauguration-day schedule, keeping hundreds of people from attending the interfaith service at Trenton's Trinity Cathedral and the noon swearing-in at the War Memorial auditorium. Cars slid into snow banks on every block, and many drivers abandoned any hope of negotiating even the slightest uphill slopes. Icicles hung everywhere, giving the state government complex an eerie appearance. The auditorium entrance, just 250 ice-coated yards from the statehouse, could be reached on foot only with the utmost care. Seventy-five diligent state workers attacked the ice with picks, bags of salt, and hot-air blowers, desperately racing to make the sidewalks safe for high heels. Still, rather than risk embarrassing pratfalls in front of television cameras, inaugural planners dispatched buses to ferry lawmakers, staffers, and onlookers from the statehouse to the auditorium.

Just after noon on January 18, 1994, Chief Justice Robert Wilentz administered the constitutional oath. The War Memorial stage was crammed with legislators, the new cabinet, former governors, and many more—a sea of white men in dark suits, punctuated by just a handful of women, including Hazel Gluck, Lonna Hooks, and Judy Shaw. The family—Kate, Taylor, and John Whitman—held the 141-year-old Bible that had been used almost eight decades earlier to swear in John's grandfather as New York's governor. As she finished the oath, National Guard troops fired a nineteen-cannon salute from the War Memorial's west parking lot, rattling frozen windowpanes and triggering dozens of shrieking car alarms.

As the artillery echoed over the icy Delaware River, Whitman began her address. "Wherever I go, whether I'm in a mall, attending a Devils or Nets game, taking questions on a call-in show, I hear the same implicit question: After the oaths, after the speeches and the parties and festivities, will you remember your promises and will you keep them. As the first statement of my governorship, to every voter in New Jersey, let me answer that question. I have just taken the oath of office you have entrusted to me. To me, this oath means one thing. I will not hedge. I will not backtrack. I will keep my promise to you my friends, to the best of my ability. . . . I did not run for governor to conduct business as usual. It is going to be different around here."

Finally, she came to the lines she had so carefully crafted and kept secret. "Four months ago, I said I would put $1.4 billion of your tax dollars back into your pocket, by cutting taxes over the next three years with the first cut coming in July. The skeptics groaned, but here we are. And I say, why wait until the next fiscal year starts in July. . . . If President Clinton and his Congress can reach backward into time and raise your taxes retroactively, your governor and your legislature can cut them retroactively."[4]

Gasps came from the crowd, and then a rising storm of applause. Most people jumped to their feet, still clapping. In the front row of dignitaries, Florio and his wife sat still, their hands clasped. Thirty feet to Florio's right, also in the front row, U.S.

Senator Frank R. Lautenberg, a Democrat, slowly rose. He fidgeted with his belt, then his shoelaces, but he did not applaud.

"He didn't know what the hell to do," said Chuck Haytaian, who sat next to Lautenberg and was planning to challenge him in the fall senatorial election. "Then he finally got up."[5]

After a moment, Whitman continued, asking Haytaian and Don DiFrancesco "to enact a 5 percent income tax cut for every family in New Jersey effective January 1, 1994—eighteen days ago." She also wanted retroactive cuts in the corporate business tax by three-eighths of 1 percent, to 9 percent, and the elimination of all income taxes for New Jerseyans earning less than $7,500 per year.[6]

The retroactive tax cuts had been hatched in a meeting several weeks before, though Larry Kudlow claimed he suggested the idea to Whitman at the Republican Governors Association conference in Phoenix. A group of close advisers, including her husband and Dan Todd, "were just kicking around what we wanted to do in that speech, and how about doing something that will really catch people's attention? And then we started flirting with the idea of going for a retroactive 5 percent [cut]," Whitman recalled later. "There had been all that speculation of, would there really be a tax cut or not, and some of the leadership being a little skeptical. . . . It would certainly catch everybody's attention, and we thought it was doable fiscally."[7]

In her speech, Whitman offered no explanations of how it would be done, only vague possibilities about reducing wasted dollars.

"Let me tell you. Once we all put our minds to it, it's amazing all the ways we can find to save money," Whitman asserted. She signed an executive order—the first anyone could remember being signed during an inaugural address—to create an Economic Master Plan Commission and offered examples of how the state squandered the dollars paid each day by taxpayers.

"Look at how the state regulates cemeteries. If you are buried with only members of your own religion, your corpse is regulated by the Attorney General's Office. But if you are buried in a nonsectarian cemetery, the Department of Banking has jurisdiction over your remains. That's right, banking. Do we really need two different state agencies to regulate the dead? From cradle to grave, our state government needs reform."

She focused briefly on education, proposing to protect the state education commissioner from political interference by creating a fixed five-year term and to approve a pilot program in Jersey City that would give parents more input into where their children went to school. And she backed the growing sentiment for mandatory lifetime prison sentences for repeat violent offenders.

"Some say crime is too tough a problem to solve. My answer to them? We're tougher. . . . It's time to make every criminal know that he or she will serve 70 percent of the court's sentence. And for three-time violent offenders, those who make a career out of crime, it should be 'three strikes and you're in,' for life."[8]

After twenty-two minutes, more than thirty rounds of applause, and quotes from Abraham Lincoln, F. Scott Fitzgerald, and Claudia Greir, a second-grade student from the town of Neptune, it was over. DiFrancesco, presiding over the ceremonies as senate president, returned to the podium, mindful that he had pushed to delay the first tax cut until January 1995. "I knew it would be January," he said, turning to Whitman and getting the day's biggest laugh. "I just didn't get the year straight."[9]

Many of DiFrancesco's Republican colleagues saw little humor in Whitman's decision to surprise them with a retroactive tax cut. They could understand why Whitman had not told the reporters, but why isolate the folks who helped her get elected?

Many were bitter and felt they were being treated like the enemy: a Democrat, or worse—a reporter. They feared it was a bad omen, a sign that perhaps Whitman planned to largely ignore the legislature and run state government by fiat.

Others, like Senator Robert Littell, chairman of the senate budget committee, took the supposed snub in stride. There would be more substantive issues to argue about, like how to find $1 billion in either savings or new revenues in the next budget. "It wasn't a surprise to me. I knew about it fifteen minutes ahead of time," he quipped. "The tax cut is doable," Littell went on, seriously, "but in order to find the votes for it in our committee, we have to know where the spending cuts are."[10]

Democrats wanted the same answers. They were badly outnumbered, but refused to allow Whitman to railroad her plans through the assembly and the senate without a fight. "We have no interest in a tax cut proposal that smacks of dubious smoke-and-mirror fiscal tactics. There is little point to providing a phantom tax cut. We have no intentions of being a party to a tax cut that gives money with one hand, while taking money away with the other," said Assembly Minority Leader Joseph V. Doria Jr., expressing the widespread fear that her tax cuts would force increases in local property taxes. Yet even Doria, a pragmatic Hudson County politician, had to admit that the governor had carried the day. "Today is Mrs. Whitman's chance to shine in the brilliant winter sunlight," he said.[11]

The celebrations would have to wait at least a few more hours. Facing a roomful of television cameras and dozens of reporters, Whitman held her first statehouse press conference, explaining her motives for the retroactive tax cut. As she emerged from her office into the outer office, a large public room used for bill signings and ceremonies, a young aide bellowed, "Ladies and Gentlemen, the Governor of the State of New Jersey." Whitman appeared taken aback. It would be the last time she'd be introduced that way, she warned her staff. It was "just so sort of grandiose and pompous, and you do that for the president. I'm not the president, I'm the governor of a state. It's important within the state, but let's not get carried away."[12]

At parties, Republicans in tuxedos and evening gowns seldom get carried away, though many celebrants at the ball that night were still giddy over the tax cut proposal. Whitman told her guests that "tonight is a night just to enjoy and to party,"[13] but most people still focused on their noontime surprise.

"If you watch the clip of her speech today, after she said if Clinton can raise your taxes retroactively, she can cut them retroactively, I was the guy in the third row who yelled, 'Yahoo!' " said Republican state senator Gerald Cardinale.[14]

Reaction to her address and her tax cuts came swiftly. Several influential lawmakers were wary about whether enough money would be found to pay for the cuts. Democrats also quickly noted that the 5 percent reduction would save about $57 for a married couple filing jointly with a taxable income of $50,000—hardly enough, they said, to spur an economic boom. But the many months of near disasters—the sloppy moments of the campaign, the Rollins debacle, the dubious reviews of the tax-cut proposal, the Democratic attacks on her character—had lowered press expectations so far that Whitman's surprise move and plain talk sparked national attention.

"As the new governor, Mrs. Whitman certainly has appealing personal characteristics—she's articulate, smart and determined to square what she does in office with what she said on the campaign trail," said a *Washington Post* editorial. "Mrs. Whitman insisted that she could enact her supply-side tax cut program 'without cutting the state services on which so many of us depend,' and 'without driving up property taxes.' That's a large challenge. The rest of the country will be watching closely to see whether—and how—she pulls it off."[15]

The *Philadelphia Inquirer,* which had ridiculed the original tax-cut proposal as a fraud, conceded that "we were skeptical when she made that promise, and we still are." The *Inquirer*'s editorial writers also conceded, however, that they were "reminded of a quote by former heavyweight boxing champ Muhammad Ali: 'If you can do it, it ain't braggin'.' If Mrs. Whitman can do it—without breaking her other promises of not increasing property taxes or reducing state services, well, we'll excuse her braggin'."[16]

The *Christian Science Monitor,* a week later, took the opposite tack, becoming the first publication to hint that Whitman might be headed for the GOP's national ticket. After a week in office and one well-received speech, the notion struck even Whitman supporters as farfetched. The pictures had barely been hung in her statehouse office, and a nationally prominent media outlet was already speculating about a potential run for the White House.

"It is hard to deny that Whitman is going to be an articulate presence in Trenton. And we suspect that national Republicans, looking for prospective presidential and vice-presidential candidates, will watch too," the *Monitor* predicted. "In last year's election, polls showed Governor Florio winning; few pundits took Whitman seriously. Judging from the latest headlines out of the Garden State, that may have been very unwise."[17]

It was not the first time that someone of national prominence considered Whitman's chances for vice-president. Lyn Nofziger, the longtime Republican strategist, had come to New Jersey during the gubernatorial race to help the youngest child of his old friend Webster Todd and been impressed by her prospects. "If she is elected governor and does a good job and is reelected governor, she's got a shot at being a possible vice-presidential candidate. I think she's got a real future, but you've got to win the first one, you know," he said during the campaign.[18]

Whitman thought such predictions were ridiculous and even embarrassing for someone who had been in office for a few days. In New Jersey, the 1996 presidential campaign seemed very far away, despite the suggestion by Rutgers professor Steve Salmore that the surprise announcement "gave her the kind of cachet that made her a national figure." Still, he was not surprised by her decision to introduce the retroactive tax cut so soon. "She had to counter the cynical arguments that she did it to get elected, and that the promise to cut taxes would be a liability if she didn't carry through," Salmore explained. "She understood that she had to do it."[19]

David Rebovich also praised the maneuver's political effectiveness, stressing that Whitman could have won the election by fifteen points if she had made the same speech five months earlier. "What it really does is outflank DiFrancesco and the moderate Republicans who thought that cut should be delayed. . . . It clearly establishes the fact that Whitman sees herself as the leader of the State of New Jersey and the Republican party."[20]

Florio, about to reenter private life as a partner in the international law firm of Mudge, Rose, Guthrie, Alexander and Ferdon, refused to talk substantively about the tax-cut proposal. Harold Hodes, however, called it "a smart political move for someone who, quote unquote, didn't know about politics. It set off the administration and with a major source of credibility," said Hodes, the veteran Democratic lobbyist. "With all the differences you have, people will still say they may disagree, but they will still say she kept her word."[21]

The new governor was just happy to have the transition behind her, though John Whitman considered it a major victory. The retroactive tax cut, he said, proved to lawmakers and reporters that she took her responsibilities seriously. To the skeptics, "that was a moment of saying the Rollins event and all this other bullshit is over. That the new government is formed and we're taking over and we're going to act," John said.[22]

Except for major occasions, John planned to stay away from the statehouse, to minimize the rampant speculation that he was already crafting the governor's budget. Before the inaugural, away from the prying eyes of reporters, he accompanied her on a tour of the statehouse's gubernatorial inner sanctum, a suite of six high-ceilinged, wood-paneled rooms that lie beyond the large outer office. The carpet in the outer office—the only room that most people ever saw, including television viewers who saw tapes of news conferences—was badly frayed from the stream of tour groups and camera crews who paraded through daily. The drapes were held together in places by gray duct tape, and the inner offices were not in much better shape. Whitman and Shaw were initially reluctant to install new carpet, worried about the image created by such a purchase in the first hours of the administration. Still, a gubernatorial office held together with duct tape was also out of place in the picture they wanted to project.

By Whitman's first full day, the duct tape, worn carpet, and torn drapes were gone, along with the slim metal lectern that Florio had used for press conferences and ceremonies. Golden replaced it with a more impressive wooden podium that had been in the outer office during the Kean years. Workers quickly installed a deep burgundy carpet and a fresh coat of white paint, and Whitman claimed the largest room as her office, a magnificent, ornate space with a fireplace and tall windows. Florio's office, a narrow room that was smaller than those used by many aides, became a study. Verniero, Shaw, their secretaries, and Whitman's secretary, Chris Leverence, filled the rest of the inner suite. Jason Volk, Whitman's all-around general assistant, sat at a desk in the outer office next to the state troopers' security post. Golden and Kenny also had prime offices in the gubernatorial enclave, though removed from the inner suite.

Whitman still had dozens of appointments to make and to push through the senate. She quickly picked nine GOP insiders to run the Garden State Parkway, and to serve on the powerful boards of the Sports Authority and the Port Authority of New York and New Jersey. She also defied tradition by removing Brendan Byrne from the Sports Authority, which ironically operated the arena that carried his name; while Whitman had no obligation to reappoint her predecessor, ex-governors were rarely removed from their positions in this manner. Adding to the irony—or perhaps the snub—Whitman replaced him with Raymond Bateman, the former GOP state senator who had lost to Byrne in the 1977 gubernatorial election.

"It wasn't a question of not reappointing certain people," Whitman said. "I had people I wanted to place on the Sports and Exposition Authority. I was pretty clear during the campaign that that's an area of concern. I wanted to ensure there were people there who understand what I wanted to accomplish."[23]

The partisan picks might have drawn widespread attention, except for Whitman's habit—which soon became a political hazard—of responding frankly to any and all questions. She came into the outer office to announce her authority appointments, but after someone asked about the Sports Authority's long-term plans, reporters left with front-page stories about the possibility of selling the nationally known Meadowlands complex, the Monmouth Park racetrack in Oceanport, and the Atlantic City Convention Center.

Whitman had criticized the Sports Authority during the campaign, primarily for refinancing its massive debt in 1992 to raise money for the new convention center, and suggested privatizing the state's sports operation. The concept fit her plan for a broad-scale spin-off of nonessential state operations, such as motor vehicle agencies.

Whitman stressed quickly that there was no plan to race the facilities to the auction block. All four of the state's professional teams—the football Giants and Jets, the basketball Nets, and the hockey Devils—played at the sports complex. While their moves from New York to Giants Stadium and the Byrne Arena had helped repair New Jersey's historically tarnished national image and boosted the local economy, there was no rule that the buildings had to be run by the state.

"We are interested in knowing, what are the possibilities of selling the arena and selling the stadium?" she said. "What is the status of the bonds, what needs to be done in order to accomplish that, to insure that the state sees the revenues to pay off the bonds associated with the original construction costs?"[24]

Whitman had not planned to announce that the properties were for sale, much less to create a statewide furor. Her response to the question about the Sports Authority's future came near the end of the press conference and had been so unexpected that a few reporters, notably for the *Record,* the prime newspaper for the Meadowlands' circulation area, had already left and knew nothing about it until the headlines appeared the following day.

To voters, the new governor's candid nature was refreshing. The statehouse reporters, accustomed to Florio's constant sparring and carefully phrased responses, were discovering a gold mine of gubernatorial quotes. Whitman felt she was just answering truthfully. But to Golden, the tendency was at once a blessing and a curse.

Golden, fifty-six, had been around politicians and journalists for nearly four decades, starting as a reporter at the *Easton Press* in 1955. Many people disliked his caustic, often bullying style and habit of intimidating—even frightening—rookie reporters into seeing the spin on a story his way. With the Press Row regulars, he was merely insulting about stories he didn't like. It was partially an act designed to produce coverage favorable to Whitman, and it worked, for no reporter wanted to deal with Golden after writing a story that put him in a bad mood. Like Whitman, Golden did not suffer fools gladly. Egos among reporters—notably columnists, who were able to express their opinions and pontificate when the mood struck—could run very high, and Golden seldom hesitated to deflate the self-importance of someone whose story he disliked. He had weak points, notably the mechanics of television coverage and the elements needed to produce flattering pictures after a lifetime of dealing with the print press, but Keith Nahigian, now planning Whitman's special events, and Mike Heid, a veteran radio reporter who joined the press staff, could handle the broadcast details.

Despite his critics and controversial style, Golden was perhaps the state's most respected press spokesman. "Like him or not, I've never known anyone who could size up a situation better than Golden," Dan Weissman said. "He knew what we were after better than we did sometimes."[25] Reporters dealing with him knew they were hearing the truth, or at least the administration's version. He prided himself on never lying to reporters, preferring to tell them brusquely a piece of information was "none of their business" rather than mislead them. Like James Haggerty, the legendary press secretary for Dwight Eisenhower, he was also known for figuratively making the trains run on time, ensuring that reporters had access to Whitman and always making himself available. Fred Fishkin, an early-shift reporter for WCBS-AM in New York, an all-news station, could always reach Golden before dawn for a drive-time interview. Reporters hearing Fishkin's broadcast, and the tape of Golden's groggy voice, played a game of guessing what time the call had come—and how many insults Fishkin endured from Golden for the early call before getting to his question.

After more than a decade working for Kean in the assembly and the governor's office, and another three years in exile as spokesman for the state Supreme Court, Golden had to endure a learning curve with Whitman. Her open style could destroy a well-planned communications strategy with one frank remark. Whitman was also too polite to refuse to answer questions from reporters she disliked. With a hectic schedule of constant appearances during the administration's first days, unanticipated questions could produce unexpected headlines.

"She's probably one of the most candid people in public life that I've ever met," Golden said. "I don't think in the beginning she appreciated the impact of what the governor of this state says in public. Not that she said dumb things, that wasn't the case. But there were a couple of times when she expressed surprise at the play stories would get. You know, 'I really didn't say anything and it's on the front page of the *Asbury Park Press*.' I said, 'You have to understand, you're governor. What you say matters. When you walk out there and say, "This is what I want to happen," the chances are it's going to happen.' "[26]

Whitman could see the degree of media scrutiny intensify as she moved into the statehouse. Reporters lurked constantly there; their offices were just one floor above Whitman's inner suite. They knew where her state car—a maroon Sable—was parked and staked out the exit from the private stairwell that led from her office to the parking lot door if they needed a quote.

"The real difference there is," she reflected, "as governor you only have to go out once a day . . . and say something, and it gets covered. . . . It gets taken with a lot more seriousness than it did when I was a candidate."[27]

There would be many more inadvertent admissions, covering a broad number of topics. While few led to permanent damage, many created controversies, including Whitman's warning three days after the inauguration that property taxes could rise in many towns and counties under her budget.

"I can't guarantee anything over areas over which I have no control," she told reporters following a speech to the winter meeting of the Republican National Committee in Washington. While state aid would not be cut because of the income taxes, that did not prevent the local taxes from rising. "There's going to have to be a level of discipline imposed at all levels of government, but my responsibility is to insure that the cuts we talk about in order to meet the [income] tax cut are not so Draconian as to require that local taxes go up."[28]

During the campaign Whitman had consistently resisted suggestions that property taxes would rise if income tax rates dropped, despite Democratic claims to the contrary. Now she was conceding that local taxes could rise, while denying any responsibility. Still, dismayed mayors of both parties worried that inflation, rising teachers' salaries, and pressure to maintain services would prompt property tax hikes, even with a steady flow of state aid.

Four days later, she met with one hundred mayors at a League of Municipalities conference. The prepared speech text was safe enough, with Whitman sticking to an admonition that "you're going to have to be as frugal on the local level as we are going to be on the state level." To the assembled reporters, however, the message was more ominous. "We don't want to reduce municipal aid. We don't want to reduce school aid. But everything has to be on the table," she said.

Rod Frelinghuysen, the assembly budget chairman, was more blatant: "I don't want anyone to leave here with the impression that property taxes are not going to rise. . . . I would suggest, quite strongly, that they will rise. It's the nature of the beast."[29]

The cries of protest were nearly universal. "Whitman has some bad news for you. She says she'll lower income taxes as promised, but your local property taxes will probably go up. So much for Whitman's tax cuts. In one pocket, out another," wrote the *Daily Record* of Morris County.[30]

Despite such clamor, Washington political reporters and network correspondents preparing for the National Governors Association (NGA) winter meeting cared more about Whitman's bold action than about a threat to local property taxes. The Rollins controversy, the drama surrounding the tax cuts, her status as the nation's newest woman governor, her comeback victory in an off-year election—they all combined to make her very much in demand even before she left for the NGA conference. National reporters called Golden each day, trying to set up interviews with the new GOP star.

"I knew immediately she was going to be besieged when she got there. I told her, 'You're going to be the center of a great deal of attention when you get to Washington, not just from your colleagues and from your peers, but a great deal of press attention,' " he said.[31]

For the national media, Whitman was a fresh face, she was telegenic, she was personable—and now she was in Washington.

"We made a list of the governors we might want, and she was at the top of our list," said Rick Davis, a CNN executive producer. "We thought she would make for the kind of guest people would tune in for and want to hear more from."[32]

A few blocks away at ABC News, spokeswoman Eileen Murphy said, "She's in the public's mind. And she really hasn't had an opportunity to express herself on the national level before."[33]

The weekend in Washington provided that opportunity, far more than Whitman expected. She was the only governor invited to three different network interview programs, ABC's *This Week With David Brinkley*, CNN's feisty *Capitol Gang*, and PBS's *Mac-Neil/Lehrer NewsHour*. No one asked about property taxes or the concerns of New Jersey mayors. Instead, the questions focused on national topics, ranging from Clinton's health care reform plans to predictions about that weekend's Super Bowl game between Dallas and Buffalo.

Whitman's strong point was not the intricacies of the 1,300-page health-care proposal Clinton sent to Congress, but television viewers couldn't tell. She espoused the Republican fears that the Clinton bill would create a huge new federal bureaucracy and embraced the position of most governors that the states should play a major role in any new system. She also proudly talked about the New Jersey health care reforms that had already instituted many principles being considered by Congress. Those reforms had been approved under the Florio regime, but viewers didn't realize that, either.

On PBS, Whitman told Jim Lehrer that "we in New Jersey

have already taken steps to . . . ensure accessibility, to ensure portability, to ensure that you're not excluded for pre-existing conditions, a lot of the things that form the basis of the federal plan."[34]

To Brinkley, she cited the GOP-controlled assembly and senate that had ratified the reforms, without mentioning Florio. "We in New Jersey enacted a package, the Republican legislature last year, a three-bill package that talked about the portability of health care, that talked about limiting an insurance company's ability to exclude for pre-existing conditions."[35]

Every major reporter wanted to talk with Whitman. NBC's *Today Show* prominently used a clip of Whitman citing the need for employer mandates in the health care reforms; CNN asked about her views on welfare reform; CBS radio wondered what the tax cuts meant for Republican governors across the country. A *Washington Post* story about Clinton watching the Super Bowl while NGA members waited downstairs at the White House mentioned Whitman before any other governor. David Broder, the dean of Washington columnists, asked for an audience.

Pictures of Whitman sitting next to the president at a White House luncheon also made front pages across the country. At most NGA meetings, Whitman would have been several seats from the president, since governors traditionally sit in the order that their states joined the Union, and New Jersey was third. At that year's meeting, the governors of the first two states, Delaware and Pennsylvania, were NGA officers and seated out of order at the head table. "You'd rather be lucky than smart sometimes," Whitman said.[36]

A few governors resented the spotlights shining so brightly on Whitman, leaving them in relative obscurity. "Because I'm female I look different than the rest of them. I'm able to wear bright clothes, and they can't, so I stand out. And I can just sense there are some of them who are just not comfortable with it," she said.[37]

Despite Golden's warnings, she was not ready for the intense focus. It was flattering, but also shocking. She was so new, so green, and so much in the public eye. Just take one day at a time, she figured, and don't get too used to the attention.

"If you listened to the introductions, while a lot of them talked about the 30 percent tax cut and getting elected on that, no one mentioned that it was the first time that an incumbent governor had been beaten in a general election. And so that kind of led me to believe from the very beginning there was more about the fact that I was female and that Ed Rollins had said what he said that brought attention to what we were doing."[38]

And, some of the national notoriety came from an unlikely story. Taro, a 110-pound Akita, had been sentenced to death by a New Jersey municipal judge two years earlier after biting a ten-year old girl on Christmas Day 1990. Taro's owner, claiming the bite was a scratch, fought to keep the dog alive, costing the state more than $75,000 in legal fees. After exhausting their appeals, the owners asked Whitman for a pardon, putting the new governor in a classic no-win situation. Legally, she could not pardon Taro. Besides, returning a potentially dangerous dog to the neighborhood was unthinkable. Meanwhile, animal lovers, watching throughout the nation, protested Taro's death-row status.

To Whitman's relief, Verniero found a solution. Taro was property, and his execution would be the equivalent of forfeiting property. Whitman had the power to waive the forfeiture—provided Taro relocated to new owners in New York who agreed to hold New Jersey blameless in regard to any future problems. Across the country, the story made headlines: Taro would live! Even ABC's Diane Sawyer, on *Day One,* the network's prime-time magazine show, updated viewers on the first night of the NGA conference. *Saturday Night Live* spoofed the fracas in a skit, and the BBC called for an interview.

By then, Whitman had been in office for fifteen days.

"We had it all," Whitman said. "And we had Taro."[39]

7

One Family

She must have had the greatest short course on political leadership ever.

—Political science professor David Rebovich in *USA Today,* February 10, 1994

FOR WHITMAN, IMPLEMENTING A PROGRAM TO MAKE NEW JERSEY truly "one family" hardly appeared to be urgent in the first weeks of her administration. Social initiatives would have to wait until the first budget was presented to the legislature in March and the cabinet selection was completed. Besides, the state had not faced a racial controversy for years—other than the Ed Rollins episode, of course.

The preachings of Khalid Abdul Muhammad, a former aide to the Nation of Islam's controversial leader, the Rev. Louis Farrakhan, dramatically changed Whitman's priorities. Muhammad, a fiery speaker known for making anti-Semitic, anti-Catholic, and anti-white slurs, was planning a late February appearance at Trenton State College. A few months before, in a little-noticed speech at another New Jersey college, Muhammad had called Jews "bloodsuckers of the black community" and insulted whites, Catholics, and homosexuals in a lengthy, often bitter diatribe.[1] According to Muhammad, Pope John Paul II was an "old, no-good pope, you know the cracker."[2] He also said that whites in South Africa deserved to die: "We kill the women, we kill the children, we kill the babies. We kill the blind, we kill the crippled . . . we kill 'em all."[3]

Despite Muhammad's rhetoric, word of his first speech spread slowly, until tapes of the talk began to circulate among reporters and Trenton State students invited him to appear at their African-American History Month celebration. Whitman feared that Muhammad's return to New Jersey would bring out hostile crowds and possibly even spark violent outbreaks. But blocking another appearance—or trying to keep him out of the state altogether—was not an option. Even his most ardent critics conceded Muhammad's First Amendment right to free speech.

Jesse Jackson and other African-American leaders denounced Muhammad's preachings. Whitman knew that words and repudiations were not enough. The nation would be watching her response and waiting for the potential racial explosion at Trenton State. Jewish groups already planned to demonstrate at Muhammad's appearance. Sitting back and just adding her voice to the denouncements would be a weak response, especially after promoting the concept "We are One Family. One Community. One State" in her inaugural.[4]

"I knew I wanted to do something that was more positive than just saying, 'Don't talk like this,' " Whitman said. "I wanted to do something that was going to be more positive and have more perhaps of a lasting impact, but that took a little more time just to determine what was the right thing."[5]

Whitman's approach was original, startling, and clearly personal. She went to see *Schindler's List,* Steven Spielberg's much-heralded depiction of German businessman Otto Schindler's rescue of 1,200 Jews from the Holocaust. Whitman was familiar with the history of the Holocaust, but the film's power, and its message of how one person can affect the lives of many others, clearly moved her. She looked beyond the story about Jews and the Holocaust to an overriding message of the devastating power of racial hatred. If she reacted that way, Whitman wondered, wouldn't others? Particularly the college students who might be susceptible to Muhammad's message and might not know about the hatred that led to the Holocaust.

She knew that just encouraging students to go watch the film in their local theater would not suffice. *Schindler's List*, a stark black-and-white drama, was not a teenage favorite. But large-scale free showings, combined with forums on tolerance, might prompt interest.

Whitman tapped Secretary of State Lonna Hooks to handle negotiations with Spielberg. Short and intense, Hooks had solid qualifications: a cum laude law degree, a federal court of appeals clerkship, and a decade working in business and for Whitman. She had the governor's full confidence, whether to cut through red tape as a business ombudsman or to represent Whitman's interests in the African-American community. A few African-American leaders complained that Hooks's ties to their community were tenuous, bringing out her ire. "Every single African-American who attains a [high-level position] has to deal with this, 'You are not black enough, you are not qualified,' " Hooks said.[6]

Spielberg quickly agreed to lend two copies of the film to Whitman. "We didn't think about him saying no. We thought, here we had the perfect situation for the usage of art, art that is going to be piercing, and challenge thought," Hooks said. "We had people here on staff who knew somebody who knew somebody. . . . They said yes over the phone."[7]

Spielberg, who would win his first Best Director Academy Award for *Schindler's List*, always envisioned it as a teaching tool. He later praised Whitman for creating a tolerance program that was copied in many states, including Michigan and California. "I've heard many teachers say," he said, " 'I'll be happy to teach

112

this for two weeks.' It can't be a two-week course. It has to be a social studies course. It has to be integrated into a curriculum."[8]

In near-total secrecy, Whitman and Hooks arranged five screenings that would begin with a tolerance seminar hosted by the governor and video-taped for distribution on college campuses. Ed Goldberg, the higher education chancellor, convened a conference on prejudice at Seton Hall University, and Leo Klagholz, the new education commissioner, organized town meetings and a new tolerance curriculum for public high schools. The first screening was held February 28, a few hours before Muhammad planned to appear at Trenton State. Whitman unveiled the program, called "Teaching Tolerance," in a Newark speech that mentioned Muhammad only once—likening him to David Duke, the white supremacist leader from Louisiana.

"If some students want to hear a Khalid Muhammad or a David Duke speak, they have the right to send out the invitations and the speakers have the right to accept or decline the offer. But when racism and hatred speak, it is incumbent upon the rest of us—the vast majority of New Jerseyans who believe in tolerance, in diversity, in equality—to exercise our First Amendment rights to confront this disease head on. As the Rev. Martin Luther King Jr. said, 'He who accepts evil without protesting against it is really cooperating with it,' " Whitman said.

She talked about Schindler's courage in defying his homeland's anti-Jewish edicts, declaring that "his is a powerful example—one that we should bring to every college campus, to every school, to every home, to everywhere people gather. I will do everything in my power to bring that message out. . . . *Schindler's List* is a good way to start."[9]

Few believed Whitman's claim that holding the first screening just hours before Muhammad's Trenton State speech was coincidental, especially after the assembly scheduled a special session for that day dedicated to tolerance. Many African-American leaders and tolerance experts criticized Whitman's decision to battle racial problems with a Holocaust film—rather than, perhaps, the TV series *Roots*—and questioned the value of an assembly session that did not focus on initiatives to help the urban poor.

"If we're going to have a special session, why not have one on what is causing so many youths to turn to drugs?" asked Assembly Deputy Minority Leader Wayne Bryant, the state's highest-ranking African-American legislator. "That, to me, would be productive."[10]

"You're always getting into dangerous territory when you start comparing oppressions," warned Margaret Klawunn, coordinator of Common Purposes, a diversity program at Rutgers University.[11]

In a show of conciliation—or a clever public relations move—Muhammad attended a matinee showing of *Schindler's List* in Princeton with his son, an aide, and four bodyguards while Whitman held her first screening twenty miles to the north. His Trenton State address turned out to be tamer than expected.

"I did not come to Trenton State university to teach black students to hate whites," Muhammad said, "but I did come to Trenton State university to teach you, black man and woman, to love your black self." He also conceded that many expected more fiery rhetoric, telling television crews, "Sorry to disappoint you guys."[12]

Eventually about two thousand college students attended Whitman's *Schindler's List* screenings, just a fraction in the number nationwide who would eventually watch the film as part of an education or tolerance program. The screenings hurt Whitman's standings with many state African-American leaders, who felt the focus on the Holocaust should have been broadened to include slavery and other atrocities. On a broader level, Whitman proved she would fight for her values. It was her first leadership test, and while critics might scoff at the specifics of her plan, few faulted her initiative. She also had an answer for the skeptics: Teaching Tolerance meant fighting all forms of hatred, not just the teachings of one outspoken extremist.

"*Schindler's List* was a magnificent start for us," Hooks said. "But coming out of it our challenge was to do things that were not going to be perceived as pandering. You have so many people with so many heritages."[13]

To Whitman, handling Muhammad was "part of being the leader of the state and showing that a state cares. . . . It was instinctive."[14] It was the part of the job she hadn't thought about, an intangible that could never be anticipated. Voters seldom considered which candidate could do a better job handling a crisis, or reacting to a disaster, or coping with tragedy. There were no questions that reporters could pose to test for such leadership qualities, or scenarios that they could present to compare reactions from candidates. That instinctive, intangible aspect of being governor, though, came up far more frequently that Whitman ever expected, forcing her to cope with confrontations like those posed by Muhammad or sending her racing to major emergencies or the hospital rooms of state troopers shot on duty.

"It's not something you particularly anticipate or think, gee, once I get into this office I'm going to do this stuff. But it is something that once it happens, at least as far as I'm concerned, it's just that's where I need to be," Whitman said.[15]

Bill Palatucci noted, "She's always the first one at the scene of an accident, getting out the facts and telling everyone it's under control. . . . She's tough, and has this iron-lady backbone."[16]

Critics claimed quietly that the notoriety motivated her, especially the prospect of heartwarming front-page pictures. Her detractors knew that openly questioning Whitman's motives for emergency room visits could backfire. They didn't want to publicly attack a governor in her first weeks in office, or appear to be petty. Instead, they whispered to reporters that the desire for publicity was genuine and the rest was an act.

"I can't believe you guys are buying this," a Democratic aide told reporters after Whitman made headlines at an emergency scene. "Whatever she says, you just put it in [stories]. Do you ever stop to ask yourselves why she keeps doing these?"[17]

The critics were unaware that many of Whitman's bedside visits—such as those she paid to Gene Johnson, a state trooper who broke his neck in an off-duty motorcycle accident—never made the newspapers. In another kind of crisis, Whitman consoled a worried wife whose husband had been taken hostage. Whitman knew the husband was already dead, but under orders of the state police, she could not tell his wife until all hostages were released and the gunman was captured. Eventually she discussed the incident with reporters, but was loathe to talk about those moments alone with the widow.

"I was just torn up for that poor woman. You know, she had the children at home and you tried to be supportive of her, but you knew how terrible it was going to be for her in just a little while," Whitman recalled.[18]

Each situation created a dilemma about whether to tell the media of her involvement. If the public focused on her role rather than on the actual emergency that prompted her presence, she might as well stay away. "I'm so afraid that people will look on it as a photo op. . . . If they're there and they catch me, that's fine, but I'm doing it for the people that are hurting or the people who are in trouble or the people who are sacrificing. I'm not doing it for the opportunity to appear in the paper having done it, and that's a very fine line. I think we've walked it so far, but obviously it can turn either way, depending on what people think."[19]

No one tried to keep the press away from Edison Township in late March, 1994; a ruptured gas pipeline exploded a fireball, killing one person and incinerating half a dozen buildings in the middle of the night. Television and radio coverage dominated the morning drive time, and local newspapers that raced reporters to the scene in the middle of the night carried dramatic photos and eyewitness accounts. Ironically, while both of her homes were within sound of the blast, Whitman was twelve hundred miles away, at her Key Largo, Florida, condominium. She was unaware of the disaster for several hours.

A few fast phone calls, a quick trip to Miami, a hastily arranged Continental Airlines flight to Newark, and a helicopter ride brought her back to Edison. While a governor rushing to a disaster scene is hardly unusual—her predecessors would have done the same—Whitman's embrace of the distraught survivors was very different from the official words of concern from conventional politicians. Her emotional response provided a human benefit to the survivors and a political bonanza for the new governor, whose spontaneous return hugs generated touching page 1 pictures and video clips throughout the region.

"There was a lot state government could do, and I wanted to be sure that we were coordinated through emergency management," Whitman said. "But it's also just part of the physical presence to show you're there and to show that you care about people. There's nothing I can do for people when they've been severely injured. I mean, I can't help them, I'm not a doctor, but I can go in and let the families know we're there for them . . . whatever happens, that we will do everything we can."[20]

Whitman kept following her instincts, handling the job in her own way—to the consternation of many statehouse veterans who tried to force her to follow past practice. "Her approach was 'Just because it was done that way doesn't mean we've got to keep doing it that way.' And there is a tendency on the part of some that continuity is all that matters, that there be a seamless transition," Golden said. "But she said, 'I'm going to do things differently. I'm not going to let the office capture me. I capture the office. And if I have a strong enough opinion on something, [if] I have a very firmly held view, I'm not going to be the least reluctant to talk about what that is. And I'm not going to use words that people want, or perceive to be weasel words or outs on certain things.' "[21]

She made both headlines and political enemies by speaking her mind, often without appearing to consider the potential impact of her words. In early February, she incensed the state's teachers by challenging their tenure system, which enabled them to hold their jobs for life unless they were laid off for budgetary reasons. "Those who are really burned out in the classroom [should not be] left there simply because they've served x number of years and they are protected forever," Whitman said. "It's not something we're going to say we're going to mandate through. . . . But to run away from it and to say that you don't want to look at it, that you refuse to even address it, I think, is a disservice."[22]

117

"These are issues the public understands," said Steve Salmore, the Rutgers political science professor. "If you're going to talk about cutting the budget, isn't one of the issues you're going to raise, going to be: 'Are you getting your money's worth?' And are the teachers really going to be able to defend the status quo?"[23]

Despite opposition by the New Jersey Education Association, the powerful teachers' union, many residents supported Whitman's stance, or at least its concept. While teachers were widely respected, they were also envied for their long vacations and job security, especially in an era of frequent corporate layoffs. Besides, Whitman had never been a favorite of the teachers, who ran a $200,000 advertising campaign against her in the gubernatorial campaign. Even before raising the certification issue, Whitman had angered the union by calling for the trial program that would offer publicly funded vouchers to Jersey City parents who wanted to send their children to private schools.

While Whitman never formally pursued her recertification proposal, she also didn't follow the statehouse tradition of bowing to the unions, or many other time-honored protocols. The growing number of women in the new administration, for example, still rankled many Trenton veterans. Nowhere was the huge influx of women more apparent than on the annual junket for state officials, lobbyists, and hangers-on sponsored each February by the Chamber of Commerce; the first trip in the Whitman regime carried a record number of female state officials, to the consternation of many men. Women's name tags on the trip, Judy Shaw noted, used to carry the initials *MRS.* Under Whitman, she quipped, "the initials have changed . . . to *CEO.*"[24]

"I was on the last chamber trip, in 1968, when women were banned. . . . Here we are more than twenty-five years later, and we have a woman governor. What more could you say than that?" asked Alan Karcher, a former assembly speaker,[25] noting the progress.

Parents frequently came up to Whitman to tell her that their daughters looked up to her. Young girls surrounded her at public events. She invariably stopped to talk with them, realizing "they haven't seen a female role model as governor, and they do consider me a role model, because I'm there."[26]

She regularly headlined at women's events, accepting awards and encouraging women to strive for equality, particularly in government. At a Women's Day event in a Metuchen school, the new governor borrowed an old line, telling sixth and seventh graders that "a women's place is in the House. And in the Senate and in the governor's house and maybe someday in the White House."[27]

She savored victories over Trenton's old-boy network, and didn't refrain from speaking her mind—including about the president. Fighting for their beleaguered health-care reforms, Bill and Hillary Clinton came to Edison to campaign for their proposal at a mid-February pep rally. It was a perfectly staged television event, with 2,500 senior citizens cheering the First Couple in a college gymnasium swathed in red, white, and blue bunting. Such events in Middlesex County, in the state's midsection, regularly attracted media not only from New Jersey but from New York City and Philadelphia, each an hour away, reaching voters in at least five states—New Jersey, New York, Pennsylvania, Delaware and Connecticut.

Presidential planners, however, hadn't taken into account Whitman's brazenness—or the possibility that she would denounce Clinton's program in front of network cameras in the briefing room set aside for White House press. She particularly disliked the president's description of the health-care debate as a battle and complained that his reforms would give greater power to government.

The infuriated White House aides cared less about the substance of Whitman's remarks than about her daring to come into an official White House facility to criticize the president. One senior White House aide berated staffers for allowing Whitman into the briefing room. Another said he considered her presence there particularly infuriating because the White House had refused pleas by local Democrats to exclude Whitman from the event entirely. A third blasted a Whitman press aide, and the Secret Service banned local reporters and camera crews from entering the briefing room, even while Whitman was speaking to the national press.

Their political differences notwithstanding, the president and the new governor projected similar personal qualities. Part of Clinton's original appeal was his common touch, the sense that he— unlike George Bush—could find his way around a K mart or knew the price of a Big Mac. Whitman had the same down-to-earth appeal. Voters might have seen Florio campaigning at a football game, but he was ill at ease with strangers and would never be seen eating in a stadium food court or signing autographs. And, in contrast to their response to her predecessor, many voters were willing to give Whitman the benefit of the doubt as she tried to sell herself and her budget-slashing policies.

"If people get to know you and like you, they don't have to agree with you on everything," Tom Kean said. "You can disagree totally with a member of the family and still support them."[28]

Flattering photos and stories about her personality and style ran regularly, reinforcing the positive impression of a governor who could have been the woman next door. The *New York Daily News* depicted Whitman "oozing sincerity, looking directly into your eyes. . . . It was classic Whitman, displaying one of her best attributes—her warmth."[29]

To mark the opening of trout season, Whitman followed her predecessors' pattern of appearing at the Pequest River, near the state hatchery in Warren County. For decades, reporters had seen the governor—Florio, Byrne, Kean—wade into the water, pose for pictures, and leave. Whitman, however, came to fish. "It was handled as an obligation. Fishing itself was hardly their wont. Whitman, however, fly rod in hand, angles for trout, not for a chance to be seen for political gain," Dan Weissman wrote in a Sunday *Star-Ledger* story about Whitman's outdoor pursuits.[30]

Name a sport—with the exception of jogging—and Whitman gave it a try. She hiked, biked, fished, swam, skied, played tennis, touch football, and softball, went whitewater rafting and horseback riding. She was aggressive and intense in each endeavor; in basketball games against state troopers and staff members, Whitman wasn't afraid to throw an elbow at any opponent. "She plays tenacious defense. She's not afraid to use her body to block the lane," said Jason Volk, who perhaps more than anyone else joined in with Whitman's various athletic pursuits. "She's as competitive as anyone else you'd meet at the pickup court."[31]

She went often to New Jersey Devils hockey games, usually spending most of the evening signing autographs for fans on Devils cheering towels, programs, scraps of paper, napkins, and jerseys. By the end of the night, her wrist would be sore, her black Sharpie marker pen nearly out of ink. "They don't think we do those kinds of things, but then they discover you're a regular person like everyone else," Whitman said at a late-season game in April 1994. She was wearing a New Jersey Nets sweatshirt and complaining about referees' calls—until the next person in line handed her a program to sign. "When people come up, I'm not going to be rude to them. It's an opportunity for me to see them, and them to see me."[32]

Even the state troopers who guarded Whitman around the clock started raving about the new boss and her common touch. The troopers had not been close to Florio, who invariably treated them politely but distantly, bidding them "good morning" or "good night" and thanking them for their help each day. By contrast, Whitman challenged them to pickup games, beat them at darts, played billiards with them—and always rode in the front seat, arguing with the trooper behind the wheel about the choice of radio station. After four years of guarding Florio in virtual silence, the troopers—male and female—were enthralled; female troopers were assigned to protective detail for the first time, guarding Whitman and Shaw. Troopers jokingly tried to argue when Whitman detoured them to favorite haunts around the region: a discount outlet called Hosiery City in Newark, a muffin shop in Manhattan, discount drugstores to pick up knickknacks anywhere in the state. She didn't often make them go clothes shopping with her, instead purchasing suits and dresses through Dan Todd's daughter-in-law, a fashion buyer; she had no favorite designer, though occasionally ordered from Herbert Grossman, a small, mid-price New York manufacturer.

She also reached out to state workers who rarely had contact with a governor in her efforts to learn the various dimensions of state government. The excursions, which included a flight on an Army National Guard F-16 fighter, had a large public relations component.

"People who are doing those jobs really appreciate it when you show an interest in what it is they're doing. It gives them a little more pride in what they're doing. There was a lot of attention within the National Guard air unit to the fact that I was down there, first female politician to go up in an F-16." Admittedly, the flight was not one of the more arduous parts of the job, and it appealed to Whitman's daredevil streak. "We had a ball. It was an absolutely fascinating experience. I didn't get sick, I didn't feel sick. It really was awesome."[33]

There were events and experiences like that all the time, many producing stories of the energetic, adventurous governor at work. She flew through a mid-air refueling, drove a snowplow through a blizzard, visited with firefighters during forest blazes, flew in a Cobra helicopter, piloted a Huey copter—under the watchful eye of pilots—and sailed through a gale on Barnegat Bay on an expedition to promote fishing.

"There's a whole litany of these things," John Whitman said to her months later, while they were relaxing in a Washington, D.C., hotel. "You went canoeing and turned over the canoes."

"I didn't turn over the canoe, everyone else turned over their canoe," she retorted.

"One of the things that I worry about is that she'll accept anyone's challenge to do anything, if it has to do with somebody in the state doing something. She won't go bungee-jumping, but other than that . . . ," John said. He had joined her on the sailing trip but stayed home for most others—including the F-16 flight.

"It's a sore subject, don't bring that up," Governor Whitman joked. "He hadn't received his [federal security] clearance. We

122

don't pull strings, that's how dead honest we are as an administration. I haven't pulled the strings to get him in."[34]

The down-to-earth style, the public relations outreach efforts, the national television appearances, the theater of the inaugural tax-cut announcement, the novelty of a woman chief executive—all these elements of her image combined to produce high marks from New Jerseyans in the first round of opinion surveys after she took office. An Eagleton/*Star-Ledger* poll in late February found that 36 percent of residents had a favorable impression of Whitman, compared to only 11 percent who disliked the governor, a ratio of more than three to one. An *Asbury Park Press* poll found a similar ratio, with 61 percent approving of her performance and 16 percent giving her poor marks. Large numbers of voters in both polls said they did not yet know enough about the governor's programs to offer an opinion; the *Press* poll also found that many were skeptical of the planned 30 percent tax cut.

Voters clearly liked her, if not necessarily her policies. As her popularity grew, her television appearances grew more frequent and in turn reinforced her image. She appeared on newscasts marking her 100th day in office, on Charlie Rose's PBS interview show, on a televised joint call-in broadcast with New York mayor Rudy Giuliani, and on numerous network interviews. The telecast of the March 15 budget address helped Whitman explain her program directly to thousands of viewers without the interfering analysis of reporters. A month later, on April 15, unofficially regarded as National Tax Day, Whitman and Bill Weld hosted a National Policy Forum—essentially a two-hour GOP propaganda program—that was broadcast nationally over cable television systems. The broadcast was boring at best, but it solidified her place in the top tier of Republican leaders.

Whitman understood, "better than any politician in New Jersey I've seen, how to use TV. . . . Not only is she getting greater exposure, she's also getting a sound bite on the eleven o'clock news," said Thomas O'Neil, a lobbyist and longtime Democratic official.[35]

"She always had a very good television presence. Some people have that and some people don't. It's not because of anything in particular, it's just something that happens," Golden said. "Her interests, her grasp of the issues, all of that comes through. And she's very comfortable at it. The camera—you've heard the expression applied to actors and actresses—the camera loves her. . . . Somehow on the tube she is gubernatorial, she is sincere, her sense of humor comes through."[36]

Mike Murphy, her media adviser, had coached her on camera angles and the medium's other technical aspects. She repeatedly rehearsed speeches slated to be broadcast, such as the inaugural and budget addresses, to get the feel of the TelePrompTer's multiple mirrored screens. Mike Heid supervised the technical details and the complicated scheduling of her radio and local television appearances; on newsworthy days, Whitman often squeezed in half a dozen live chats with New York and Philadelphia television anchors during evening drive-time broadcasts. As she sat in a straight-backed chair in the outer office, camera crews rapidly set up and then tore down their equipment, one after another.

"Other than learning how to talk into a camera lens with nobody else around and looking engaged and warm and speaking to the person whose voice is disembodied in my ear, it's pretty straightforward. . . . It's me and the camera and the person who's asking the question," Whitman said.[37]

She didn't like television's time-limited format or its requirement to explain problems or solutions in a sound bite. She wanted to provide detailed explanations—impossible in an interview that might last two minutes. "It's very difficult, and it also makes it difficult to problem-solve in one sense, because people want to hear a very complicated issue presented in fifteen seconds, which you really can't do, so you have to simplify it. And then people tend to think, 'Well, that's it, it's that simple right there.' You've defined it in fifteen seconds, so how can it be that difficult to solve? And it kind of feeds on itself. We are a society that expects quick fixes. We do expect, you know, simple answers to complex problems because we're used to that kind of can-do attitude of the United States. But partly, in order to get people's attention, at least in political terms, you have to talk and boil everything down to a very concise sentence or two to get their attention."[38]

As part of his role in planning special events, Keith Nahigian worked to enhance Whitman's visual image for still photographers and television crews. Whitman was more telegenic than photogenic, remarking in an interview that "there is no such thing as a good picture of me."[39] Nahigian was young and ambitious but cared little about the details of the budget plan or Whitman's relations with the teachers' union. Instead, with Golden's oversight, he concentrated on ensuring that Whitman looked good on all cameras at all times, focusing on little details such as the number of microphones on Whitman's podium. For scheduled appearances, he insisted on just one microphone; a jungle of mikes with TV and radio logos would clutter the picture and distract viewers' attention from Whitman. And there were always colors to worry about. A blue dress on David Brinkley's ABC News program, for example, could make her disappear against the set's blue backdrop.

"You have to think ahead. It's hard with a female candidate or governor. Males you don't have to worry about anything. Females you do. It's a TV world. . . . Every TV camera is 250,000 people. So if there's four video cameras back there, that's a million people. She's speaking to a million people with this one shot. So you better make sure everything looks good here," Nahigian said.[40]

Many voters, however, did not need network broadcasts or newspaper critiques to form an impression about their new governor. For months, she had been wowing crowds at town meetings and virtually every other appearance. At dinner events, she regularly walked back to the kitchen to shake the hands of cooks and waiters; at public functions, she insisted on saying hello to police officers working overtime to provide security.

Her outreach efforts were a result of Whitman's instinct, her political common sense, and lessons learned from Jim Florio's mistakes. The widespread anger at his 1990 tax hikes came only partially from the actual tax hike; many voters never paid any additional income taxes. They resented what they saw as Florio's arrogance in refusing to explain his tax increases to the public. Veteran political pundits understood the extent of Florio's self-inflicted damage and told the reporters that part of Whitman's success—aside from the charisma that appealed so strongly to voters—came from her determination not to repeat Florio's failures.

"At the least, New Jerseyans will say, 'She tried to explain her position and she listened to people who had questions and complaints,' " Rebovich explained.[41]

"In terms of communicating with the general public, she has shown a lot of political savvy," said Clifford Zukin, an Eagleton professor. "It's not yet clear what she wants to do, what her agenda is. But her message is simple and it's getting through."[42]

Whitman's outreach efforts took many forms. With Debbie Poritz, her attorney general, she toured the state's youth detention centers, talking to inmates as part of a review of the state's ailing juvenile justice system. In Trenton, she presided at more than a dozen roundtables with experts on topics ranging from transportation and business concerns to health-care reform and welfare. Most helped Whitman learn about state issues or communicate her goals and visions. Several meetings also produced tangible results, such as Whitman's decision on the advice of thirty environmentalists and industry officials to halt the awarding of environmental research contracts to out-of-state schools.

"Did we get a good listen? Yes," said Marie Curtis, head of the New Jersey Environmental Lobby. "She was unique in that. She did not interject her own ideas and opinions. She listened to everyone. Except once, when people complained about the situation with the research money. She asked what it would take to change that, and people said, 'a word from you.' She turned to (Environmental Commissioner Robert) Shinn and said, 'that's the word.' "[43]

Taxpayers were also urged to help Whitman cut the budget by attending a town meeting or writing or calling with ideas for savings through a program she called Your Tax Dollars. While some suggestions—such as serving prisoners meat collected from deer killed on state highways or establishing tax deductions for pets—

were simply absurd, other sound ideas, such as a suggested audit of the state's telephone bills and elimination of duplicate health-care coverage for husbands and wives both employed by the state were considered. Democrats called her outreach effort a public relations gimmick, noting that only a minuscule portion of a $15 billion budget could be reduced by taxpayers' suggestions.

Yet no one disputed the success of Your Tax Dollars in enhancing support for Whitman's tax-cut policies. Columnist Steve Adubato, after hosting a televised forum with Whitman, wrote that the audience left with a very different attitude about the new governor. "She shows her sense of humor, avoids making any commitments on a potentially controversial issue, and gets points for asking average folks their opinions on what to do. . . . How much does all of this warm and fuzzy stuff count? Listen to Jim, a cop and graduate student from Plainsboro: 'Even the people who tried to stick it to her about their program possibly being cut came away satisfied and with a smile. She didn't give us a lot of meat, but was saying to people, 'I'm going to listen.' That matters.' "[44]

The public relations campaign also helped Whitman solidify support among wary Republican legislators for the first 5 percent income-tax cut. The senate, led by the cautious Don DiFrancesco, would be a far more formidable hurdle than the assembly, where few Republicans defied Chuck Haytaian. Many members of DiFrancesco's caucus insisted on knowing how Whitman planned to pay for the cut, a request they viewed as very reasonable. He led a delegation of twenty-four Republicans; with twenty-one votes needed for passage, he could not afford to lose more than three votes on any issue. Legislators, sensitive to their constituents' feelings, also wondered whether they should be trying to lower property taxes instead of income taxes, especially after both the *Asbury Park Press* and Eagleton/*Star-Ledger* polls found that more residents wanted property tax cuts rather than income-tax rate reductions.

From an economic perspective, Steve Forbes and Larry Kudlow remained convinced that the income-tax cuts offered the best chance to bolster the state's lagging business environment. They wanted New Jersey to compete with the Sun Belt states for new business, but the state was not even competitive in the Northeast. Even with the initial income-tax cut, the state's top rate would be 6.65 percent, far above that of many of its neighbors.

"Just take a look at Pennsylvania, where the business tax is worse than New Jersey's and probably as bad as New York's. But companies are moving there anyway and Pennsylvania is doing better than we are. Why? Because its top income-tax rate is 2.8 percent," Forbes said.[45]

Trying to keep their caucus unified, senate leaders upstaged Whitman and their assembly counterparts by coming up with their own plan for paying for the cuts, drawing on surplus funds in the budget for the current fiscal year, which would end June 30. DiFrancesco refused to criticize either Haytaian or Whitman for pushing a tax cut they might not be able to pay for, telling reporters, "Don't get me into any more trouble than I'm in now. . . . We just think it would be speculative if we just proposed cutting taxes today without telling you that we are not going to affect school aid, we are not going to affect municipal aid, we are not going to affect property taxes. . . . We could not stand here today and propose that we eliminate $285 million without telling you that it can be funded through a process in the budget as it exists today."[46]

The plan, which eventually formed the basis for financing the first cuts, undercut most remaining opposition. Despite any qualms, most Republicans knew they would vote for the bill when it reached the assembly and senate floors. After years of ridiculing Florio's 1990 increases, they could hardly oppose a tax cut, and they were leery of rejecting Whitman's top priority in her first weeks in office. They'd be much tougher, they promised each other, in scrutinizing the full budget Whitman would unveil March 15.

The assembly vote came first, with many Democrats joining the GOP in passing the bill. It was an easy decision for the Democrats: at this early stage, they could vote for tax cuts but blame

Whitman if the budget reductions caused too much pain—or any property tax hikes.

"We are taking her at her word that she can incorporate this tax cut without hurting state aid to municipalities and education so property tax increases can be avoided," Joe Doria, the assembly minority leader, said.[47]

The senate followed the lower house's lead three days later and passed the cut by a wide margin, again with substantial Democratic support. The bill's signing ceremony in the ornate assembly chamber produced the expected bevy of Republicans congratulating each other and jockeying for position in front of a dozen television cameras recording the brief event. Despite a noticeable absence of Democrats and any real news beyond the expected ceremony, the day prompted a series of flattering headlines for the governor.

The *Trenton Times,* the leading newspaper in the state's capital city, proclaimed, TRIUMPHANT WHITMAN MAKES TAX CUT OFFICIAL,[48] with two large front-page pictures. The *Asbury Park Press* headline said, TAX CUT WILL GO DOWN IN HISTORY.[49] The *Atlantic City Press* stated, WHITMAN STARTS TO MAKE GOOD ON CAMPAIGN'S INCOME TAX PLEDGE.[50]

Yet the celebration was somewhat restrained by Whitman's refusal to discuss spending cuts or reveal how she would close the huge revenue gap in the upcoming budget. She was partially motivated by a fear that the news would leak before her budget address. There was also a simpler reason: it just wasn't finished. Whitman, state treasurer Brian Clymer, and their top staffers had less than two months between the inauguration and March 15 to decipher Florio's current budget, determine their own priorities, select programs to cut, and find revenues to close the widely anticipated structural deficit. Every incoming governor had trouble with the schedule, but the difficult transition—and the Florio team's understandable disregard for the upcoming budget—complicated the process.

"It's almost an impossible task when you first come in to work on your first budget because most of the budget that's in place is not yours. It's somebody else's already far down the road and you have a couple of months to sort all through it and make it into some kind of policy document. And we tried to do that," said Jane Kenny, Whitman's policy chief. "We had to do things very quickly."[51]

They didn't like what they found. Florio's proactive, big-government approach clashed with Whitman's repeated calls for "smaller, smarter government." Florio, like many chief executives on every government level, had relied heavily on one-time, non-recurring revenues in his budget, forcing the Whitman team to replace them with tax increases, more one-shot fixes, or spending reductions.

The budget's sheer size also created difficulties. With a $15 billion budget and more than 66,000 workers, New Jersey was larger than most *Fortune* 500 firms. Besides the long list of cabinet departments, the state had dozens of autonomous or semi-independent authorities, boards, and commissions with budgets tied into the state's spending plan, including the massive Port Authority operation.

"You know, you couldn't get your hands around it, and you were uncovering things all the time," Whitman said. "You were uncovering fiscal practices that just were not good and sound ones, and we were going to have to make some changes. We were going to have a tax increase in this state if half of the promises that we found had been made were actually carried out. It was just going to have happened. And it was hard because everybody saw it as being my budget but it really wasn't my budget."[52]

The built-in obstacles were formidable. The state constitution required a balanced budget by July 1. The federal government, as well as many state governments, such as those of New York and California, regularly ignored deadlines and operated without a budget, but most experts thought that practice would be illegal in New Jersey. No governor had ever tested the law, and Whitman had no plans to be the first.

The state also faced an April court deadline to absorb into its prison system thousands of prisoners housed in overcrowded county jails, or begin paying sharply increased rates for their daily

The populist touch of campaigning by bus was a hit with New Jersey voters in 1993.

Candidate Whitman makes a point while debating New Jersey governor Jim Florio in October 1993.

Talking on the air with controversial talk-radio host Bob Grant on WABC-AM in February 1993. Whitman would later repudiate Grant and criticize his divisive tone.

Whitman reading *The Little Engine That Could* to a group of children at a Toms River child-care center. Many saw this story as a metaphor for Whitman's determination.

Whitman with her adviser Hazel Gluck in October 1993. The two women would do much to challenge the "old boy" network in Trenton.

Campaign advisers Lyn Nofziger (*left*) and Ed Rollins.

Rollins's post-election claims to have paid money to suppress the African-American vote cast the shadow of racism over Whitman's gubernatorial victory and created her first major crisis.

Whitman explaining her bold tax-cutting budget at her inauguration day press conference on January 18, 1994. State Treasurer Brian Clymer is behind her.

With the possible exception of jogging, Whitman is very competitive in almost every recreational sport.

John Whitman gives his wife a hand during a vacation on the Jersey shore in August 1994.

With her children, Kate and Taylor, during a party in October 1994 at Drumthwacket, the official governor's residence

Joking with former New Jersey governors Tom Kean (*center*) and Brendan T. Byrne

Her ability to empathize with victims of the gas pipeline explosion in Edison in March 1994 convinced many people that Christie Whitman was a different kind of governor.

food and board. Interest payments for bonds issued by the Florio administration were scheduled to triple in the next year, and the state supreme court was considering a decade-long challenge to the legislature's method of dividing money among poor, wealthy, and middle-class school systems. A superior court judge had already ruled that the state needed to give urban districts an additional $450 million to close the gap between city and suburban schools; most state officials expected the supreme court to uphold the order.

Looming above everything else was the question of a second tax cut. Reporters and columnists openly speculated that Whitman would contend that the first retroactive cut took her off the hook for another reduction in 1994. She had an ally in the difference between the regular calendar and the state's fiscal year—which ran from July 1 to June 30—that was little understood by most voters. A 5 percent tax cut spread through all of 1994 would give taxpayers the same financial boost for the year as a 10 percent tax cut that began July 1, enabling Whitman to claim she had kept the first part of her promise.

From a political standpoint, this made sense. Republican lawmakers openly balked at the prospect of cutting favorite programs, especially local aid that could validate the Democrats' warning about property taxes. Given the other budget problems, she could credibly claim that the first tax cut had been accomplished and that a second was targeted for 1995. Many also believed that five years of working on Somerset County budgets could not substitute for the hands-on expertise needed at the state level. Whitman had improved her once-superficial grasp of macroeconomics, a problem while trying to justify the tax cuts seven months earlier, but that did not mean she could find billions of dollars in hidden cash or wasteful spending.

The staffers closest to Whitman—Jane Kenny, chief of staff Judy Shaw, and chief counsel Peter Verniero—had also never produced a state budget, and Clymer was a transportation expert who knew little about New Jersey. Jim Florio had served in Congress and the state legislature, and Tom Kean had been assembly speaker, yet neither had been able to cut taxes. Indeed, income taxes went up in the first year of each man's term. So, the reporters asked, how could Whitman do it?

"I was surprised that people . . . were [as] surprised as they were that I was going to try, that I was committed to it," Whitman said. "I definitely wanted to do 10 [percent]. . . . My sense of it is, we needed to do it as fast as we could do it reasonably because the political will to do it was not going to last forever. Because you do come to a point, there is no question of it, that when you reduce revenues, you've got to reduce expenditures. We should, and I believe that we should be reducing expenditures anyway, but it does certainly put a lid on things. Everybody was going to see that, and the choices are difficult because there's a case to be made for almost any and every program. . . . I was determined to get to the 30. I wasn't sure we were going to get to the 30, but I certainly wanted to get the 10 there so we'd have 15 [percent total]. . . . My intent always was to get to the 30, no question about it, but I just wasn't sure we'd be able to make it."[53]

Budget meetings, usually shrouded in secrecy, began immediately after the inaugural. Clymer brought his top staffers and number crunchers from the Office of Management and Budget. The staff troika, plus Golden and Michael Torpey, Verniero's chief deputy, sat in on most meetings, though the economic kitchen cabinet—Forbes, Kudlow, and John Whitman—avoided the statehouse. After resigning in early March from the investment firm of Bear Sterns and starting a new job as economics editor with *National Review* magazine, Kudlow was preparing to go public about his long battle with drugs and alcohol, and Forbes was running his magazine and fighting for conservative economic causes. Each day reporters maintained their surveillance of Whitman's office—there were only so many entrances—waiting for one of the three to appear.

"We all got banned from Trenton really for just that reason," said John Whitman. "If you found all of us sort of sneaking around in the corridors, it would have reinforced this view that there was a cabal in the back room who was running things. So we actually did it on purpose. We kept everybody out of there."[54]

Away from the statehouse, Forbes provided a long-term perspective. At Whitman's request, Clymer occasionally briefed him on their progress. "He was very useful in bringing that outside perspective, some of that New York, Wall Street perspective, the big business perspective. He'd look at it and put it in a context of what was happening nationally, the trends that were happening. It was a good way to benchmark our progress."[55]

The meetings went seven days a week, often past midnight, and always behind tightly closed doors, frustrating reporters and infuriating GOP legislators. The lawmakers had automatically assumed they would be part of the planning process; a few even were forced to cancel private meetings they had scheduled to give contributors a preview of Whitman's plans.

If no one was sure what to expect from Whitman, Clymer was a total mystery. The secrecy was okay with him. With only two months to learn the state, analyze its financial problems, and fulfill the long list of Whitman promises in a balanced budget, the prospect of nosy reporters and antsy lawmakers parading through his office carried little appeal.

"There's a time and a place for everything. This is her budget," Clymer said. "If you're trying to bring a budget to closure, and you're starting to put out major elements of the budget, then what you're doing is giving one special-interest group versus another the opportunity to have a pre-budget shot at what the recommendation is going to be. And I don't think it benefits anybody when you get down to the last couple of weeks to try to close the budget while you've got open negotiations going on."[56]

Rumors about impending cuts produced quick responses from the affected groups. The only figure publicly mentioned—a potential 13 percent cut in higher education appropriations—sent college presidents scurrying to protect their funding through a public relations campaign. Administration officials quickly claimed that the proposed cut was a worst-case scenario and illustrative of why they refused to release information.

"It's not a question of hiding anything from them. It's just that we've seen what's happened already, with one working document getting out there and everybody getting panicked that this in fact, this is what's going to happen, and they react to that," Whitman said.[57]

"The fact that I didn't tell anybody, that we were able to keep it a secret, I think that surprised a lot of people. It was a bit like the inaugural address with the 5 percent retroactive [tax cut]. We kept that under wraps too, for a real reason. We wanted the surprise factor," Whitman said on another occasion. "It's not that I like sneaking up on people. There are just times—on an issue that's very important to me or to the administration—I do want that opportunity to present it in the context in which I would like to see it."[58]

She knew that the Republican legislators resented being excluded, but she was tired of hearing their complaints that the tax cut could not be done. The budget speech, for the first time in history, would be broadcast in prime time, over major television stations. Until then, everyone—especially the lawmakers—would have to be patient.

"You can say we sandbagged them a little bit," she said. "And maybe we did."[59]

8

Tax Cut II

On a national ticket she could help Republicans where they particularly need help. . . . Whitman is making waves and Republicans nationally are taking notice.

—George Will, *Newsweek* columnist and ABC News analyst, April 2, 1994

FOR GENERATIONS, STATE BUDGET ADDRESSES—IN TRENTON AND most other state capitals—traditionally have been largely colorless, government-by-the-numbers affairs. Legislators feign interest as they sit through the speech, applauding on cue if they are in the governor's party. After all, lawmakers usually know most of the highlights, and the budget's line-by-line details are not discussed in the speech anyway. Typically, only professional politicians or lobbyists watch on television, if the speech is televised at all.

Whitman's first budget address, on the night of March 15, 1994, promised to be different. It was more than the decision of

WWOR-TV, a national cable superstation, to broadcast the speech in prime time or the still-novel experience of watching a female governor in action. In the statehouse assembly chamber, a range of emotions—anticipation, giddiness, frustration—ran through the crowd. In contrast to the ho-hum atmosphere of past years, there was a sense of excitement and urgency.

Republican lawmakers were ecstatic after hearing last-minute confirmations that Whitman planned another income-tax cut. Anxious reporters constantly glanced at their watches, knowing every moment drew them closer to deadline. Traditionally, budget addresses began at 2:00 P.M., but Whitman's 8:00 P.M. address would leave many reporters with very little time to decipher the budget for their audience. A handful of people, notably Ed Goldberg, the higher education chancellor, worked to hide their anger. Whitman's staff waited until just before 6:00 P.M. to tell Goldberg that the budget eliminated his department. In six weeks of budget planning, no one had consulted him, largely to prevent his supporters from organizing opposition. The shutdown of the public advocate's department that represented taxpayers in utility and insurance-rate cases was also a surprise, though Republicans had complained for decades about lawsuits it filed against the government on behalf of taxpayers.

After the weeks of secrecy, Whitman was ready to move forward. Her hair was coiffed, done by Cindy, her regular hairdresser from the Far Hills shop called Express Yourself. She finished her customary prespeech snack of chocolate and bananas in her office just before walking over to the assembly chamber. The cabinet, her husband and brother, and her top aides were already seated in the gallery's front rows. Just after 8:00 P.M., the red light glowed on the camera perched in the assembly chamber's center row.

"I asked to give this speech at this time because you deserve to hear directly how your tax dollars are being spent," Whitman said.

"With this budget, we begin the process of remaking government. Of making the machinery of government smaller. Smarter. Faster. More responsive to you, and less costly. We have no other choice. Taxes in New Jersey—the cost of running the machinery of government—are too high. High taxes drive jobs out of New Jersey and discourage new businesses from coming in. They make it hard for young families to buy homes and for senior citizens to keep them. They force our children to look for jobs and opportunities far away from their home."

She laid out the second round of tax cuts, calling for another 10 percent reduction for families with taxable incomes under $80,000 and smaller cuts for residents in higher income brackets. The cuts, if approved by lawmakers, would boost the total reduction to 15 percent for most families starting January 1, 1995.

"Make no mistake: I will call for a third tax cut next year. For democracy to work, those who ask for your vote must keep their promises. I will keep mine," she said.

"Not everyone will be happy with this budget. You will hear complaints about particular cuts, questions about why I kept my promise to cut taxes. But tax cut or no tax cut, we would have had to cut spending this year. . . . With this budget, we must stop spending more than we take in."

The tax cuts had their price. About six hundred workers would be laid off. Eleven hundred more jobs would be lost through attrition and the spin-off of state-run day care centers to nonprofit agencies. Some cuts, notably the elimination of the two cabinet departments, shocked much of the audience. New Jersey Network cameramen and technicians televising the speech listened as Whitman talked about a $2 million funding cutback that could lead to their own dismissals.

"Speaking of better ways to spend our money, public television cannot truly be independent as long as it is funded by government dollars. With this budget, we begin a two-year transition to making New Jersey Network financially and politically independent, like its sister stations in New York and Philadelphia. Government ownership of the media went out with *Pravda*."

With a few exceptions, state and municipal aid levels would not change, avoiding the widely feared deep cutbacks but preventing towns and school systems from keeping pace with inflation without property tax increases or spending cuts. The state would save close to $700 million by ending its traditional 2 percent subsidy for public-employee pensions and by changing the funding for employee health benefits to a pay-as-you-go-system. The biggest change—which would reduce costs by more than $2 billion during her first term—came from revisions in calculating how much money had to be set aside each year for pension benefits for public workers. In plain, straightforward language, Whitman conceded, "Yes, we will have to make tough choices about our spending priorities.

"But that's what a budget is. You make those choices every month when you pay your mortgage or rent, buy food, and pay your utility bills first. Then you see if you have enough money left over to go on vacation or out to the movies. I'm talking about common sense—a sense all too uncommon in government. You don't spend more money than you are taking in. Government shouldn't either."[1]

Supporters called it the finest speech of Whitman's brief career, blunt and simple, without lofty quotations or flowery rhetoric. Republicans milled around the assembly chamber after she left, happily slapping each other on the back and grinning at their political good fortune. Party leaders were full of sports clichés, with Don DiFrancesco calling the address a "home run" and Chuck Haytaian labeling it a "touchdown."[2]

Democrats, mindful of public anger over President Clinton's federal tax hikes and remembering the political pain of the Florio era, were at a loss. They disapproved of many of Whitman's proposals, especially the cabinet department shutdowns. Party leaders also worried that the bills for the pension changes would have to be paid by future generations and insisted that the budget guaranteed property tax hikes. Their immediate dilemma was simpler: they were surrounded by whooping, applauding Republicans, and criticizing a popular governor or the largest tax cut in state history wouldn't play well with voters.

For Senator Bernard Kenny, the ranking Democrat on the senate budget committee, there was little time to consider a response. A veteran legislator, articulate and well versed in the budget, he was overpowered by the emotions of his GOP colleagues as he went on the air to give the Democratic reaction to the speech.

"She looked great, she had everybody there, everybody was applauding at every other sentence. I was feeling very alone and isolated as I stood before NJN's cameras. I had to suck it up to make the case about why this was wrong, thinking, 'This is hard,' not because I didn't believe in what I was saying, but the political euphoria on the Republican side was so overwhelming that it was hard for me to make the case against it," he said.[3]

Democrats knew that they would have to pick their battles. They were badly outnumbered by Republicans in both houses, and criticizing a governor growing more popular each week would be difficult. They would have allies on several issues. Public workers would fight the pension changes, educators were angered by the treatment of Goldberg and the higher education department shutdown, and students feared pending tuition increases. Fighting the tax cuts, though, would probably be hopeless.

"I realized then that this thing's going to happen, that nothing's going to stop it," Kenny said. "Politics is a lot like the laws of nature, in that there are actions and reactions. I just had the feeling that there had to be a reaction to what happened [during Jim Florio's term] in the early nineties and that Governor Whitman was going to be the enforcer of that reaction. It had nothing to do with the policy side, it had to do with the law of nature and politics."[4]

Joe Doria, the top assembly Democrat, predicted that "she's going to be successful. But if it results in higher property taxes, I don't know how New Jersey's taxpayers gain. . . . Whitman will probably win some praise on Main Street tonight, but the litany of speculative fiscal maneuvers in her budget may jeopardize New Jersey's standing on Wall Street in months to come."[5]

News stories quickly noted Whitman's reliance on fiscal gimmicks, including hundreds of millions of dollars in one-time revenues and the reduced pension funding. Reporters also wrote about the budget's tactical blunders, such as predictions that the sale of two state-owned seaside marinas could fetch $7 million, or plans to use $15 million from a fund that paid medical bills of children with catastrophic illnesses and insufficient insurance coverage. The marinas' value, Clymer's staff eventually learned, was less than $1 million, prompting guffaws from Whitman's critics. DiFrancesco, who helped start the children's illness fund—which was widely hailed as one of the best efforts of New Jersey state government—adamantly refused to allow the raid on its surplus cash. Such errors came from inexperience or the rush to form a new budget: Clymer was unacquainted with DiFrancesco and his deep commitment to the children's program; the marina sale simply was a mistake made during a hurried planning process, he later admitted.

Yet none of the complaints remotely approached the ferocity of the feelings against Florio four years earlier. The anti-Florio demonstrators fought against tax hikes, an issue that every state resident seemed to take to heart. A smaller but vocal group of public employees fought Whitman's proposal, but their protests could be dismissed as self-interest. Once again, the only budget issue that touched everyone in New Jersey was income taxes—and under Whitman, they were going down.

Voters reading the headlines or watching television news summaries of the budget found out about the tax cuts but learned little of the budget's details. From the perspective of Whitman's public image, the coverage was magnificent, trumpeting lower taxes and a smaller state budget.

In an editorial, the *New York Times* noted: "Popular, yes. Prudent, no. . . . She has delivered what she promised New Jersey voters. She is cutting taxes without at the same time cutting school and municipal aid in a way that forces property tax increases."[6]

"It was supposed to have been a horror show," wrote Chris Mondics, the *Philadelphia Inquirer*'s Trenton bureau chief. Instead, the budget "had little in the way of apparent bloodshed. Apocalypse Now it wasn't." While Mondics did not ignore Whitman's efforts to employ gimmicks and one-shots, he realized they were maneuvers "that actuaries and accountants quibble over, but that hardly ignite raging political brushfires."[7]

For most New Jersey voters, and political leaders in Washington and elsewhere, the message was simple: Whitman pulled it off. The headlines and newscasts talked of record tax cuts. Only professional politicians or readers with a deep interest in government waded through stories heralding the dangers of underfunded pension accounts or debating whether the state should have a higher education department. As media studies had repeatedly proven, most readers relied on headlines, story leads, and pictures for their impressions.

"The things that she did well were easy to explain," said Mary Caffrey, a statehouse reporter. "The things that she did that were harmful were very difficult to explain. They were extremely complicated and difficult for the media to get their arms around."[8]

This phenomenon gave voters an impression that Whitman's first 100 days in office were a cause for celebration. Striving for balance, most newspapers and television stations noted that Whitman's early successes were more of style than of substance and that her fiscal policies were not examples of sound long-term planning.

But for voters reading headlines or looking at pictures—of Whitman smiling, Whitman waving, Whitman with little children—the 100-day analyses were just short of spectacular. David Wald, the *Star-Ledger*'s chief political reporter, penned a Sunday column titled GOVERNOR PROJECTS THE IMAGE OF WINNER 100 DAYS INTO HER TERM,"[9] while Jim Goodman's critique on the same day in the *Trenton Times* stated WHITMAN RIDING HIGH AFTER 100 DAYS.[10] The *Asbury Park Press* even ran a three-part series examining Whitman's promises and popularity. And the *New York Times* fell into line four weeks later with FOR WHITMAN, APPLAUSE IN THE EARLY ACTS.[11]

Even what was perhaps the most biting analysis, by the Associated Press's Ralph Siegel, conceded that Whitman was superb in dealing with media queries about her programs. The praise came first, before criticisms of Whitman's reluctance to talk about specifics or answer probing questions.

"Once a couple of papers start writing how great Christie is, then the other editors start asking, 'where's our story saying how great Christie is?' " noted Herb Jackson, now of the Asbury Park

Press.[12] Reporters bristled at suggestions that their critiques were the product of "pack journalism," common among political writers covering the same person over an extended period. However, many privately agreed with Steve Salmore's assessment that "it's more prestigious covering a popular governor. Your story is more likely to be on the front page, you're more likely to be asked for your opinion by other reporters. It has to have an impact, it's a more fun story."

Salmore also believed that the traditional focus of New Jersey newspapers on state government helped Whitman by giving stories about her successes more prominence than similar write-ups received in other states. "This is a small state. The major newspapers, the *Star-Ledger,* the *Asbury Park Press,* the *Bergen Record,* have no major cities. The *Star-Ledger*'s beat is not Newark, it's New Jersey, and the top [political] reporters for all these papers are in Trenton," Salmore explained. "The reporters covering [New York Governor George] Pataki are not the top reporters for the *New York Times.* They're in New York. For the Chicago papers, they're certainly not going to be [at the state capital] in Springfield."[13]

National political writers also jumped on the Whitman bandwagon; the clamor about the rookie Republican from New Jersey had not abated since her Washington debut. For George Will, the nationally syndicated conservative columnist and ABC News analyst, the growing praise warranted a trip to Trenton.

"A New Jersey governor is an American Caesar, the nation's strongest chief executive. Whitman is New Jersey's only statewide elected official, wielding line-item, conditional and absolute vetoes, so she has power commensurate with the clarity of her program," Will wrote upon his return. Her economic program, he said, "contrasts tellingly with the president's. And it could catapult her into Republican plans for defeating him."[14]

Back in Trenton, Will's prediction initially struck many as incredible. Yet other top Republicans also joined the chorus singing Whitman's praises and speculating about her prospects against the expected Democratic ticket of Clinton and Al Gore in 1996.

One voice came unexpectedly, almost from the grave. Richard

Nixon, a New Jersey resident for the final years of his life, died in late April. Whitman, who knew the Nixon family and had attended the Chapin school in New York with his daughter Tricia, flew to California for his funeral. "He was certainly right there for me in the Senate race and came forward when a lot of other people weren't and provided an extraordinary opportunity for me to access his knowledge," she said.[15]

Now, three weeks after his death, Nixon gave Whitman another boost. *New York Times* columnist William Safire, a former Nixon aide, wrote about a final talk with his onetime boss about the GOP's 1996 prospects. Nixon might not have been widely respected for his ethics, but no one could match his political acumen. " 'We should have a woman on the ticket. It doesn't do anything for the Democrats, but would do plenty for Republicans, . . . Has to be a governor. Executive experience,' " Safire recalled Nixon saying.

In his column, Safire wrote that Nixon "grinned at the thought of the New Jersey governor as vice-president."

"He liked the way Governor Whitman, daughter of a Republican state chairman, rose to a crisis: 'She showed great presence during the Rollins flap.' "

"What should she do?" Safire asked the former president.

" 'Get to New Jersey's issues—crime, welfare, drugs. Be progressive but conservative. Travel abroad to get New Jersey business; that's always a good excuse. Then come back and talk to the New York Economic Club.' "[16]

William Kristol, who was Dan Quayle's chief of staff before becoming a GOP conservative guru and publishing *The Weekly Standard,* took the prediction even further, proposing a 1996 "Dream Team" ticket of former Joint Chiefs of Staff chairman Colin Powell and Whitman.[17]

"Admirers drool over the qualities that would make her an ideal opposite number to Al Gore: same fortysomething vintage, the right gender—women's votes will be decisive—impressive work rate, telegenic skills," wrote the *Economist* magazine.[18]

In Washington, a political novelty-store chain, Political Americana, even began selling buttons proclaiming CHRISTIE WHITMAN—PRESIDENT 1996. "We have a sense who is salable and who isn't," said Mort Berkowitz, president of the New York firm that manufactured the buttons. "She's hot. People like her."[19]

Talk of a national role for Whitman was not limited to novelty shops. At a City Hall press conference with Whitman, New York mayor Rudolph Giuliani asked her, "Has the general called yet?"[20] PBS interviewer Charlie Rose asked her pointedly, "you've not looked in the mirror and said . . . 'President Whitman?' "[21] And a May conference in Plainsboro, attended by both Whitman and Powell, became the perfect setting for pictures and speculation about the Dream Team. "We were going over who calls whom when we decide to do this," Whitman quipped.[22] A few days later, Powell sent her a note with his telephone number.

Whitman kept insisting she was not interested in national office, but was always careful never to close the door on the possibility. Again and again, she stuck to the same script about how much she loved her job and about her commitment to New Jersey. Reporters kept up the pressure, and she kept up the denials, occasionally growing testy when the question was asked once too often.

"I have the best job in the world. It is a wonderful job to be governor, particularly the state of New Jersey. It's a great state. It's got all the problems that every other state has, but we get them a little faster and a little sooner because we're the most densely populated state in the union," she told Rose on PBS. "If we can solve the problems here, that can be a model for other people, but we've got to do it."

Rose didn't give up so easily. "So, if someone like Governor [Pete] Wilson from California, he gets reelected and then he become the nominee and says, 'Governor Whitman, I need you, it would be a great ticket.' You would tend to say, 'I've got unfinished business in New Jersey?' You'd sort of Sherman-like say, 'I don't want to be on the national ticket in 1996, thank you very much?' "

Again, the stock denial: "I want to do a job for New Jersey, and we've got a lot to do. We just started."[23]

Despite the constant denials, the nationwide attention rapidly became part of Whitman's political persona. Larry Sabato, a University of Virginia professor and a widely quoted pundit, said Whitman resonated "in a media age where symbols are everything. If someone fits the symbolic requirements, they are projected onto the national scene, whatever they have under the cover. . . . Is this the way it used to work? No. You'd have to serve as governor for a number of years and accomplish a good number of programs before you'd be considered."[24]

Everyone around Whitman understood the practical advantages in being touted for 1996: widespread exposure, greater prestige, increased credibility at home, and easier access to prominent figures in Washington and among the media elite. They also understood the political and media factors that had brought her so far, so fast. Still, they shook their heads in amazement.

Ironically, perhaps the most critical analysis of the press's love affair with Whitman came from her own husband. "There's a difference between form and substance, and what's missing is any substance from the political pundit's point of view," argued John Whitman. "How can you conceive of becoming the vice president or the president of the United States or anything like that when you've been a governor for a year, or two months . . . and you haven't held a major elected office before, and you haven't run some major corporation or been a general in the army?"

He scowled while pondering the power of pundits. While they had elevated his wife to the level of potential presidential contender, their unquestioned influence and the press's increasing dependence on them disturbed him.

"This is the fabrication of this new group of people who think they're a political elite, who were creating images. And all they're interested in is image as opposed to substance," he complained. "Billy Kristol's remarks . . . amounted to 'She'd look good on the ticket, or she would make us look good,' or something like that. No concept of whether it would be good for the country, or whether these people could manage their way out of a paper bag."[25]

To Dan Todd, competence mattered less than the political strengths that a vice-presidential candidate brought to the national ticket. Not that he thought Whitman couldn't do the job. "Let me be the old gray-haired cynic," he said. "The fact that she'd only been in the office for three months doesn't even figure. . . . It never would surprise me, whoever is the vice-presidential candidate."[26]

On one issue, the governor, her husband, her brother, and most senior aides shared the same sentiments: the vice-presidential speculation carried both risks and rewards. "It was a help because we were viable with our [federal] policy requests, with our input. We were certainly players. We were not like a typical freshman governor probably. . . . We felt we had an ear and that she could walk into a room and knew that she would be listened to, and so from that point of view, it was really good for New Jersey," Jane Kenny explained. The downside was that "it does make people not understand that we are very committed to this state, and that everything that we're doing is so we can leave a good legacy in the state."[27]

Whitman knew that the glow could not last and that the national media scrutiny had only begun. She realized that many potential candidates, such as Gary Hart and Joe Biden, had faded from the national scene largely because of intense press attention.

"Just wait until the national media gets hold of her. She needs to place a call to Geraldine Ferraro," Sabato said, recalling the former congresswoman who became the first woman on a major national ticket when she ran with Walter Mondale in 1984. Although Ronald Reagan's overwhelming reelection victory that fall had little to do with the harsh treatment given to Ferraro and her husband, Ferraro never recovered politically from the debacle. "The media will regurgitate the Rollins incident and rake it over seventeen ways till Sunday. Then they will go over her record and those early [negative] media stories will be pulled up," Sabato said.[28]

If there were complaints from voters about the national publicity, they did not register in polls of Whitman's popularity. New

Jerseyans enjoyed sharing her national prominence. No New Jerseyan had been president or vice president since Woodrow Wilson nearly eighty years before, but too many residents had heard the lines about living near highway exits or the mountains of garbage near the Meadowlands sports complex. To humorist Dave Barry, they lived in the "New Jersey Turnpike State." A little state pride—such as the glow of a nationally heralded political star—was very welcome.

On May 15, the first statewide poll after the vice-presidential speculation began found that 78 percent of voters approved of Whitman's performance, with 19 percent giving her negative marks. The *Asbury Park Press* survey noted a significant jump in Whitman's ratings since her budget address, with no major difference in the perspectives of Democrats and Republicans, men and women, or people of different ethnic backgrounds. Most also approved of her outreach efforts: 61 percent believed Whitman held the town meetings and other forums to stay in touch with voters, while 35 percent contended they were designed to produce free publicity.

"I'm always nervous, though, when you see numbers that high. There's always a great possibility for them to start going down," Whitman said.[29]

Democrats contended that most voters focused only on Whitman's image rather than on substance—or lack of it. "At this stage of an administration, style means a lot, and even I rate her excellent on style. As to substance, probably the fairest grade is incomplete," said B. Thomas "Tom" Byrne, the new Democratic state chairman.[30]

Democrats also took the talk about Whitman's future lightly, reminding reporters of similar speculation about other New Jerseyans in the past. Many top Democrats considered Bradley a leading contender for a national ticket before he almost lost to Whitman in 1990. Republicans had weighed a Tom Kean national candidacy in the late 1980s, and even Jim Florio was briefly mentioned as a possible contender before his tax program crashed around him.

"I've heard that with every person elected in New Jersey in the last twenty-five years," said Representative Robert Torricelli, a Democrat, who ran for the U.S. Senate in 1996. "When I worked for Bill Bradley, people said, 'Don't take long-term leases, because we'll be campaigning in New Hampshire.' . . . There are people in Trenton who are convinced that the nation revolves around it, like people once were convinced that they were at the center of a flat world." Torricelli, a wily politician, knew all about Whitman's attributes: "She's very personable. I've worked with her on a few issues and I like her. But her success or failure is not going to be based on whether people like her. She is in a very high-stakes gamble."[31]

The gamble was over Whitman's budget. Although Washington pundits cared little about the upcoming legislative debates, Torricelli and many other New Jersey politicians knew Whitman would have to struggle to get the budget approved intact—and a major loss could derail her national success story.

Whitman's high approval ratings only went so far when maneuvering through the statehouse's political minefields. It was little known outside Trenton, but Whitman had yet to charm her own legislators. It had happened before: Jimmy Carter was initially liked by voters but disliked on Capitol Hill. Ronald Reagan's success partially came from the ability of his first chief of staff, James Baker, to deal effectively with Congress. A rejection of Whitman's programs by Republican lawmakers in her own state could indicate to party leaders that she might not be ready for the big time after all.

The hard feelings, particularly between DiFrancesco's GOP senate caucus and the Whitman staff, had grown over a stretch of months, partially reflecting the differences between running a government and leading a state. First, many senators were angry over the surprises in both the inaugural and the budget addresses, especially the elimination of the Higher Education Department. Phone calls to Kenny, Verniero, or Shaw often went unreturned for days. Republican lawmakers' requests for assistance on items they considered routine—such as minor patronage appointments they expected to be rapidly filled—were often rejected. Despite Whitman's assurances that legislators were part of the budget process, she also refused to consider compromises in major decisions such as the Higher Education Department shutdown.

"It was a policy decision of mine, based on discussion prior to making the announcement. I did make that policy decision. That was what I was elected to do as a leader. I may not have all the answers on the best way to effect that change, but the change is going to happen," she said.[32]

Whitman, Shaw, and others in the inner circle were also sensitive—overly so, some felt—to sexist slights by legislators who were having difficulty adjusting to women running state government. At least a few lawmakers, on both sides of the aisle, still believed that Whitman was not up to the job—a belief that Whitman was well aware of and resented.

The consensus, Golden said, was "that she was going to be easy to push around. That she didn't have the experience. Tom Kean came out of the legislature, Jim Florio came out of Congress. They had been through the rough-and-tumble, and she was a Republican freeholder in Somerset County. That really isn't hard to do, get elected as a Republican in Somerset County. And there were some people [thinking], well, she hasn't been through this. She hasn't walked through the fire. And therefore, she's really not going to be that difficult to deal with."

Golden had worked in the statehouse long enough to recognize the legislators' doubts. While many feminists openly called him a chauvinist, he also realized that some lawmakers believed they could easily handle a female governor. Legislators, he said, were convinced that "we can get out of this, this woman is not going to stand and fight, this woman is not going to stand up when she has to."[33]

"It was difficult for a lot of men who were politicians for a long time to accept a woman," conceded John Bennett, the senate majority leader. "Frankly there were a lot of people that felt she would not have the capability of getting anything through the legislature, even though it was her own party. In both houses, it was male dominated, politicians who had been in office for a very long time."[34]

A few statehouse veterans, such as Kean, saw the tensions coming from the start. "I had an advantage that she doesn't have. I had been in the legislature for ten years. They were friends of mine, a number of them," Kean warned during Whitman's first hours in office.

"If there are any suspicions, if there are any feelings that either side is hiding stuff or not telling the truth or that they have their own agendas, separate and apart, that can be a very great problem. One of the top things the governor has got to do over the next two or three months is get to know the legislature, get to know them as people," Kean said.[35]

She made early outreach efforts to Democrats until GOP lawmakers protested their involvement, leaving the minority party cut out of any future decisions. Within a few weeks of the inauguration, however, Republicans started balking at not being any more involved than their Democratic colleagues.

"I would prefer that she be in the office on a legislative day and meet regularly with the legislative leadership," DiFrancesco said. "You've got to do that. Even if you don't agree on anything, you should do that. Face-to-face meetings are much better than no meetings, regardless of the outcome of the meeting. And I used to go into these meetings with Kean, and we'd have Democrats, we'd have Republicans. . . . She should do that."[36]

Whitman's frequent policy roundtables also generated resentment. Legislators felt shut out as they watched businessmen, environmentalists, academics, and even lobbyists regularly parade into Whitman's office. "They don't vote on bills, you know?" said DiFrancesco. "Certainly, she's very capable. But if you haven't sat in one of those chairs, it's hard to visualize, to think of what's the mentality of the legislator. Well, they liked to be talked to when somebody is asking for their vote."[37]

Many legislators felt ignored—especially Republicans who had been early Whitman supporters. Yet complaining publicly could be risky. In the assembly, Haytaian functioned as Whitman's floor manager and did not tolerate rebellion in his caucus. Senators realized that their constituents—especially in solidly Republican districts—would not sympathize with their complaints. There was a danger that their version of internal battles with Whitman would be viewed as insiders whining about access. So, most senators kept their feelings largely to themselves.

"Almost every senator resents [Whitman's] style of never schmoozing, never asking their opinion," said a veteran GOP lawmaker. Like several others, he was upset that the "front office" took weeks to respond to his request for a constituent to be given an unpaid seat on a minor state board. "When you go to them and ask can you get this person, for them it's minuscule, for the senator it's everything."[38]

"You should, generally speaking, either look that person in the eye and say, 'You got it,' or the next day call him back and say, 'We've taken care of this,'" DiFrancesco said. "That was not happening, and that's a mental thing. . . . Everybody has something they're concerned with. One guy might like to have a job for somebody. Another person might like his bill signed into law. But you have to know these people to know what's important to them. And you don't get to know them unless you talk to them."[39]

Everyone knew that the inexperience of the Whitman troika—Shaw, Verniero, and Kenny—caused many of the problems. With rare exceptions, such as Golden's return to the communications director slot, no one could come to the statehouse knowing how to run a governor's office. The very nature of the positions required on-the-job training, and a reasonable number of miscues were to be expected. The first chiefs of staff for Florio and Kean lasted less than a year, and both governors went through a slew of chief counsels.

"They were just feeling their way, and every administration feels its way in the first year. There is no administration that I have worked with that comes in and like that, snap of the finger, is on board riding high, everything is working well. I mean, it takes time," Haytaian said.[40]

Many of the troika's predecessors, however, had either known the legislators before taking their jobs or, in Trenton vernacular, "worked the hallways" to familiarize themselves with the legislature. Shaw and Verniero took a different approach to their jobs, focusing on managing the executive branch rather than schmoozing with the legislative branch. Many lawmakers contrasted Verniero with Robert DeCotiis, Florio's second chief counsel, who became a statehouse legend by constantly negotiating and cutting deals with the veto-proof GOP majorities. Verniero saw himself as Whitman's attorney rather than as a deal maker. His starched-collar, formal style also contrasted sharply with DeCotiis's gregarious, backslapping manner. Verniero had no intention of mimicking DeCotiis's style and quickly grew weary of the comparisons. He was too polite to complain to reporters, so he tried another tactic. "Hi, I'm Bob DeCotiis," Verniero told reporters, a grin spreading across his face.[41]

Shaw concentrated on administration rather than the office's political components and spent long hours on the road with Whitman, trying to get a better feel for the boss's style and priorities. They hadn't known each other very well before the transition. While the interaction helped their relationship, it often took Shaw out of the office's day-to-day flow. She was a self-admitted policy wonk trying to do a good job, even if that meant delaying decisions to make sure they were right. Like Kenny and Verniero, she had little interest in high-level Statehouse politics and hoped to leave that to others.

The problems were also exacerbated by Whitman's insistence on approving details of agreements with the legislature, as well as her system of three co-equal top staffers. Neither arrangement led to quick or simple decisions. For legislators, the setup marked a disturbing contrast to Florio's term, when they would negotiate with DeCotiis and arrive at a deal—or a decision to talk again that night over a fine Italian dinner in Trenton's Chambersburg district—before anyone left the room. Now they could leave a negotiating session without even an indication of what a final agreement might look like. On major decisions, all three top aides often became involved, routinely prolonging the process. Even advisers from the nonpartisan National Governors Association warned that the system probably wouldn't work.

Whitman understood that GOP legislators needed time to adjust to her management style. She realized that they were also exercising less power, after virtually controlling state government with a veto-proof majority during the final two years of Florio's term. Her understanding, however, could only go so far.

"We try to accommodate and be sensitive to their needs within the parameters of what I have defined as good government and what I think is the right kind of budget procedure. And we've eliminated some programs that were favorite programs of people on both sides of the aisle, because they didn't make sense or they weren't doing what they were supposed to do," Whitman said.

"You'll talk to some people who sound as if they've never been in this office, and they've never had anyone they wanted appointed," she continued. "We kept pretty careful check. We can tell you who they've recommended and how many of their recommendations have been appointed. We can tell them."[42]

Whitman's staff carried their own grudges and complaints, including that the legislators were being unfair. At Lorenzo's—Trenton's top restaurant for insider power meals—Kean's former top aides assured Shaw that the legislators' assertions of how much better they had been treated in Kean's day were exaggerated. Whitman aides were also angered when several Republican lawmakers took ideas developed by Whitman staffers and released them as their own proposals or tried to play the top aides off against each other. "If they didn't like the answer they got from me, they'd go to Peter. If they didn't like the answer they got from Peter, they'd go to Jane, or whoever, in whatever order. That took a lot of our time," Shaw said.[43]

However, Whitman had no plans to change the system or the staff. She had warned that the new administration would not conduct "business as usual"—and told legislators they would have to get used to a new approach. "When I go to them representing the governor on a point, they can take that to the bank that it's not going to change, that they can take me at my word that I'm speaking on the governor's behalf," Verniero said. "They would feel a whole [lot] less comfortable with that if they knew that I was swinging on a vine, flying without a net with her approval. . . . I would think that people outside of the governor's office would be very comfortable with our system because they would know, and hopefully they do know, that when we say something on the governor's behalf, we're speaking with her full authority behind it."[44]

Only a few stories about these squabbles were reported in the media, since most readers would consider it "inside baseball." The resentments, however, were real and threatened to disrupt her legislative agenda. Several initiatives that were important to Whitman—especially the Department of Higher Education shutdown—generated little interest in the legislature. The education community didn't want the plan approved, the *Star-Ledger* waged a campaign against it, and hardly anyone except Whitman would mind if it were rejected by resentful lawmakers.

DiFrancesco found it increasingly difficult to round up votes for Whitman, and had an equally hard time hiding his frustration with the front office's refusal to work with his caucus. "When I'm trying to get twenty-one votes for something that they want, I need action on things. I need this guy to get his answer. I need this guy to get his, or she's got to go to this fund-raiser and I have to have answers. So if it takes you three months to get your answer, you're so turned off it doesn't matter," DiFrancesco said. "There may be no logic to the whole thing, but you want that person's vote, you've got to deal with them. And they need to do better on that."[45]

9

Media Darling

Nearly two years after American voters punished George Bush for breaking his anti-tax pledge, Christine Todd Whitman, New Jersey's governor, is helping restore the Republicans' reputation as the tax-slashing party.

—*Boston Globe*, July 9, 1994

FOR ED GOLDBERG, WHITMAN'S PLAN TO CLOSE THE DEPARTMENT OF Higher Education marked an abrupt turnabout from the administration's very first days. Whitman had hailed him as a "strong leader" for quickly denouncing Khalid Muhammad's hate rhetoric and for creating standards for responding to bigoted speech on college campuses.[1] The assembly also passed a glowing resolution honoring Goldberg. Certainly, his place on the Whitman team appeared solid.

Then came March, and the governor's surprise announcement that his department would be eliminated. No part of Whitman's budget plan created more resentment inside the statehouse. The savings from closing the Higher Education Department and replacing it with a new commission of college presidents—about $4.6 million in the first year—was negligible in a $15 billion spending plan, but the message that Whitman was serious about her push for smaller, smarter government was clear.

"This is maybe what she had in mind when she said there would be no more business as usual," columnist Adrian Heffern wrote. "No wonder Democrats in the legislature are storming in protest and Whitman's fellow Republicans are having nervous twinges. Here's a department that took them nearly thirty years to build, and she's acting to reduce it overnight to a mere commission. It's shaking the foundations of their whole world."[2]

The solid opposition of educators and the hostility of GOP lawmakers threatened Whitman with her first legislative defeat. Don DiFrancesco and other party leaders gave the issue a low priority and knew most voters were not paying attention to it. They could retaliate against the months of apparent snubs by voting against the plan while still supporting the tax cut and budget, GOP legislators calculated. With the department's demise scheduled for July, a few legislators wondered if Whitman might capitulate, swapping concessions on higher education for guaranteed votes on the budget and tax cut.

Whitman tried damage control. She muzzled Goldberg by keeping him out of cabinet meetings and banning him from hearings on the shutdown plan. While she could not stop Goldberg from testifying as a member of the public, she kept him from speaking as an administration official. Whitman might be candid with reporters, but she would not tolerate public dissent within her administration. Staffers were also warned that leaks would be punishable by dismissal; several aides were grilled by senior staffers after stories appeared about the poor relationship between the troika and Republican lawmakers. While Whitman seldom became angry, aides said she was clearly annoyed by the negative stories.

The *Star-Ledger,* though, could not be silenced. The newspaper's veteran education writer, Robert Braun, believed dismantling the department would ruin the state college system by eliminating oversight and coordination between the different schools. The newspaper's longtime editor, Mort Pye, opposed Whitman's plan and gave Braun the freedom to focus on its flaws. Through much of the spring, the *Star-Ledger*'s staunch opposition to Whitman's proposal filled news stories, columns, and editorials.

"There is more vendetta than vision in the plan to destroy higher education oversight," Braun wrote, without identifying the vendetta's origin or target. "Not one credible, disinterested person of stature inside or outside higher education favors Gov. Christie Whitman's plan."[3]

Braun's stories regularly reached the front page, giving credibility and visibility to his contentions. To Whitman, they were extraordinarily one-sided, venerating Goldberg and ignoring her perspective. The *Star-Ledger* occasionally pushed for special causes—whether an annual Christmas charity drive or the construction of the Meadowlands sports complex—but few could recall the newspaper ever pushing a single issue for so long, so vehemently, and against the stance of an incumbent governor. For years, statehouse reporters had joked that the *Star-Ledger* viewed itself as an extension of the governor's office, routinely floating trial balloons or advancing gubernatorial causes. Whitman didn't play that game. Possibly, some speculated, Braun's stories were the newspaper's retaliation.

"You can sense the reporters who have an agenda, and who will absolutely take anything that is said or done by this administration and twist it or do whatever they have to do to make it fit their agenda. Whether the outcome is what they wanted or not, they will conveniently ignore. They will pick up one side, there's no question. And there are other reporters and papers that are more interested in getting a story and doing a story. That doesn't mean they are always complimentary. It doesn't mean that I always have wonderful editorials from those papers and those writers," Whitman said.

"At least I have a feeling that I'm being treated fairly. At least I have the opportunity to have whatever the program is reported for what it is, and then people can agree or disagree and take potshots. [To] my mind, that was always the difference between reporters and editorial writers. Reporters were supposed to report the story and the facts, and editorial writers were to give the opinions. And you see in some papers there's not much of a line between reporting and editorializing."[4]

The stakes for Whitman were enormous. If Braun's stories resonated with readers, the tenuous legislative support for her proposal might evaporate entirely. The *Star-Ledger* reached into seventeen of the state's twenty-one counties. It was also required reading in Trenton, where Braun was well known in the education community.

Reasoning with Braun appeared unlikely to help. He seldom called for Whitman's version of events anyway. Instead, Golden wanted Whitman to meet with Pye in Newark, telling her that "we have to get this thing straightened out."

"You're not going to get Mort on your side. He's so far exposed on this thing now that he's not going to change it now. But he has to know what our position is here. He has to know what our view is of his coverage. He has to know that. And you can't do it with a phone call," Golden told her.[5]

They took the extraordinary step of asking for a private session with Pye. Braun—who won a major journalism award that year, primarily for his coverage of the troubled Newark school system—did not come to the meeting. Pye appeared skeptical, telling Whitman that the *Star-Ledger* knew that the administration's stance on the Higher Education Department shutdown would not change—and that calling for comment to stories would yield the same answer.

Whitman recalled telling Pye, " 'Look, you've got to understand what our side to this is. There is another side.' That wasn't coming through the paper that there was another side. Did it make a difference? . . . It always helps a little bit. And I think it probably did temper things a bit. It's probably always useful to let your opinion be known. I don't tend to shout and pound the table, and that's not what we did," Whitman said.[6]

Many people close to Whitman did not want her to meet with reporters whose coverage they considered unfair. While they conceded that the coverage of her had improved since the campaign and that most reporters respected Whitman's privacy, to John Whitman the media still went too far. He would not tolerate coverage—no matter how positive—that went beyond the family's public life. While reporters were allowed on the farm, he insisted that the house stay off-limits to all journalists, without exception. He disliked giving interviews, although he occasionally granted requests from magazine writers or reporters who Golden felt would be fair in their coverage. He knew that as the state's First Husband, getting into angry confrontations with reporters was politically unwise. But he urged his wife—he often called her Chris—to ignore writers who stepped over the privacy line or consistently wrote stories he considered unfair. Don't call on them at press conferences, don't talk to them. Pretend they aren't there, he urged her.

"There are some people who, no matter what you do, were going to pan what you did. And from my point of view, after they did it four or five or six times, I kept saying to Chris and Carl, 'Well, just cut them off.' They'd say, 'No, we can't do that,'" John said.

He knew that he was inclined to anger and that the reporters would "often drive me beyond the bend. My style is not suited to . . . the political process. . . . I wouldn't put up with the games. But then nobody would elect me governor either."[7]

John was not alone in pushing an "us versus them" mentality. Several top staffers urged Whitman to stop being so accessible to the press and to rethink her policy of regularly granting all interviews. Within Whitman's inner circle a battle raged between advocates of accessibility and those who proposed a virtual news blackout.

Whitman never saw much of the coverage. Each morning, well before dawn, staffers assembled a file of clippings of articles about the state, the administration, and national policy and politics, distributed in brown folders to senior administration aides. The diligent clipping staff included every pertinent story, no matter how small or how far inside the newspaper. The system saved Whitman time but failed to give her an accurate impression of what voters saw, since most newspaper readers scanned front-page stories and skipped many inside pages. Jason Volk would often sift through the package for Whitman, reducing the number of stories from hundreds each day to dozens.

"Let's say there were fifty clips in that batch. If forty-nine of them were fine and one was critical, that's the one they'd say, 'See, this proves my point that they're just out to get you.' They played that card over and over," Golden said about staffers wanting Whitman to stop dealing with reporters.[8]

Whitman listened to the advice but never seriously considered following it, refusing to succumb to the emotional temptation. Judy Shaw called her a "flat line" in terms of keeping her emotions in check.[9] She rarely, if ever, displayed anger or joy in public. Some attributed this to her upbringing in a public and political environment; others, noting that John had a similar background, speculated that the self-control was a very personal quality. Either way, Whitman didn't plan on losing her temper over a reporter's story. The price was too high.

"If I were to do that as a female governor," Whitman pointed out, "a lot of [people would say], 'Aw, she can't take it.' If . . . I started to complain about bad press or people beating up on me, it would be like the poor little woman whining, and I'm sensitive to that. . . . I don't let it get under my skin. . . . If you start responding emotionally every time you get mad at a question, then the emotions will start to control you, and that's bad for decision making and then everything else. . . . The other side of it is, I always figure the media has the last word. It doesn't behoove me to get into a spitting contest with the media, because I will never have the last word in that. There's always one more line that can be written in a story, or one more something, and so it just isn't worth it. It's not my style, and I'd lose anyway."[10]

John prevailed in isolated instances. When the *Trentonian,* a Trenton tabloid featuring daily pinups, wrote a story criticizing the condition of a rental house the Whitmans owned, he went to the newspaper office to complain. But both Whitmans had to learn to live with what they considered "stupid questions," part of the cost of public life. After Whitman underwent laparoscopic surgery to remove an ovarian cyst in November 1995, a television reporter asked a surgeon to display the instrument he used to remove the noncancerous tumor. Moments later, another reporter asked whether the operation would prevent Whitman—who was forty-nine—from bearing more children.

"I don't think that was an irresponsible question. I think it was an unthinking question," John said. "Reporters are people too. If this reporter had thought for more than two seconds about it, he wouldn't have asked the question. It didn't strike me that it was asked maliciously. And everyone in the whole room knew it was stupid. But we all do stupid things from time to time. And that kind of thing doesn't bother me. The malicious stuff is what bothers me."[11]

Golden urged her to ignore the simplemindedness of some questions. He had been around long enough to know she would get questions that "are just remarkably stupid. I mean, there are reporters, the Nobel Prize for physics isn't in their future. It's just the way it is. I said, 'If you just want to smile, that's fine, but the worst thing you can do is show up a reporter in front of his colleagues. . . . They don't need you to say, "what a dumb question." They know it's dumb. You just answer it.' "[12]

Still, she was tempted to speak out. "There will be a time sometime in the future maybe where I will just finally say, 'That's the stupidest question I've ever heard, or the most insulting question.' I've come close on occasion. But it isn't worth it. It just isn't worth it."[13]

She had a few firm rules in dealing with reporters, whether radio or television, newspaper or magazine. No one received special treatment. Reporters she liked and trusted were given the same access and same answers as any who occasionally provoked John's anger. She would not give exclusive interviews or leak stories, and while her brother, her husband, and top aides occasionally spoke off the record, Whitman refused to do so.

"It's because of my father, because he said, 'It's not fair. . . . Reporters have to earn a living. They have to convince their editor every day that they've got something worth writing and having printed in the paper, and it's not fair to give them something off the record and ask them not to print it.' . . . So I've never done it," Whitman said, adding she would never want to be a reporter. "I wouldn't want to try to write a story every day that was meaningful and convince everybody that you had the right thing."[14]

Whitman's strengths with the media were her instinct and Golden's advice. He stood by her side at press conferences, cutting questions off after ten or fifteen minutes with a loud and emphatic "Thank you." Whitman would then turn around and walk the three feet to her office door, preventing reporters from asking follow-up questions—the so-called "second question" that the Associated Press's Ralph Siegel criticized her for ducking in his analysis of Whitman's first 100 days in office.

Most reporters felt that they didn't know Whitman very well and that she maintained an invisible wall between herself and them. Florio, near the end of his term, arranged a quiet, off-the-record dinner with his wife and a few reporters and their spouses, in a better-late-than-never effort to develop a rapport with the press corps. Despite suggestions from reporters to Golden that Whitman do something similar, she wasn't interested.

"I don't think she's open with any of us," Jim Goodman said, citing the national profiles of Whitman as evidence. "Look at these quotes. There's nothing there that she doesn't want said." Goodman, who had been around far longer than most other reporters, said he had never seen anyone more controlled in responding to the media or in relationships with the press. Her refusal to chat with reporters after the formal end of press conferences infuriated him. Even if Goodman could get near the governor, Volk would block his path. "People have gotten used to the idea that they can't talk to her, so they don't try. If you want to get to her like that, you have to plan it," Goodman said.[15]

Yet reporters with specific questions could often arrange a brief, private interview by checking with Golden. On out-of-town trips, Volk and Keith Nahigian would ensure that local reporters would get a few minutes each day with Whitman. "But it's a far cry from the day when I showed up at her farm and Dan Todd [and] John and Christie Whitman showed up to greet me. I get the sense that we're less crucial," Michael Aron said.[16]

Aron's farm visit—just a reporter and a camera crew—came during the campaign's early days, when Whitman needed media coverage. As governor, it took her a long time to accept that her every utterance would be reported and scrutinized—and that more and more reporters from major publications or networks wanted to talk to her.

"It wasn't that we were pushing her, it was they wanted to talk to her because she gave a different angle on a show. . . . She was fresh, she was different, and she wasn't a suit, so every single discussion that came up for every different show, it was 'See if you can get Whitman,' " Nahigian said.[17]

Whitman and Golden vehemently insisted that she always gave the same answers, whether to a national columnist or the Trenton reporters she saw every day. Indeed, the quotes were often similar. On some subjects, especially the tax cuts and the vice-presidential speculations, statehouse reporters saw that the direct quotes in the local and national stories were nearly identical.

Yet there was a major difference between the state and national coverage. National writers, whether from magazines or the networks, were almost invariably doing a single, one-time story. They had neither the time nor the space to look at every facet of her administration. The next week or the next month, they would move on to another subject. This approach almost ensured that their coverage and perspectives were superficial—and often very flattering. By contrast, reporters covering Whitman full-time had to give readers a far more thorough and in-depth explanation of both her achievements and failures. "The national press treats her differently than we do. They have a broader, more general view of her, and they treat her with more deference than we do. She's the darling of the national media," Dan Weissman of the *Star-Ledger* said.[18]

Both in New Jersey and around the country, Whitman's tax-cut plans prompted a large number of stories as the deadline for the budget's adoption drew closer. Statehouse reporters wrote about 25,000 government workers protesting the pension and health care changes in the statehouse plaza and about Democratic warnings that the changes could cost the state billions of dollars by the year 2008. In contrast, George Will, in an *Esquire* column about Whitman, did not mention a single criticism of the budget and tax program.

Many national stories also focused on Whitman as the leader of the national tax-cut movement, ignoring earlier efforts by other Republican governors. A front-page *Wall Street Journal* story about the growing effort to roll back state taxes typified the national coverage. Only Whitman was mentioned in the headline, and only her caricature appeared on the front page. Other governors with substantial tax-cutting programs—such as Michigan's John Engler and Massachusetts's William Weld—were cited in passing.

"Gov. Whitman is, in fact, in the vanguard of a kind of mini-revolution: the 1990s Republican tax revolt. Unlike the 1980s tax revolution promoted by Ronald Reagan, though, this one isn't being masterminded in Washington. It's breaking out in state-houses around the country," the *Journal* story said.[19] Only the last six paragraphs cited her budget's potential drawbacks.

Stories in other national publications followed the same pattern. A prominent *New York Times* story on the first day of the new budget year portrayed Whitman as the leader of the gubernatorial tax cutters, under a headline stating ONCE WHITMAN'S BUDGET PLAN WAS RIDICULED. NOW OTHER GOVERNORS FOLLOW HER LEAD. "Other governors have imitated Mrs. Whitman's politics and policies right down to the catch phrases," the *Times* wrote.[20]

George Will, in his late March column promoting Whitman for vice president, had compared her tax-cutting efforts to those of Ronald Reagan. By summer, the comparison became trendy. "Observers say Whitman's victory . . . has increased the pressure on conservative Republicans and some Democrats to retake the political heartland with a new wave of tax-cut pledges unseen since the days of Ronald Reagan," the *Boston Globe* wrote.[21]

Democrats tried to use the Reagan comparisons against her, hoping memories of the huge federal deficit accumulated in the 1980s would remind voters of the dangers of Whitman's program. "In her own way, she's the women's movement answer to Ronald Reagan. She's borrowing from the future, like public employees' pension funds, but they're going to be paid for one day by future taxpayers," said Bob Torricelli,[22] the New Jersey Democratic congressman.

"She's a very good salesperson," conceded Tom Byrne, the state Democratic chairman. "Where I have problems with her is the substance. Whitmanomics is Reaganomics brought to the state level. The parallels are pretty striking. Reagan transferred fiscal burdens to the states and when that ran out, he borrowed from the next generation by tapping the Social Security fund. Whitman is transferring fiscal burdens to municipalities and when that game runs out, she borrows from the next generation by tapping into the pension fund."[23]

Many political experts thought the Democratic strategy badly backfired and enhanced Whitman's national reputation. Regardless of the consequences of Reagan's fiscal policies, he was still beloved by tens of millions of voters who felt that Reagan symbolized the 1980s boom days and America's return to fundamental values. His eighty-fifth birthday, in February 1996, was treated as a major celebration by the media. "Even his political enemies could not dislike him," said actor Charlton Heston, a longtime Reagan friend.[24] Reagan and Whitman shared a common fiscal theme: cut taxes and shrink the size of government. Their philosophies were simple, straightforward, and easy for voters to understand, while the potential long-term consequences of their budgets were far more complex and diffuse. Other governors shared their economic vision as well, and Whitman knew that stories praising her as the leader of a tax-cutting revolution on the state level were misleading, and often wrong. She recognized that Weld, Engler, Wisconsin's Tommy Thompson, Arizona's Fife Symington, and others had made substantial strides in cutting taxes and spending before her election. Whitman credited them often, insisting she was part of a movement rather than its leader.

Within the national GOP establishment, Weld, Thompson, and Engler were major forces, frequently working with congressional leaders and lobbying for state interests on a range of issues. Weld became widely known for his strong advocacy of homosexual rights, achieving hero status in the gay and lesbian community. By 1995, Thompson chaired the National Governors Association, a powerful insider position, and Engler headed the Republican Governors Association.

For reporters writing about the surge of GOP tax-cutting governors, though, Whitman's saga was more interesting. "Obviously the fact that she was a woman and a very attractive personality played into it. She made a very strong and favorable impression. Even when she was quite new in office . . . she knew a lot. As long as you were willing to sit and listen, she could talk in substantive ways about the state budget, state programs, welfare reform ideas, etc. She was a very substantive person, beyond being this sort of political star that we all wrote about," said David Broder.[25]

She stood out as the only female governor in a sea of dark-suited men pushing significant cuts. The male governors tended to blend together, and their tax cuts were generally more complex.

"I felt a little awkward," Whitman said about receiving more notice than "these other people who had done a lot more than I had in terms of having been governor longer and seen programs through and made changes."[26]

While Whitman's program included a few smaller cuts, such as the elimination of income taxes for residents with a very low income, other states targeted several different major taxes, making the savings harder to quantify in a story lead or sound bite. A few states that cut local property taxes also increased sales or other taxes, complicating the bottom-line analysis further.

New Jersey Democrats still contended that Whitman's income tax cuts would yield little real savings if they resulted in higher property taxes. Feeling ignored, they often became emotional in their attempts to attract attention. "The governor has tried to pull the wool over people's eyes by telling them she'll put money in their pocket. The reality is she's putting money in one pocket by taking out more from the other pocket. Where I come from, we call that theft," said Ronald Rice, a Democratic state senator from Newark.[27]

Unfortunately for the Democrats, just as the pension fund reshuffling could not be easily explained in a headline or brief television report, their property-tax argument was hard for voters to understand. Millions of New Jersey residents did not recognize the direct link between state and local taxes. Voters never realized that Florio's huge state tax increase had largely stabilized local property tax rates or that the rapid growth of government under Tom Kean had partially caused the explosion in property taxes in the 1980s.

Democrats also suffered from a credibility problem. Whitman was fulfilling her promise to actually cut income taxes, while Democrats were warning about something that might or might not occur. Whitman kept telling taxpayers that their mayors and school boards were responsible for local tax increases—a claim that was far easier to understand than the Democratic efforts to link the different taxes. The legislature's votes on the income-tax cuts would also come before any property-tax hikes: local tax bills were scheduled to be mailed in July, weeks after the state budget adoption.

Yet Whitman realized her original proposal could not survive intact, given her troubles with Republican lawmakers, the battle against the Higher Education Department shutdown, the anger of public worker at the pension changes, and the Democratic focus on property taxes. A late compromise with GOP legislative leaders provided extra funds for local aid, delayed the end of the state's public employee pension contribution by one year, and eliminated the planned raid on the fund that paid bills for severely ill children. The changes would secure needed Republican votes without fundamentally altering the budget's overall structure.

Whitman also waged her own public relations campaign for the tax cuts, setting up a grassroots coalition led by Republican congressman Dick Zimmer and airing commercials on forty-nine radio stations paid for by the Republican state committee. "You elected me to make some tough decisions about cutting taxes and spending so we can get New Jersey moving again. . . . Some special interest groups are unhappy, but my plan puts the taxpayer first," Whitman said on the commercials.[28]

Republican senators grumbled that the administration had waited too long to negotiate specifics with them. With the vote margins on several bills still very narrow, Peter Verniero and Judy Shaw prowled statehouse hallways hunting for last-minute votes. The most likely converts were given private audiences with Whitman, who focused the charm she used with voters on the wavering Republican senators. "The same ability that she had to maintain high rankings in the polls, she had . . . as a communicator one-on-one. If she says, 'I need your vote on something,' it's hard to say no to her," said John Bennett, the senate majority leader.[29]

The bills easily passed in the assembly and narrowly squeaked by in the senate. The tax cut became law a week later in a setting designed primarily for photographers and television, at Perth Amboy's Proprietary House, the last standing colonial royal mansion. More than two hundred years earlier, William Franklin, the state's royal governor, was arrested at the site for opposing the Revolutionary War and the colonists' fight against British taxation. On a hot oppressively humid afternoon, children in woolen colonial garb and a man dressed as Franklin—in white wig and tights—watched Whitman try to compare her tax cut with the War for Independence.

"Every revolution forces each man and woman to choose sides. . . . In 1994, we have taken the taxpayers' side," she said. "Those who say we cannot cut taxes side with a government that has grown too big and spends too much. Last year, I promised to cut the income tax by 30 percent. Within a year of my inauguration . . . we are halfway there. . . . And make no mistake. We will cut taxes by 30 percent."[30]

The average weekly savings for a family with a taxable income of $60,000 would be less than five dollars per week, prompting Democratic charges that the cuts were not worth the risk of rising property taxes. But there was no clear proof yet that property taxes were rising.

"There was a real sort of reaction that yeah, maybe it isn't a huge sum of money, okay, but she kept her promise. And that really had an impact. People in this state, like people in this country, quite frankly, [have] become so accustomed to be[ing] misled, deceived perhaps, that they've gotten extraordinarily cynical," Golden said. "People say, 'Yeah, it doesn't make any difference who you vote for.' . . . And I think that her actions in the first six months did a lot to say, 'It doesn't have to be that way. You don't have to think that way about government. Yeah, we know you've been misled and deceived and all the rest. But I'm different. I'm going to do this differently. I promise you something, I'm going to do it.' "[31]

The efforts to spread the word about Whitman fell largely to Golden. He sifted through endless media requests, occasionally arranging a series of interviews for her in New York or Washington. In early July, less than a week after the tax-cut signing, she met in Washington with the *Los Angeles Times* bureau, discussing issues ranging from tax cuts to tolerance. The next day's headline, however, focused only on Whitman's belief that the party should drop its longtime opposition to abortion from its 1996 presidential platform.

In a story reprinted throughout the country via the *Los Angeles Times–Washington Post* News Service, the *Times* wrote that Whitman "called on the GOP" to abandon its abortion plank and warned of the increasing power of the party's conservative wing. "I would hope . . . there's going to be enough of a voice to get that plank knocked out of the platform entirely," she said in the interview. "It's not a partisan political issue, and it doesn't belong in a party platform. . . . People like the religious right . . . can only win in caucuses and . . . in conventions and platform committee meetings."[32]

Conservative leaders, she warned, could hurt the party's chances for victory if they repeated the right-wing tone of the 1992 convention at the 1996 gathering in San Diego. She had missed out on voting against the abortion plank in 1992; although she had attended the convention, Whitman wasn't a delegate. Maybe the party needed a repeat of Barry Goldwater's debacle in the 1964 campaign, Whitman theorized. She had worked for Nelson Rockefeller in the primaries that year and now remembered the lesson of Lyndon Johnson's landslide victory. "We've got to understand what it takes nationally and that's why I say it may take another year like 1964 to really convince people that extremism, as perceived or real, is not going to win. It cannot win nationally," she said.[33]

Whitman's views were well known in New Jersey, a predominantly pro-choice state where abortion was seldom a political issue. An entire generation of Garden State governors and U.S. senators from both parties had supported a woman's right to decide the matter for themselves. Whitman was too fresh on the national scene for her views on all issues to be widely known throughout the country, but neither the governor nor Golden expected that the *Los Angeles Times* would focus so strongly on her offhand comments.

Pro-life Republicans were furious. Congressman Christopher Smith, a veteran Garden State Republican, accused Whitman of encouraging "bigoted scare tactics."[34] In New Jersey and elsewhere, pro-life forces began organizing to protect what they saw as the heart of the GOP.

"Where has this woman been living for the past fourteen years? In a cave? The Republican party, under a fiercely pro-life traditional values president named Ronald Reagan, swamped this country in two elections. . . . His successor, George Bush, rolled to victory too on a pro-life platform. He lost the second term, not because of abortion, but because he betrayed a solemn tax pledge and because of a stagnant economy. I dare Christie Whitman to confront Ronald Reagan and denounce him as a religious right-wing extremist who cannot win a national election," columnist Ray Kerrison wrote in the *New York Post*. "Christie has erred seriously with her intemperate assault on people of faith. That's too bad. She launched her term with purpose, strength, good sense, and flair. Now she sounds like just another Upper West Side Democrat," Kerrison added.[35]

The pro-life furor increased when California's Republican governor, Pete Wilson, echoed Whitman's stance less than twenty-four hours after her *Los Angeles Times* interview. Wilson, who was facing a difficult reelection battle, paralleled Whitman on many issues. Although he raised taxes in his first year in office to close a massive deficit, Wilson shared Whitman's socially moderate, fiscally conservative philosophy. Political writers were already speculating that they might make an attractive 1996 ticket. They were also frequently grouped in stories with Weld, whose views were also similar, prompting discussions of the rise of the "three W's"—Whitman, Weld, and Wilson.

Wilson's support for Whitman's pro-choice stance increased the prospect that the GOP could split over the issue at the 1996 convention. For the pro-choice groups, Whitman appeared ideal as a national leader: prominent Republican women were rare, pro-choice Republican women were rarer, and a pro-choice Republican woman who was a potential vice president was almost too good to be true. "This opens her to a leadership position in the Republican party," said Roger Stone, a GOP consultant. "It is essential for the party to make a change if we are going to be viable in 1996."[36]

Whitman strongly favored taking abortion out of politics and ending the tendency of Republican conservatives to use abortion as a "litmus test" for evaluating candidates.[37] She became frustrated, however, with the rabid attention to her pro-choice stance, especially since she had said nothing new to spark the controversy.

"I'm concerned that that gets seen as my only role and only issue, and that's not true by a long shot. Am I comfortable with the position that I have on that issue? Absolutely. Do I feel that if there were to be a fight at the convention, would I be there as a spokesperson for those who would like to see more open language or no language on the issue? Absolutely yes, I would do that. Am I seeking to be the spokesperson for the pro-choice wing of the party? No, there are lots of spokespeople for that," Whitman said. "I always have a concern that, because I'm female and because I am pro-choice, I kind of get tagged as if that's my issue and that's my only issue. And obviously my concerns are broader than that. But I'm still not going to back away from what I feel on that issue."[38]

She also grew frustrated that reporters, more interested in the 1996 presidential horse race than the policy ramifications of her positions, insisted on linking her views with the vice-presidential speculation. Her position on abortion and other social issues—such as her support of affirmative action and homosexual rights—made her anathema to the conservative wing.

"The assumption was that she was trying to get on the national ticket, which was a false assumption to begin with," Golden said. "So if you accept the false assumption she's trying to get on the national ticket, then you buy into the theory that being pro-choice would keep her off the ticket. It sort of becomes circular.

"She never took the initiative," Golden went on. "She never went out and gave a speech in which she said, 'Here is where I stand on this issue, and here's what the party ought to do.' It was always in the context of questions, largely media questions, and it was always in the context of everything from the Christian right to the individual candidates like Dole or [Pat] Buchanan or Powell or somebody like that."[39]

She hoped the frenzy would slowly subside, but the timing of her *Los Angeles Times* interview—just before the National Governors Association summer meeting in Boston—precluded any chance she might quickly fade from the limelight. Coincidentally, magazine profiles of Whitman in *Esquire, Vogue,* and *Mirabella* were also published in mid-July, enhancing both her visibility around the country and the media's interest in her at the Boston conference.

Given the months-long planning schedules of monthly magazines, editors could not have foreseen that their stories would hit newsstands in a week that saw Whitman dominating newspapers' front pages. For their millions of readers around the country, the magazines offered the first in-depth look at Whitman. By any standard, their stories were flattering. George Will, in an *Esquire* issue about "Women We Love," compared her to former British prime minister Margaret Thatcher, "without all that abrasiveness."

"Actually, *love* is a bit strong," Will wrote. "As is well known, we conservatives are incapable of tender feelings, and anyway, conservatism teaches that love is a disproportionate response to things political. But I'll say this: I'm fond of Christine Todd Whitman, the governor of New Jersey, and not just because she kept her promise. (Said she'd cut taxes. Did. Retroactively. Remarkable.) Rather, what recommends her is her steely ability to cut to the heart of things. . . . Make that *mighty* fond.

"She is not only a woman, a biological fact," Will continued, "she is a lady, a social artifact. It is supposedly retrograde to remark about such things, but she is well born and bred and it shows. She has that certain diffidence and confidence that can come with the security of a comfortable upbringing. So she can say, with unfeigned indifference, 'They hate me anyway,' when asked about the opposition of the teachers' union to her support for Jersey City's school-choice voucher program. And about that tax cut: 'I didn't say, "Read My Lips." I'm just doing it.' "[40]

Vogue and *Mirabella* were just as flattering. *Mirabella* wrote, "Whatever happens, her stunning upset [over Florio] has established Whitman as the new GOP superstar. . . . Especially as a woman, the governor is just what the doctor ordered for a party trying to recover from the self-inflicted wounds that put it on the critical list in 1992." *Vogue* focused primarily on her upbringing, calling her a "patrician with a populist touch" and noting that "so far, every political trick has worked to Whitman's advantage. When her honesty gets her into trouble with interest groups, it pleases the crowd."[41]

Golden knew the stories would be published in July and expected that Whitman would be the target of another media frenzy at the governor's conference. He had been to more than a dozen NGA conferences since 1982 but had never seen media crowds like those following Whitman. "There was such a level of [national] interest that it was almost mind-boggling that it had reached that point. . . . I don't want to suggest this is pack journalism, but it got to be, 'Well, if George Will is interested in her, maybe I should be too.' And some columnist, 'Well, if Bob Novak is interested, maybe I should be interested too.' And it took on that kind of atmosphere. . . . We wound up turning down a lot of invitations from people simply because we just couldn't do it."[42]

For the first time, Whitman was seen as something more than a government figure. Admirers began to use the term "celebrity," conveying a status usually accorded to rock stars or sports heroes. Camera crews followed her everywhere, and Bostonians asked for her autograph. When Steven Spielberg addressed the governors about tolerance and the impact of *Schindler's List,* pictures of the pair chatting were beamed around the country. "When you read about Christie Whitman, it's like reading about Lady Diana or John F. Kennedy Jr. She's a celebrity, not a politician. She has succeeded in being above being a politician," said State Senator Joseph Kyrillos.[43]

Whitman publicly tried to dampen the intense media attention, noting that Will's *Esquire* testimonial faced a full-page picture of Lassie, another selection in the magazine's "Women We Love" issue, and that Madonna, in leather bra and panties, was on the magazine's cover. "If [the magazine profiles] had any impact at all, it was not a particularly positive one for governing," Whitman said. "We weren't talking substantive policy in any of those. Those were profiles, and to the extent that that raises your profile, it raises scrutiny, and it raises jealousy among those who haven't been in those kinds of things."[44]

Republicans, though, were serious about pushing Whitman closer to stardom. Dozens of GOP candidates from around the country asked for her help in their fall campaigns, hoping her popularity could sway voters or attract contributors to fund-raising events. Several governors also encouraged the vice-presidential speculation, and Weld even mentioned Whitman as a contender for the top spot on the 1996 ticket.

Bob Dole and Newt Gingrich, the House Republican leader, also praised her leadership potential. While both opposed abortion and knew Whitman's position on the issue, they spoke glowingly of her future in the party. Although Dole was planning his 1996 presidential campaign and would not talk about Whitman's prospects to be the vice-presidential nominee, Gingrich openly touted her for the ticket. "She has been seen around the country now as a very exciting addition to where we're at on national policy. She's emerging very rapidly as a serious national player," Gingrich said.[45]

Whitman's success in pushing through a 15 percent tax cut in less than six months inspired Gingrich as he formulated the Contract With America that would become a centerpiece for the GOP's upcoming fall congressional campaign. He was also impressed by her appeal to voters and by the prospect that Whitman could help the party's eventual nominee—whether Dole, Powell, or anyone else—beat Clinton in 1996.

"If you were putting together a list of vice-presidential candidates," Gingrich said, "she'd be on the short list."[46]

10

Campaigning Coast to Coast

Two weeks before an Election Day on which Republicans
could win big, Whitman has become perhaps the trendiest
name in politics.

—*Newsweek,* October 31, 1994

ABOUT ONCE A DAY, KEITH NAHIGIAN TOOK "THE LIST" OUT HIS DESK
drawer, read it over and shook his head in wonder.

The List's official title was "Document Listing, Out of State
Political." Its purpose was to compile the hundreds of political
invitations that came from around the country asking Whitman to
appear at an event or campaign for a Republican candidate. Its
length, by the fall of 1994, was close to two hundred items and
growing daily.

"Can you believe this? All these people want her to come in for
them. It's absolutely amazing," Nahigian said. "There's no way
she could ever go to all of them, that's all she'd be doing. Every-

one thinks that she has all this time, but she has to pick and choose the ones that are really important."[1]

The requests featured events of all sizes and political importance, ranging from an offer for Whitman to speak at a Montana Republican Party awards dinner, to invitations for fund-raisers hosted by Bob Dole, Pete Wilson, and Jack Kemp. The Mexico City Republican Leadership forum wanted her to speak at a luncheon; the Republican Woman's Club of Myrtle Beach, South Carolina, asked her to deliver a keynote address at a fund-raiser.

Republicans running in the 1994 election dominated The List, with thirty-six governors, thirty-four senators, and the entire House of Representatives on the November ballot. New Jersey's off-year gubernatorial election schedule enabled Whitman to campaign for other Republicans in a congressional election year without having to worry about her own race, and of the other prominent Republicans equally available, very few were as prominent as Whitman—or as popular.

Pete Wilson's request typified the invitations. He was facing a difficult reelection campaign against Democrat Kathleen Brown, daughter of former California governor Edmund "Pat" Brown and sister of Jerry Brown, the perpetual presidential hopeful. Wilson hoped that bringing Whitman to the West Coast would blunt Brown's sizable lead among women voters and help erase the stigma of his unpopular 1991 state tax hike.

Still, Wilson knew that Whitman was not a household name in California, despite the national media exposure. An *Asbury Park Press* reporter, talking to voters about Whitman outside the Los Angeles Hard Rock Cafe, found only a handful who knew much about her; one person thought she was the prosecutor in the O. J. Simpson murder trial. Wilson also realized, though, that Whitman was well known in the state's political community. A Whitman appearance at a rally or expensive fund-raiser would lure top reporters and wealthy contributors who otherwise might stay at home.

"Those who did know her were very enthusiastic," Wilson said. "She had great courage in pushing her conviction that the tax cut was needed for New Jersey. She was very tough-minded and very disciplined, and she stayed with it when it got tough. I find that very appealing."[2]

Whitman had the final say on choosing the events, picking campaign appearances in Pennsylvania and New York, and whittling down the list of out-of-town invitations from farther away. She would not go to New Hampshire, site of the nation's first presidential primary, for fear of encouraging vice-presidential speculation, and did not want to be out of the state for extended periods. The best way to maximize her exposure and minimize her time away from Trenton, staffers calculated, was to combine appearances into campaign swings that jammed appearances in several states into a few days.

Nahigian planned these whirlwind trips, creating an arduous schedule that exhausted everyone—troopers, aides, reporters, and eventually even Whitman. On the first trip, just before Labor Day, she attended fund-raisers in Dallas, Houston, Austin, San Antonio, and Phoenix and toured a model juvenile-justice facility in Fort Worth in just two days, before heading for California.

In St. Louis, the first stop on the eight-city tour, she stumped for the reelection of Senator Christopher "Kit" Bond, a family friend who had attended Princeton University with Dan Todd in 1960. He praised Whitman as a national star, a tax cutter, and a prominent woman official, before lightheartedly revealing another motive for the invitation. "You have no idea how tough it is to attract some media attention in St. Louis on a Saturday," Bond said.[3]

In Texas, Whitman starred at several expensive fund-raisers for Senator Kay Bailey Hutchison, a longtime Todd family friend, and at a $10-per-person barbecue for George W. Bush, the son of the former president who was challenging the Democratic incumbent governor, Ann Richards. Other than Hillary Clinton, Whitman and Richards were perhaps the nation's most prominent female political leaders, creating a natural rivalry of sorts. Richards had also campaigned for Jim Florio in 1993, and Whitman didn't mind returning the favor for Bush—or any other Republican.

For Whitman, fidelity to fellow Republicans came naturally. Web and Eleanor Todd had taught their children about loyalty to family, to friends, and to the party. Now that she could help others, Whitman felt compelled to campaign for GOP candidates in need. "What helped the candidates," Whitman reflected, "was that I was kind of a novelty, and that would help them raise money, because people would come to see 'Who is this?' That's the reason they had me there."[4]

On the campaign trail, just as candidates tailored stump speeches to fit the audience, Whitman could change personas to fit each situation. When she spoke to women's political groups, she was the nation's only Republican female governor, talking about the importance of women in government, in business, and in American society. "There's the five W's of politics. When Women Work, We Win," she told two hundred pro-Wilson women at a Los Angeles fund-raiser. "I'm a great supporter of women candidates, I want to see more women in positions of power, and certainly Pete Wilson is one who has opened the door for women in ways that other governors did not."[5]

The next morning, she transformed herself into the gender-neutral chief executive. "I was here to promote Pete Wilson. Not because I'm a female here supporting Pete Wilson, but because I'm another governor here supporting Pete Wilson," she insisted at a press conference.[6]

Whitman acknowledged that she molded her political identity in each situation. "It goes with the territory. It happens every day. It's happened all my life. I mean, it happens to every female who is doing things in a male-dominated world, and most of the world has been male-dominated until recently. You're a novelty, and you get used to such. As long as you can . . . turn it and use it to your advantage, as long as you can use it for what it is you're trying to do, I don't make any apologies for it. I'll take advantage of low expectations. I'll take advantage of fascination. I don't care what it is. If I can turn it around, I'll do it."[7]

She was evaluated at each stop by dozens of curious reporters and party leaders who had heard about the golden rookie from "back east" and wanted to judge her for themselves. There were also always a few transplanted New Jerseyans, anxious for a glimpse of the home-state star, or local natives with friends or relatives in the Northeast who had told them about Whitman.

"Texans are very aware of the rest of the world. We don't like taxes, we don't have income taxes, we don't want income taxes in Texas," said Elizabeth Diono, who moved to Dallas from New Jersey in the early 1970s, at the Dallas barbecue for Bush. "She has worked hard to lower taxes in New Jersey, and for this we love her."[8]

Most events were staged for the party's local elite, with price tags that reached as high as $5,000 per person. They were the rich and powerful, the kind of people who gave lots of money to political campaigns and whose approval could bolster the prospects of a rising star; the type who felt at home in a posh Houston mansion at a $500 per plate brunch for Hutchison or mingling with Whitman and Wilson's wife, Gayle, at an expensive Beverly Hills cocktail party.

Working the crowds and making small talk in knots of conversation, Whitman was at her best. In places like the gold-plated, mirrored Verandah Ballroom in Beverly Hills' posh Peninsula Hotel, she moved from group to group, extending her hand—she seldom carried a glass—and projecting amiability and intelligence. When she addressed the group, it was briefly and without notes.

Her performances were widely noticed. Belva Davis, host of KRON-TV's *California This Week* program in San Francisco, admitted that she had not expected Whitman to be so impressive in their half-hour television interview. "She's hit a nerve, she's attractive, she's female, she beat an old-time Democrat," Davis said. Not only had Whitman cut taxes, she was "very, very articulate, and those are the winning combinations that it takes to get elected these days."[9]

Whitman knew she was being closely watched and judged. At each stop, Democrats looked for inconsistencies and emphasized such negatives as the Rollins incident, which, more than one alleged, implied the governor and her staff tolerated racist attitudes.

Meanwhile, Republican leaders wanted to see how she handled criticism and whether she lived up to her good PR.

The biggest test came on September 1 in San Francisco at the prestigious Commonwealth Club, a ninety-one-year-old bipartisan public affairs forum that regularly produced many national headlines and headliners. In 1992, it had been the site of Dan Quayle's famous "Murphy Brown" speech. Whitman's text dealt largely—and safely—with philosophical matters, employing quotations from a German novelist and the Declaration of Independence. Afterwards, in an extended question-and-answer session, Whitman worked hard to avoid endorsing Quayle's comments while, as a loyal Republican, supporting his push for family values. ("You noticed that? I thought I had done that very well," she said later.)[10] Commonwealth Club members were not yet ready to help pack her bags for the White House, but her performance—particularly her precise, pointed answers to club members' questions during that informal give-and-take—impressed many in the audience.

"If she decides to run for vice president, I hope they don't give some old dog for president," Beth DeAtler, a San Francisco real estate investor, said after the Commonwealth speech. "I wouldn't want her to lose."[11]

Despite the hectic schedule, she enjoyed the campaigning and the chance to publicize her administration's efforts, whether on tax cuts, making the state more open to new businesses, or juvenile-justice reforms. The constant push dictated by Nahigian's timetable left no time for relaxing, except after an evening's last event, when Whitman chafed to get away from the troopers' protective custody and to unwind playing darts in a tavern or relaxing in a coffee shop. The troopers' standing orders were to stay with Whitman everywhere, particularly in uncontrolled situations on the road. To Whitman, the troopers' determination to keep her under wraps was a challenge too tempting to resist: finding a way to escape—"to get out of the fishbowl"[12]—quickly became a favorite activity on out-of-state trips. If successful, according to the unspoken rules of the game, she would call the troopers, who would then sheepishly retrieve her.

Whitman often recruited Nahigian and Jason Volk as accomplices, instructing them exactly how they fit into her plan.

She performed her most daring escape at Yale University, climbing out a second-floor bedroom window and down the side of the building. Volk was waiting to help her over a wall and a fence before they walked about a mile into New Haven. The troopers had assumed that no one—not even Whitman—would dare a second-story escape. "They wouldn't believe we had gone. We had to call down to New Jersey, because the phone was busy in the [troopers'] room, to tell them to call the room and tell them we were gone, and even then they didn't believe it," Whitman recalled, a big smile on her face.[13]

She particularly enjoyed the less-structured events, away from the pomp of a Commonwealth Club speech or the formality of a $1,000-per-head fund-raiser. In a park rebuilt by a youth conservation corps twenty miles north of San Francisco, Whitman demonstrated her farm skills for the cameras, raking eucalyptus leaves with the Wilsons. By himself, Wilson would not have attracted the television crews over the Labor Day weekend. Whitman was the draw—especially after raising more than $100,000 for Wilson at a closed-door fund-raiser the previous night. "I only wish that her duties permitted her a longer stay in California. I'd like to keep her sixty more days," Wilson said.[14]

Other candidates, in other states, felt the same way. Around the country, under Newt Gingrich's leadership, Republicans fought to take control of the House, the Senate and a majority of statehouses. The GOP pushed its Contract With America, a sweeping legislative proposal that promised tax cuts and less regulation, much as Whitman had done in New Jersey. Gingrich frequently cited Whitman as a precursor of what he hoped would be a Republican revolution, prompting even more GOP candidates to ask for her help as Election Day approached.

"I'm going to be out there saying a lot of these candidates have been suggesting the kind of things that I suggested during the campaign, gotten about the same response that I got during the campaign and I'm there to say, 'But it can happen.' Not all politicians just say things during campaigns and then walk away from their promises," Whitman said.[15]

To Haley Barbour, Republican National Committee chairman, "a very special element of her appeal was that when she said she was going to cut income taxes, the press—particularly the liberal press—called it impossible. . . . When we have a president whose words have nothing in common with what he does, a governor who stands by her word despite the derision of the liberal press is a very popular spokeswoman at campaign events."[16]

Her attacks on Bill Clinton grew more frequent and strident, charging that he and the Democratic-controlled Congress found ways to tax the money she saved New Jersey taxpayers. During a five-day, six-state trip through the Midwest, she campaigned for more Republican stars, including Governor John Engler in Michigan and Fred Thompson, the former actor, in Tennessee's heated Senate race. Once again, she maintained a grueling pace, with stops in Cleveland, Indianapolis, Flint, and Detroit in one day. This trip had a difference: candidates began talking about how they wanted to emulate Whitman and her tax-cut programs, even calling themselves "Whitman Republicans."

Republican gubernatorial hopefuls in neighboring states—George Pataki in New York, John Rowland in Connecticut, Tom Ridge in Pennsylvania, and Ellen Sauerbrey in Maryland—openly invoked Whitman's tax cuts as a model for their own economic plans. Pataki, for example, wanted to cut taxes by 25 percent over four years, while Sauerbrey planned a 24 percent cut over four years. Rowland promised to eliminate Connecticut's income tax, which supplied a third of the state's revenues.

The so-called Whitman Republicans were a new breed for the party, combining Goldwater Republicans' support for smaller government and Rockefeller Republicans' tolerance on social issues. Political scientists postulated that Whitman Republicanism, advocating tax cuts, business-friendly policies, more efficient government, and an inclusive social outlook, was suburban in its origin. Its biggest advocates, they said, were aging baby-boomer professionals who had been raised in the liberal, freethinking days of the 1960s and who now earned large salaries in the 1990s.

"Suburbanites are anti-tax, they're for welfare reform and tough on crime, and their looking for someone to make government work," said Stanley Rothenberg, a Washington analyst. "At the same time, they're very reluctant to buy into the conservatives' moral agenda. . . . They're nervous about intolerance, they're nervous about the rhetoric about gays and abortion and school prayer that they're hearing from southern and western Republicans. Right now, Christine Whitman has come to stand for their values."[17]

Newsweek, in an election story with a cartoon and a picture of Whitman, called the new breed of governors "Volvo Republicans," reflecting their suburban strength. This group, *Newsweek* said, included most of the tax-cutting governors, with Wilson given honorary membership for supporting tax cuts, despite his 1991 increases.[18]

While Whitman was the newcomer and Weld, Wilson, and Engler were finishing their first terms, she was the model for other Republicans to emulate and the celebrity who attracted the television cameras and national political reporters. In October, in New York, Whitman headlined at a black-tie dinner that raised $2 million for Pataki, while President Clinton starred at a nearby dinner that produced $2.5 million for Democratic incumbent Mario Cuomo, producing stories about a showdown of the nation's top political stars.

Her reputation clearly extended beyond the New York and Philadelphia media markets. At an appearance for Sue Collins, a Maine gubernatorial hopeful, "we got more out of her visit than we ever hoped for," said Steve Abbott, Collins's campaign manager. "We led the six o'clock and seven o'clock news on all the Portland stations that night. We got 157 people to a $250-a-head fund-raiser. If we'd charged that much and had any other Republican except George Bush or Ronald Reagan, we couldn't have put together that kind of crowd."[18]

Just two days after her appearance, Hillary Clinton stumped in

Maine for Collins's Democratic opponent, inevitably prompting comparisons between the two nationally prominent female leaders. To David Broder, at least, Whitman fared well in the face-off. "In some ways, Whitman's message has even more authority. Hillary Clinton's power derives from her husband's position; Whitman's is a direct gift from the people. But there is little to choose between them as campaigners. Both are extraordinarily deft, tailoring their message to the needs of the candidates they're helping, managing to be forceful and feminine," Broder wrote.

Broder, who also noted that "Whitman has as good a chance to be facing Vice President Al Gore in some October 1996 debate as any Republican you can mention," stressed that the governor and the first lady espoused dramatically different views of government's role. Whitman pushed for her view of a smaller, smarter government that spurred growth through tax cuts; Hillary Clinton favored an activist government that invested in education, welfare, and health care.

"If someone could arrange it, these two could have a great debate," Broder said.[19]

Whitman took the celebrity status and flattering media coverage in stride and laughed off the label of Volvo Republican, claiming she always drove American cars. It was harder to be comfortable with being the mother of an entire political philosophy. "It was sort of embarrassing, because you've got the Bill Welds, you've got the [Ohio Gov. George] Voinovichs, you've got the Englers, you've got people who have been out there before I was visibly doing it, and there have been people long before us who personify the kinds of things that I've been talking about and we've been doing here," Whitman said.[20]

As the election approached, calls from Republican candidates became even more frequent, and more pleading. With the exception of an occasional one-day excursion, though, Whitman could not go on the road again. At home, Chuck Haytaian faced an uphill battle to unseat Frank Lautenberg in the U.S. Senate race and needed Whitman's help to sway undecided voters. Democrats complained that her place was in Trenton, not on the campaign

185

trail trying to promote herself for higher office or stumping for GOP hopefuls who were strangers to Garden State voters. "I guess it all depends if you want to be governor or vice president. The [staff] help is figuring out the budget, and she's off traveling," Tom Byrne quipped.[21]

While her popularity soared around the nation, Whitman faced a long series of miscues that endangered her standing at home. The administration's most serious blunder to that point came in late summer, when the long-simmering controversy over lobbyist Hazel Gluck's influence suddenly threatened to become a major scandal.

Gluck, whose business was flourishing, held a unique status within the Trenton beltway, based on her former partnership with chief of staff Judy Shaw, her friendship with Whitman, and her longtime working relationship with half-a-dozen other top aides and cabinet commissioners. Her access to the governor and top state officials prompted many Democrats and lobbying competitors to allege that she had an unfair, and possibly improper, position within Whitman's world.

Whitman owed much of her early success to Gluck, who had dropped her own plans to run for governor to support Whitman's bid. Her lobbying business unquestionably benefited from Whitman's success, though the governor noted that Gluck was also impeded from pursuing certain clients because of the potential conflict.

"It really wasn't fair in the sense that she wasn't communicating with me on a regular basis. We weren't talking policy issues. We weren't talking individual decisions. She wouldn't do that and I wouldn't do it either, and she knows that. So that to a degree was unfair, but I guess it was natural," Whitman said.[22]

Gluck didn't openly battle the perception of power, which regularly brought in new clients. If the state's political community wanted to believe she had access, why fight it, provided she clearly kept her business interests distinct from her friendship with Shaw and any political advice she gave to Whitman. Gluck turned away potential clients who wanted to hire her solely to put in a good word with Whitman or Shaw and rejected prospects whose priorities contradicted those of the administration. Still, she realized there were risks, to herself and to Whitman, from the unexpected and from critics who feared the impact of Gluck's influence.

"You never know what's going to happen, as careful as you're going to be. . . . If I make a mistake, I'm going to get killed and it's going to spill over on the governor. And that's the last thing I want," Gluck said.[23]

Ironically, the eruption over Gluck's role involved a client of her son's rather than anyone she represented. Michael Gluck, an attorney and a lobbyist, worked as a consultant for the long-troubled Essex County welfare system. After years of alleged corruption and mismanagement, Human Services Commissioner William Waldman believed the state should temporarily take over the system, much as the state had seized control of school districts in Paterson and Jersey City. Waldman, a respected veteran who had also served in Jim Florio's cabinet, met repeatedly with Jane Kenny, Whitman's policy chief, about the proposal. By August, Waldman believed he had the governor's office's approval and started the takeover process.

The apparent misunderstanding between Kenny and Waldman—which surfaced when the takeover order was issued—was just the start. Michael Gluck, hearing of the impending takeover of his client, called Shaw, who knew of the proposal but had not heard of any final decision. Kenny, in Amsterdam for a conference that week, could not be reached, and a Human Services courier was en route to Newark with the order. In a scene that would do honor to a Hollywood thriller, Shaw ordered Waldman to dispatch a second messenger to intercept the takeover order. Whitman, who knew a takeover was being considered but knew nothing of Waldman's order, hedged about the sequence of events at a press conference several days later. She stood by the decision to delay a takeover, based on her belief in less intrusive government and a hope that state assistance could help Essex officials solve the problems in their welfare system.

The bigger problem, she realized, was the administration's re-

187

lationship with Michael Gluck, the reaction to his call to Shaw, and the perceived role of lobbyists within Whitman's realm. "I still to this day believe it's been the right decision to have made. It was the right decision to make at that time. But knowing that it was Michael, you just knew there were going to be people who were going to question it because it was dramatic. It probably would have gotten some attention, but not nearly the attention it got because of the personalities involved," Whitman said later.[24]

Democrats, other lobbyists, and Hazel Gluck's critics within the administration charged that the episode carried the imprint of improper influence. Senator Richard Codey, an Essex County Democrat, called for a senate committee hearing to determine "whether behind-the-scenes manipulations are hindering improvements to the county welfare system." He specified, "Something doesn't sound right when a lobbyist can call the governor's office to get a state takeover order by the human services commissioner called off, particularly when he is in line to make money from the deal."[25]

In an editorial, the *Star-Ledger* wrote that "it appears that New Jersey is experiencing a bald, bold, brazen case of government by lobbyist. Someone who is not a part of government is playing a major part in the business of government. Mrs. Whitman should know this cannot be allowed to continue."[26]

The episode threatened to tarnish the reputations of the principals, and stunt the governor's growth as a national celebrity. A combination of factors, though, minimized the damage: Republicans controlled the legislature, preventing any formal hearings; at the height of the summer vacation season, Trenton was nearly deserted, and few readers paid much attention to a flap over a lobbyist; the murky sequence of events prevented most reporters from quickly deciphering what exactly had happened.

Another, not insignificant, factor was Whitman's widespread popularity, which dampened the enthusiasm of many editors for negative stories about her. Whitman's charm and high approval ratings gave her a benefit of the doubt her predecessors seldom enjoyed. The same events during Florio's administration, reporters postulated, might have prompted an investigation by the attorney general's office or a grand jury. "It would have been federal, because it was a welfare program. If it were Tom Kean, there might have been legislative hearings," said Dan Weissman, among the writers surprised by the public's lack of interest in the episode. "There were no calls for it, and it just went away.[27]

In a *Trenton Times* column, Jim Goodman wrote that "something's fishy" but concluded that "none of this is likely to hurt Christie Whitman. She has won the confidence of the voters by making good on her tax-cutting promises and by putting herself on the side of the people against so-called special interests. She has a way with people that other politicians would kill for."[28]

Whitman's political luck stayed with her. The year's most critical newspaper evaluation of her fiscal policies, a damning analysis that warned that future generations would have to pay for her tax cuts, was published in the *Washington Post* on Labor Day—barely causing a ripple in the nearly deserted nation's capital. The retirement of Associate Justice Robert Clifford created the first opening on the state supreme court in a decade, giving Whitman an opportunity in her first year that Florio never enjoyed in his entire term.

The selection of supreme court justices, on both the state and federal level, often created political quagmires, but Whitman's choice of appellate court judge James H. Coleman was widely praised. Legal experts considered Coleman a thoughtful and intelligent jurist who would not permit personal views to sway his votes on abortion, capital punishment, or the state's ongoing court battle over school funding. Coleman's selection also provided a political bonus for Whitman: he was the first African-American named to New Jersey's supreme court, producing acclaim from many who had been critical of Whitman's record on minority appointments.

Whitman's national political standing was also bolstered by her role in the state government's response to the rape and murder of a young Hamilton Township girl. Megan Kanka, just seven years old, was allegedly killed by a released two-time sexual offender living across the street, whose criminal history was unknown in the neighborhood. The public was outraged, as they had been a few months earlier when six-year-old Amanda Wengert of Manalapan was killed by a teenage neighbor whose record of sex crimes against young children had been sealed because they occurred when he was a juvenile, and six-year-old Latasha Goodman of Asbury Park was raped and killed by a neighbor.

Whitman's juvenile justice reforms already proposed the disclosure of juvenile records in certain situations, and she strongly supported the immediate call for police registration of released sex offenders. Despite reservations about potential legal pitfalls, she also backed the concept of telling communities about certain paroled offenders living in their neighborhoods. At memorial observances for the children, rallies for the proposed new laws, and bill signings in her office, Whitman often appeared on television consoling the girls' families. As the mother of a teenage girl, she could identify with their grief and understand the fears of other mothers around the state.

"You and your families have taken, and turned, the darkest days in yours or any families' lives, and turned them into a statewide, even a nationwide campaign to protect children," Whitman told the girls' parents at a somber bill-signing ceremony attended by a crush of media. "I don't know where you get the strength and the courage to do what you've done, but because of you, we're changing laws and hopefully going to save lives."[29]

The package of bills came to be known as Megan's Law, in memory of Megan Kanka. Although several other states, including Louisiana, Washington, and Alaska, already had similar safeguards, publicity from the New York and Philadelphia media outlets branded all notification and registration programs as Megan's Law. Across the country, Whitman was praised as a law-and-order supporter. Conservatives hailed her for pushing through stern measures, while legal experts supported her insistence on delaying the bills for a few weeks to enable chief counsel Peter Verniero and Attorney General Debbie Poritz to redraw provisions that could face constitutional challenges. The entire process, including the legal reviews, took eighty-nine days.

"That, by government standards, is lightning speed. . . . If we had waited four or five, six, seven, eight months, I think there would have been a tremendous amount of pressure. But I would say we moved decisively but not precipitously, and our conclusions were validated by the Supreme Court," Verniero said.[30]

In many situations, Whitman managed to turn a negative event into a political advantage, or at least avoid being damaged by her mistakes. At the height of the campaign season, an *Asbury Park Press* photographer saw Whitman flying in the state helicopter that she had criticized Florio for using and that she had promised a year earlier to sell. A suggestion in the Your Tax Dollars program had prompted Whitman to designate the $4 million helicopter for emergency medical evacuations instead; the bids for the retrofitting were not yet finalized, and Whitman flew in the helicopter four times on a busy travel day. Joe Doria and other Democrats ridiculed Whitman's folly for using the helicopter, noting that "she's the one who made it into an issue, and now she's got to live with it. She's created a problem for herself."[31] Yet the incident did little damage to Whitman's reputation for keeping promises.

"Deep down, Doria knows his charges fell on deaf ears. For now, Whitman is in what athletes call 'the zone.' She can't miss," wrote Steve Adubato.

"Am I making too much of the 'Whitman Mystique?' Maybe. But if it's no big deal, why do so few politicians have it? Janice Ballou, director of the Eagleton/*Star-Ledger* poll, says: 'She's got that Tom Kean/Ronald Reagan syndrome.' "

As a result, Adubato concluded, "Whitman is getting the benefit of the doubt on everything. When she uses the taxpayer-supported helicopter (that she said she wouldn't) to get around on a busy day, most folks say, 'No big deal, who needs a governor who's so frazzled from sitting in rush-hour traffic like the rest of us?' When tuition goes up, sure, some students gets peeved (who cares, they don't vote) but their parents don't blame Whitman. Property taxes go up and your mayor points the finger at Whitman? That won't work. All people know is she's cutting their taxes and that their whining mayor should do the same."[32]

Haytaian hoped Adubato and the other columnists writing

about Whitman's popularity and political luck knew what they were talking about. He trailed Lautenberg in most polls, even though Republicans were surging in races around the nation. Lautenberg, a little-known two-term incumbent, had been considered vulnerable for several years, but Haytaian was not making much headway.

He tried focusing on his sponsorship of Whitman's tax cuts and on a push for a flat federal income tax that would eliminate most deductions while setting a single rate for all salaries and wages. At Whitman's request, Steve Forbes helped Haytaian push the flat-tax proposal, appearing at a series of newspaper editorial boards. Forbes was not yet well known enough to voters to be a major asset, but he was very effective in explaining his flat tax to skeptical editors.

"This is not a boon to the rich. It's an opening for people who want to get ahead," Forbes told the *Asbury Park Press* editorial board, trying to explain why his plan would not tax capital gains or investment income. "When you go to an orchard, you don't chop the tree down; you want to tax the apples on the tree. Why do you put a tax on capital? Why do you destroy your seed corn? You can tax the fruits of that seed corn, why are you trying to destroy your base of capital?"

Forbes spoke passionately, without notes but with obvious feeling. The flat tax, he believed, would rescue America's economy, spur investment, reduce the income tax form to the size of a post-card—and give thousands of tax accountants new lines of work. "They'd be busy keeping the books of all the new businesses that would be started," he said.[33]

Haytaian's biggest asset, however, was Whitman's popularity. He tried to call on her help sparingly, hoping that a series of late October appearances would be more effective.

"She did whatever he asked her to do. One of the things you have to be very careful of when you're a governor—and I went through this with Tom Kean—you use that resource to the best of your advantage. But you have to be very careful that it doesn't

192

appear as if the governor has become the candidate. So you can't overuse it," Golden said.[34]

Haytaian had two major problems: Lautenberg's large personal fortune and New York radio host Bob Grant. Whitman occasionally appeared on Grant's program and had received his strong backing in the 1990 Senate race against Bradley and the 1993 gubernatorial campaign. As Election Day approached, allegedly racist statements attributed to Grant forced Haytaian to decide whether to stand by his political ally or risk angering Grant's loyal, conservative national following.

In a *New York* magazine story Grant was quoted as calling African-Americans "savages" and advocating sterilization for welfare mothers.[35] The state's African-American leaders recalled that Whitman had immediately denounced Khalid Muhammad for racist language, and they insisted she and Haytaian do the same to Grant. "Yet, rather than being denounced by the leaders of our state, Bob Grant is invited by our governor to her inauguration [and] to the governor's house and [she] attends his birthday party," said the Rev. Reginald Jackson of Orange, a prominent minister. "What hypocrisy. What a double standard."[36]

Whitman and Haytaian made different choices. The assembly speaker denounced racism while avoiding comment on Grant. Whitman publicly promised to stay off his radio program, throwing the controversy onto front pages throughout the region.

"Bob Grant is someone with whom I agree on a lot of economic issues and a lot of other issues and that's been fine. But the rhetoric of late has been disruptive to what I consider very important for the state of New Jersey, which is 'Many Faces, One Family,' and the tolerance that we are trying to promote, and that's where we differ," she said.[37]

Grant, in his caustic style, directed a message to Whitman on his radio show: "I am deeply hurt over this. . . . You obviously feel my use is no longer of value. You have been elected. You are getting national attention, and Bob Grant can be cast aside like a pair of shoes that you needed on a rainy day but now you throw them out."[38]

For Whitman, the controversy offered no easy solution, one of the few times in her administration that she was unable to win political points. African-American leaders were angry that she ever had any connection with Grant, his conservative listeners branded her a traitor, Lautenberg exploited Haytaian's failure to sever all ties with Grant, and her critics reminded voters of the Ed Rollins episode.

"There was no way of winning on that," Whitman said, noting that she had never heard Grant make racist comments. "It was not that I kind of took on Bob Grant. A lot of people felt so strongly and so loyally about him that they perceived what I had done as . . . walking out, turning my back on a friend and a supporter. They couldn't separate out the issue that I was concerned about, but it was precisely because he did have such influence that what he said mattered. And they took it very personally . . . and a lot of them said that. 'You know, you're calling me a racist.' They believed it was okay to talk that way about groups of people and to label people. And that's what we have to face overall on an ongoing basis, and that was perhaps the most disturbing part of the whole thing. . . . I wasn't interested in labeling and calling anybody a racist—Bob Grant, the ministers, the people who listen to him. But I want people to be honest and face up honestly and hear themselves and see what they're saying," Whitman said.[39]

The African-American and Democratic protests against Haytaian, Lautenberg's spending advantage, and the powers of incumbency produced a 70,000-vote victory for the Democrat, raising questions among New Jersey politicians about whether Whitman's popularity could help other Republicans. Ironically, some analysts said Whitman's success in cutting taxes might have hurt Haytaian by removing the intensity from the issue for many voters. "Anger is a stronger emotion than gratitude," Rep. Dick Zimmer theorized.[40]

Across the country, Whitman was far more successful from a personal political standpoint. With the defeat of Ann Richards in Texas, she emerged as the nation's only female governor. Incumbents and challengers, Republicans and Democrats—every woman gubernatorial candidate on the ballot lost her election. The media loved anyone who was unique—and Whitman had suddenly become the nation's highest-ranking female chief executive, boosting her political worth even higher.

"She's the right person in the right place at the right time. She's a woman in a party that has an enormous gender gap. She's governor of a large swing state that Republicans need to win if they want to capture the presidency," said Larry Sabato, the University of Virginia pundit.[41]

Despite Haytaian's loss, she received credit from Barbour, Gingrich, and other party leaders for helping Republicans sweep to a national landslide that gave the GOP control of both houses of Congress for the first time since 1954. She raised $3.5 million for Republican coffers, and eighteen of the twenty-one out-of-state candidates she campaigned for won their races.

The victories enthralled Whitman, who repeatedly stressed that she was part of a larger team that propelled Republicans to victory. Yet she was concerned about the landslide's potential by-products, particularly the conservative social proposals in Gingrich's Contract With America, such as school prayer and sharp reductions in welfare benefits.

"I support the principle of laying out what you want to do, and I certainly support the basic context of a small government and a less intrusive government. . . . Line-item veto, balanced budget amendments, term limits I support. But I certainly could not support unequivocally every aspect of the legislation behind each idea in the contract," she said.[42] Whitman's priority was pushing for the inclusive philosophy she believed was vital to the party's success in 1996 and beyond—and she had no intention of backing down to anyone who wouldn't accept her.

"She and Weld are good people. They are good friends, but they are never going to be president or vice-president. They are liberals on social policies," said Mississippi governor Kirk Fordice, a devout conservative. "You people in the media are making all this fuss over Whitman. She's the darling of the media, but she's a liberal. Anyone who thinks she can be the vice-presidential candidate is crazy. That's just bull!"[43]

Fordice's attitude wasn't atypical. Many conservative Republicans, especially in the South, viewed Whitman with suspicion, prompting her to fight even harder for her inclusive views.

"I think there is certainly room for Newt Gingrich and me in the Republican party," Whitman said. "My only concern is with those who don't believe there is room. . . . This party cannot write people out of it."[44]

11

Whitman 1, Clinton 0

That she is, at least for the moment, the GOP's crown princess became clear when the party leadership chose Whitman . . . to deliver their response last week to President Clinton's State of the Union address.

—*Chicago Tribune,* January 29, 1995

EACH DECEMBER, *PEOPLE* MAGAZINE SELECTS ITS TWENTY-FIVE MOST intriguing people of the year. The popular issue boasts *People*'s largest circulation each year, selling more newsstand copies than usual to readers attracted by the luminaries on the cover. The stories are shallow and rarely critical, but the significance of being selected is far greater than that of anything in the written text. To millions of Americans who care little about politics, *People*'s annual list denotes true celebrity status.

In 1994, *People*'s picks included Pope John Paul II, Princess Diana, Michael Jordan, Heather Locklear, O. J. Simpson, and

Tonya Harding. Only three political figures made the list: Bill Clinton, Newt Gingrich, and Whitman.

"When Christine Todd Whitman was elected . . . no one thought she would turn into a one-woman political slogan. But in a year of right-wing arias, dozens of candidates happily declared themselves 'Whitman Republicans'—socially liberal, fiscally conservative," *People* wrote.[1]

People wasn't alone. *Ladies' Home Journal,* the nation's sixth largest magazine, picked Whitman—along with Caroline Kennedy Schlossberg and Barbra Streisand—among its most fascinating women in a special issue. *Glamour* featured her in its "Women of the Year" story. *Newsweek,* commemorating the swearing-in of the new-GOP dominated Congress, selected six officials for a picture essay on the nation's most influential Republicans. Gingrich was there, of course, along with Bob Dole, Rush Limbaugh, Bill Kristol, the former Dan Quayle aide who was among the first to suggest Whitman as vice president, Ralph Reed, head of the powerful Christian Coalition—and Whitman. She was the only woman, the only state official, and the only pro-choice supporter on *Newsweek*'s list.

If Whitman harbored ambitions to be a national candidate in 1996 or later, the magazine publicity was ideal, exposing her to millions of people across the country. Every time Whitman's supporters assumed that her popularity had peaked, it surged even more. Many of her staffers, notably the younger aides, were giddy over the national exposure. As 1995 began, they asked each other just how high she could go. Whitman's more experienced staffers knew they should enjoy the good times—because a downfall could come at any time. "My judgment is that these kind of things are fleeting," Carl Golden observed. "You enjoy . . . the Andy Warhol fifteen minutes of fame and then you move on. Her fifteen minutes has extended into two years. She sort of disproves Warhol's theory, I guess."[2]

Jim Florio, Tom Kean, and Bill Bradley had their share of positive coverage over the years, prompting speculation about a future on a national ticket and influence beyond New Jersey. All three had been mentioned as candidates for cabinet jobs. None, however, had received nearly as much nonpolitical exposure as Whitman was enjoying. "That gets you to the people you can never reach," noted Don DiFrancesco. "I can't imagine being able to get into *People* magazine. That reaches so many people that don't care about politics. Even if it's just the name, it's an easy name, and it's a female name."[3]

Even Whitman, with her innate realism and the pessimism she learned from her father, expected a downturn. So far, her luck had been brilliant, but how long could it last?

"I'd be a liar if I didn't say it was flattering to have things written, but it's also scary because you don't have any control and you don't know what people are going to say, and some of the things are not all that complimentary." Whitman reflected later. "You've got to be careful when those kinds of things start to get written about expectations and what that does to people's expectations, because it can get so much hype they can see you as something you're not. . . . [Good publicity is] always nice and it's always satisfying, but then there's tomorrow and there's a reality of today and yesterday."[4]

With so many stories focusing on Whitman's tax cuts, voters' expectations rose about the potential benefits of her program. The praise and copycat proposals from Republicans across the country produced the impression of a magic-bullet cure for all economic ills. The income and corporate tax cuts, coupled with Whitman's efforts to reduce red tape, apparently helped improve the state's business climate, business leaders said. However, it was difficult to distinguish between the impact of tax cuts and the national economic recovery that brought lower unemployment, inflation, and interest rates and a booming stock and bond market. As 1995 began the state's 6.1 percent unemployment rate was higher than the national average of 5.4 percent, and the 60,000 jobs created in her first year fell far short of the pace needed to meet Whitman's first-term goal of 450,000 new jobs.

Critics also continued to insist that the tax cuts were forcing local property taxes to soar. An offhand comment by Whitman that the full 30 percent cut might take four years instead of the three originally promised had fueled skepticism about whether her policies were more show than substance. Democrats insisted that Whitman's own doubts proved that her goal was not feasible.

For Democrats, emphasizing any rise in property taxes still offered the best hope to derail the Whitman juggernaut. Most of the state's large cities had prominent Democratic mayors who could get coverage of their warnings of local tax hikes caused by Whitman's program. An Associated Press study found that property taxes rose an average of 5 percent the prior year, two points above the inflation rate and significantly higher than the increases in Florio's final two years.

The critics also finally found a few national reporters who were willing to write about their property-tax predictions. During her first year in office, Whitman's meteoric rise had dominated her coverage. The national media, however, eventually take a more critical look at people who become suddenly prominent. This pattern showed itself repeatedly in the 1980s and 1990s for political figures who burst onto the national scene, including Whitman's adviser and friend Steve Forbes.

Similarly, national publications took a new look at Whitman's economic program as she started her second year. While calling Whitman one of the country's most influential Republicans, *Newsweek* wrote about the fears of New Jersey mayors and school boards that "if the governor reduces state aid to towns and school districts, they'll be forced to raise local property taxes—an act tantamount to political suicide."[5] A *Money* magazine story published just before Christmas also cited the potential for property-tax increases, based on the lack of local aid increases.[6]

The most damning stories came from Bob Herbert, a liberal *New York Times* columnist who felt Whitman's policies were fiscally dangerous. In a series of columns, he bluntly made his case. "While this cut-at-will policy is great for Mrs. Whitman's ego and ambition, it has some dire consequences for New Jersey. The income tax is not a problem in that state; the property tax is. And while Mrs. Whitman is dismantling the income tax in the service of her political career, property taxes are soaring," Herbert wrote.

He also slammed her use of pension fund recalculations. "She needs cash now, and if mortgaging the state's future is the way to obtain it, so be it. She needs to cover her tax cuts. She wants to be vice-president. When the bills ultimately come due, as they will, she will be gone. She hopes."[7]

New Jersey reporters focused on promises Whitman had so far failed to keep, such as pushing through the "three strikes and you're in" bill and her vaunted school voucher program. The three strikes bill, which would give mandatory prison terms to repeat offenders, and the school voucher proposal, designed to provide parents with government funds to help pay for private schooling, were both mired in the legislature.

Yet the critical stories had a negligible impact on Whitman's national rise. The Herbert columns on the *New York Times* editorial page were seen by fewer people than the newspaper's repeated page-one or metro-section front-page stories praising Whitman. The *Newsweek* story about property-tax hikes also told readers that more than 60 percent of New Jersey voters approved of her performance, and even a Herbert column began by telling readers that Whitman was bold, aggressive, and politically astute and had the potential to be the first female president.

Democratic lawmakers in Trenton repeatedly vented their frustration over what they called Whitman's "Teflon coating."[8] The same substance, they said, had protected Ronald Reagan from constant criticism about his fiscal policies.

"I don't think you could get much better press than she's gotten. When you compare it to Florio, it's wonderful," said Bernard Kenny. Much of it, Kenny realized, came from Whitman's "very attractive charming demeanor. She has the political persona that is first class. Whatever it is, she has it. You either have it or you don't, and she has it."[9]

To Larry Sabato, it was a simple matter of press perspective and personal popularity. "She's in the protected category. It's a combination of gender and ideology. It's a very sturdy shield. She's a woman and she's a moderate Republican," he said. "Even though the press denies it, they have good-guy and bad-guy categories. If you're Christie Whitman, your motives may be sanitized. If you're Al D'Amato or Jesse Helms [GOP senators], your motives are always suspect."[10]

The biggest test would come over the new budget to be unveiled in January 1995. State Treasurer Brian Clymer and his staff had more time to develop a spending plan than they had during the hectic weeks between the inaugural and the first budget speech—but they also faced more obstacles to piecing together a balanced budget. In July 1994, the state supreme court ruled that New Jersey's school-funding formula still did not meet its criteria for closing the gap between the state's wealthiest and poorest school districts. The court gave Whitman and the legislature until the 1997–98 school year to meet its mandate; with nearly three years to develop a solution, Whitman and Leo Klagholz, her education commissioner, decided to reexamine the state's overall education goals and curriculum before determining how much money had to be spent. Critics called it a stalling technique, noting that redrafting the curriculum would take at least a year, while Whitman supporters insisted that pouring more money into a failing system would be foolhardy. Clearly, though, a down payment on the supreme court's order was needed in the budget.

There were other financial problems looming, including the pending expiration of a law that paid for the bulk of the state's highway and mass transit projects. Many Republicans feared that Whitman's tax-cutting image could be destroyed if she approved a proposal to raise the gasoline tax that could both pay for the transportation fund's annual cost and help close the deficit in the general budget. While Whitman's first budget substantially reduced dependence on one-time revenues, she still had to find just under $1 billion to stay even in the next fiscal year.

Whitman also wanted to start spending for her social initiatives, notably the sweeping juvenile justice reforms that she considered a cornerstone of her administration. The reforms, developed by Attorney General Debbie Poritz and a panel of experts, proposed providing quality education to teenagers in detention centers, increasing mental health and other assessment services available to judges, hiring more minority police officers, and creating more host homes or group homes as detention alternatives.

Poritz, who had a major role in planning many Whitman initiatives, including Megan's Law and the "three strikes" bill. At age fifty-eight, she was older than most of Whitman's team—and among its most respected members, particularly for her legal expertise and attention to detail. Her juvenile justice recommendations, which took nine months to prepare, were immediately embraced by Whitman; their biggest drawback could be the cost of implementing the proposals.

"Will there be more money required, probably. Is that a good investment to make for the people of this state, undoubtedly. . . . If we can divert young people before they get into crime then we will end up saving lots of money in the long run," Whitman said. "The definition of whether something is going to go forward or not seems to be entirely, 'How much more money?' " she added.[11]

The biggest issue was the question of the next income-tax cut. Politically, she couldn't stop now. Halting the cuts in mid-stream, or delaying the full 30 percent reduction until the last year of her term, would undermine similar efforts by other GOP governors, notably the Whitman Republicans who based their programs on her success, and anything short of another full cut could cause her to be seen as a failure by the press, Democratic critics, and voters nationwide.

Despite the fiscal problems, Whitman looked back on her first year with satisfaction. She realized there could be problems ahead: as the *Asbury Park Press* wrote in a year-end review, "Whitman's biggest problem in 1995 may be gravity. When you're near the top of the hill, the easiest way to go is down."[12]

She understood that "the nature of the job is such that the decisions that I'm going to have to make, that it's my responsibility to make, are going to tick off a lot of people. . . . The other side of that question is, will we doing everything with a weather eye always on the polls and trying to stay popular? I know that can't happen."[13]

Whitman also insisted on staying positive, using her first State of the State address on January 10 to deliver a good-news, upbeat review of life in New Jersey. The annual speech, broadcast on New York and Philadelphia television stations and on C-SPAN, resembled a pep rally for her economic programs. From a policy perspective, business and industry cheered her unprecedented promise that cabinet departments would institute a money-back guarantee of making permit decisions in a timely fashion. At the regulation-heavy Department of Environmental Protection, for example, land-use and other permits would be issued or denied within ninety days of application. The new program, combined with her tax cuts, would make the state more competitive in attracting businesses, she insisted.

She also promised there would be another tax cut, the size unspecified, in the budget to be unveiled two weeks later. There would be no increase in the gasoline tax, she said. Instead, the transportation trust fund would be refinanced by using more revenue from the current gas tax and by extending a car and truck registration surcharge scheduled to expire in 1997. Democrats immediately charged that the surcharge extension was the equivalent of a new tax, despite Whitman's assertion that "we're not increasing those fees, we're extending them, these are not new taxes."[14] Environmentalists also complained that the new permit process would ruin safeguards and eliminate most protection standards.

The critics might as well have been talking to themselves, because few voters were listening to their complaints. Whatever their position on her policy initiatives, lawmakers and statehouse veterans—from both parties—quickly lauded Whitman's speech: a master political stroke; a public relations bonanza; political theater at its best; a half-hour, nationally-televised "Whitman for Whatever" commercial, and another step toward wherever her national political fate might lie.

Whitman had used the State of the State message to reinforce her role as New Jersey's head cheerleader. "Together, we sent the

204

message, across the state, across the country and around the world, that New Jersey is Open for Business. People are noticing. They are noticing not only our success, but what we did to get there," she told her audience.

"A year ago, the governor of New York looked at New Jersey and laughed. He said our plan to cut taxes to stimulate economic growth would never work. Well, today, New York has a new governor, George Pataki. And he has a copy of our New Jersey plan right on his desk. Nobody's laughing at New Jersey anymore."

Reminding voters of her national acclaim, Whitman added that "the nation is watching New Jersey. We have a message to send, a message of excellence, of compassion of hope." Legislators from both parties gave her a standing ovation for insisting that "the message, quite simply, is that the best of New Jersey is the best of America."[15]

The applause kept coming, even when Whitman signaled for quiet. She had little bad news for anyone, except perhaps a handful of Democrats who had hoped Whitman would discuss their favorite subject, property taxes—and who insisted on continuing to compare her to Ronald Reagan. Six months before, New Jersey Democrats had focused on the similarity between her fiscal policies and the former president's. Now they harped on the two Republicans' frequent emphasis on the upbeat aspects of their respective administrations.

"This is a Ronald Reagan special, where you wrap yourself in the flag, say the country is the greatest country in the world. Here we're saying New Jersey is the greatest state in the union. . . . All we talked about are platitudes. Warm and fuzzy platitudes. There was no substance, no initiatives, really little there other than to make you feel good," said Democrat Robert Smith, the assembly deputy minority leader.[16]

Indeed, many budgetary questions remained unanswered. While the transportation trust fund dilemma appeared to be solved, Whitman offered no clues about the education funding problem or how she would close the revenue gap. John Lynch, the senate's top Democrat, charged that "the governor's obvious theme is that when in doubt, announce another income tax cut. It's simple and it makes for a good sound bite, especially when you're talking to a national audience and not to the New Jersey residents who have to pay the bills."[17]

Once again, Whitman was keeping a secret from the legislature, the public, and the media. She knew the size of the next tax cut when she delivered the State of the State speech but had no intention of telling anyone outside her inner circle until her budget speech on January 23. Just after New Year's, Brian Clymer had brought his fiscal 1995–96 financial projections to Whitman's office for a meeting that would finalize the budget's parameters. Clymer regularly tracked the state's tax revenues and had been running computer programs for months projecting what the impact of a new 5, 10, and 15 percent income tax cut would be. With revenue from sales taxes up sharply and with reasonably rosy economic conditions forecast for the year ahead, he surprised everyone in the room by suggesting that they complete the 30 percent tax cut in the upcoming budget. After enduring "I told you so" barbs from Democrats over her comment that the tax cuts might require four years, Whitman needed little prodding to finish the program ahead of schedule.

"Brian is very even, very steady, but before the meeting that day he was gesturing at me, like he's really excited, to come over," Jane Kenny said. "He said, 'Jane, I want to tell you something. If we do this and this and that, I think we can do the whole [remaining] 15 [percent].' "[18]

As they had done with the retroactive tax cut unveiled in the inaugural address a year before, Whitman's staff treated her go-ahead for the final 15 percent cut as a state secret. The speculation among lawmakers and reporters about the size of the impending cut had the same largely skeptical tone as that before the first budget address, with most estimates putting the next cut between 5 and 10 percent. A 15 percent cut was not even discussed by most statehouse insiders. It was too implausible, too unlikely.

Yet the 15 percent cut was not the biggest secret being kept by Whitman's confidants. A week after the State of the State speech,

Whitman received an unexpected phone call at Drumthwacket from Haley Barbour, the Republican national chairman. Would Whitman, he asked, represent the GOP by delivering the party's response to President Bill Clinton's State of the Union address the following week, on January 24?

The offer was stunning, and historic. No governor and no woman had ever given a State of the Union response. Typically, white male members of Congress in dark suits followed the president; Bob Dole, for example, had responded to Clinton in 1994 (and would again in 1996). Nor had the response ever been delivered from outside Washington, but Barbour suggested using the statehouse, possibly the ornate assembly chamber.

The idea of asking Whitman, Barbour explained, came from Speaker of the House Newt Gingrich. The opposition party leaders in the House and Senate alternated in picking who should follow the president's address, usually choosing themselves, and 1995 was Gingrich's year. However, the new Speaker, facing daily criticism for a book deal that promised to pay him millions of dollars, felt he should find someone else to deliver the response. Handing the selection back to the Senate—especially when the GOP controlled the House for the first time in a generation—would be unthinkable.

Gingrich's Contract With America called for a smaller federal government that would return power to the states. Why not draw attention away from Clinton by asking a governor to give the Republican response, he wondered. From a policy perspective, there were many qualified choices, including Bill Weld, John Engler, Pete Wilson, and more. Whitman, though, was the strongest. As a woman, she would automatically present a dramatic contrast to Clinton. As a moderate, she could reassure millions of voters who were afraid that Gingrich's Republican revolution would make dramatic social changes. As a chief executive, she had kept her word to · cut taxes, in another contrast to the president. And she was the only governor considered a national celebrity.

"We wanted to send a signal about what kind of team we are. We wanted to send a signal about how broad-based we are. . . .

207

Our answer is not going to come from Newt Gingrich. Our answer is not going to come from the U.S. Capitol. Our answer is going to come from Governor Christie Whitman. . . . How would you like to be President Clinton's speechwriter and figure out, 'How do we precede her?' " Gingrich said.[19]

Whitman was stunned. This call was unlike any other she had ever received or even anticipated. She needed a few minutes to grasp the significance of Barbour's offer, to realize that "he was talking about doing *the* response to the State of the Union."[20]

The speech's timing would be ideal, coming just one day after Whitman planned to reveal her largest income-tax cut yet in the budget address. Barbour and Gingrich, who knew nothing of Whitman's budget plans when they picked her, had stumbled into a political gold mine. In their response to the president, Republicans would offer the nation a top official who not only kept her promise but beat her own deadline in finishing a sweeping tax-cut program.

The shock value of the unique selection would also increase the interest in Whitman's speech. Even her supporters, upon hearing the news, were stunned. "Oh, my God," said GOP strategist Bill Palatucci, who like many others praised Gingrich's choice once he absorbed the surprise. "She is at her best on TV, the camera loves her. She comes across very well, very comfortable."[21]

There were many details to be decided, such as where she would speak. Whitman favored her private office, perhaps in front of the fireplace, which would give a warm, homey feeling in a controlled setting, away from nosy reporters. Barbour pushed for the assembly chamber, with lots of cheering Republicans. The conversations went back and forth, with Whitman explaining the realities of Trenton to the party leaders. "I cannot give this kind of address in the chamber without inviting both sides of the aisle. I mean, this is the people's house, and you can't not have Democrats there," Whitman told Barbour, adding that she would not be able to stop Democrats from booing or hissing the same lines Republicans would applaud.[22] Yet it was the assembly chamber that best presented the image of a setting away from Washington—and the impression the Republicans were hoping to leave with voters.

As usual, the Republican response would focus on the GOP's priorities, not the president's proposals. Whitman, Gingrich, and Barbour quickly agreed that it should be upbeat, touting the tax-cutting accomplishments of Whitman and other Republican governors. An early draft from GOP writers in Washington was rejected as too bloated, too unlike Whitman's clipped speaking style.

Mike Murphy and a speechwriter from Barbour's office worked on drafts in the parlor at Drumthwacket over the weekend; down the hall, in the library, Peter Verniero, Judy Shaw, and statehouse speechwriters were revising the budget address. While the two teams worked separately, their themes had to agree; certainly, Whitman couldn't contradict her budget address in the State of the Union response. Later, Verniero praised the Washington writers for their willingness to work with the Whitman aides. "They were genuinely helpful. She made a lot of changes, and actually they understood her phraseology. They had obviously done some research. And it was not a case of her having to deliver a speech which the National Committee had written as sort of a take it or leave it. It was not that way at all."[23]

The budget speech shocked state leaders and provided new material for television network anchors who would introduce Whitman to the nationwide audience the next night. Democrats, who almost unanimously expected a 5 percent tax cut, speculated that Whitman had enlarged the tax cut after learning that she would deliver the Republican response to Clinton's address. To Verniero, who handled the budget briefings for reporters with Clymer, the insinuation that Whitman put a "one before the five" was insulting.[24]

"It would presume a manipulation of the budget for the sake of a single speech, a rather offensive presumption for someone to make about her . . . particularly when you're dealing with other people's money. Her whole approach to budget making is that we're dealing with other people's money. We are trustees of the taxpayers. It's their money, it's not ours. And we have to spend it prudently," he said later in an interview.[25]

In a virtual repeat of her first budget speech, the surprising nature of Whitman's tax-cut announcement overwhelmed voters' impressions of her proposal. The secret had been so well kept that even most of the cabinet didn't know what was coming. Besides the completion of the income-tax program, Whitman called for reducing corporate taxes for businesses earning under $100,000 per year and eliminating the sales tax that Florio had imposed on Yellow Pages advertising.

"The tax cuts are working, even better than I thought. Our job growth has put tax revenues in the state coffers faster than we expected. So why wait to reinvest in New Jersey's future? Why wait to return as much money as we can to taxpayers? Why wait until next year to keep a promise we can keep right now?" Whitman asked.[26]

Union leaders and Democratic lawmakers, though, stressed that Whitman's cuts would be felt by many people. More than 800 employees were targeted for layoffs, 300 jobs would be lost through attrition, and 2,200 workers would have to fight for their jobs when businesses took over privatized state operations, such as motor vehicle agencies and centers for developmentally disabled adults. State workers would have to start paying for part of their health-care coverage, and taxpayers faced $19 million in fee increases, including a new five-dollar surcharge for renewing drivers' licenses or car registrations in person. While the poorest school districts would receive $100 million more in state aid—a down payment for the supreme court mandate—more than 150 wealthy districts faced cuts in their allocation.

"Once again, Governor Whitman is proposing a tax cut without corresponding cuts in spending. We have tax cutting, but we don't have budget cutting," charged Assemblyman Joseph Roberts, the Democratic assembly budget officer. "New Jersey has benefited so much from the improving national economy that she should publicly thank President Clinton when delivering the Republican rebuttal to his State of the Union address tomorrow night."[27]

Bob Purcell, president of the Communications Workers of America, the state's largest employee union, asserted, "This budget shows the dark side of Christie Whitman. It reminds me of a Doctor Jekyll and Mr. Hyde where in one breath she says it's terrible when someone loses a job, and then she comes out with this budget."[28]

Not surprisingly, Democrats also complained about property taxes and the parallels they saw between Whitman and Reagan. Even less surprisingly, hardly anyone listened in the euphoric statehouse atmosphere. Whitman's staffers felt that their more difficult speech was behind them, since the State of the Union response would be half the length of her twenty-eight-minute budget address. Republican legislators facing reelection in the fall celebrated the prospect of campaigning on a record of more tax cuts.

In the assembly chamber that night, CNN technicians created a state-of-the-art television studio, with hundreds of yards of cable, a dozen monitors, and five cameras. The chamber's dark polished woods gleamed in the bright television lights; the yellow and gold trim reflected the spotlights. The long black microphones normally used by DiFrancesco and Chuck Haytaian when they appeared on the podium with Whitman during gubernatorial speeches were removed, since Whitman would appear solo and technicians complained they appeared to be antennae protruding from her head.

Around the statehouse, no one could remember a two-day period with so much national attention focused on Trenton. Reporters from major newspapers, photographers from *Time* and *Newsweek,* and network camera crews roamed the hallways, hoping to catch a glimpse of Whitman and constantly wandering into Golden's office looking for scraps of information. Whitman's tax cuts—for the second straight year, the largest in state history—would have made headlines even without the State of the Union response. The combination brought Whitman exposure that was unprecedented for a New Jersey governor, in every corner of the country.

On January 24, the television coverage started before dawn, with appearances by Whitman from Drumthwacket on network morning talk shows, and would last until the final reviews of the State of the Union speech and her response on ABC's *Nightline* at midnight.

"A wide American audience got its first look at the woman [Republican congressman] David Dreier called 'the epitome of what the new Republican party is—visionary, upbeat, and committed to reducing the size of government,' " the *Los Angeles Times* wrote.[29]

Whitman spent much of Tuesday rehearsing her speech on TelePrompTers, posing for pictures in the assembly, and relaxing with her top staffers and family. For the first time anyone could remember, Dan Todd and John Whitman were seen in the statehouse on consecutive days. They had two of the coveted seats in the front ring of the assembly chamber for the State of the Union response, along with Kate Beach, the governor's sister; Haytaian and DiFrancesco; Shaw, Verniero, and Kenny; Tom Kean; Virginia Littell, the state party chairwoman; and two other party leaders, state GOP finance chair Clifford Sobel and Turnpike Authority chairman Frank McDermott. No Democrats had been offered front-row seats. Steve Forbes sat in the second row. Jason Volk, as always, stayed close to the governor, coming into the chamber just before the address and sitting near the podium, holding a copy of the speech in case the TelePrompTers failed.

Clinton began his address just before 9:15 P.M. Whitman, her husband, Kean, and the staff troika watched the president on the color television in Haytaian's office, just off the assembly chamber. The president was scheduled to speak for between thirty-eight and forty minutes, White House aides advised the networks, giving Whitman an estimated starting time of about 10:00 P.M. Clinton started strongly, promising to work with the new Republican congress and backing a series of themes generally associated with the GOP. By the top of the hour, however, he was rambling from subject to subject with no indication that he soon planned to finish.

In the assembly chamber, the largely Republican crowd cheered whenever the president appeared to finish—and then groaned as he moved to another topic. In Haytaian's office, Whitman listened to the president and to John's banter about the length of the speech, trying to keep her nerves under control. "You try to think of it as just, I'm going to go out and give another speech with TelePrompTers in the assembly chamber. Obviously you know it's a little different than that. But what made me nervous at the beginning was that the president's speech was so like my speech," she later recalled.

"His first minutes were right on the themes that I was going to be hitting on, and there was going to be zip contrast, and I was sitting there saying, 'Okay, what do I do now? Do I completely blow this speech . . . and ad lib?' Because that's disastrous. I had a very tight time frame in which to give my response. I mean, I didn't have a whole lot of time, I couldn't go on for hours. And [I] was starting to [get] very nervous [about] how this was going to be anything that would set the party apart."[30]

Clinton calmed Whitman's nerves by going on and on. Her speech might not be better than the president's, she knew, but it would certainly be shorter. By 10:35 P.M., when Clinton finished, he had spoken for eighty-one minutes—the longest State of the Union address in memory—and for the moment, at least, the audience's mind was on its length, not its content.

"Before I begin, let me assure you, I am not going to ask for equal time," Whitman ad-libbed.

Her response was just twelve minutes long. Whitman stuck largely to the concepts of lower taxes and smaller, smarter government that had propelled her to the national forefront, ignoring many of the other themes of the Contract With America. There was no mention of the social issues, such as abortion and school prayer, that threatened to split the GOP at the 1996 convention. Instead, she focused on the accomplishments of six of her fellow Republican governors—Weld, Wilson, Engler, Thompson, Symington and Allen—as proof of the "revolution of ideas" breaking out across the country.

There was a clear contrast between phrases contributed by Washington—the flowery oratory of Capitol Hill—and her own plain-spoken style. While talking about the most recent national election, she said voters "rejected the tyranny of expanding welfare state policies, the arrogance of bigger and bigger government, the frustration of one-size-fits all answers." Talking about her own programs, Whitman's words were far more down to earth. "I was told that tax-cutting policies were a gimmick," she informed millions of viewers who knew little about New Jersey.

"I've heard we couldn't do it, that it was impossible, that it would hurt the economy. But I had given the people of New Jersey my word that we could cut their taxes and we did. In the first year, with the help of the New Jersey legislature, we cut businesses taxes. We reduced income taxes, not once, but twice. We lowered state spending, not recklessly, but carefully and fairly. Just yesterday, I announced the third wave of income tax cuts, another 15 percent, taking us to a 30 percent reduction to put more money in the hands of families like yours."

Whitman also took a few light shots at the president—it was, after all, a response to Clinton. "While at times tonight, some of the president's ideas sounded pretty Republican, the fact remains that he has been opposed to the balanced budget requirement, he proposed even more government spending, and he imposed the biggest tax increase in American history."[31]

After Whitman's speech, Democrats returned the salvos. Loretta Weinberg, New Jersey's senior Democratic assemblywoman, complained that Whitman turned the chamber into a partisan rally. In Washington, Bob Beckel, a frequent network commentator and the manager of Walter Mondale's 1984 presidential campaign, said the GOP response was "awful." He commented, "She reminded me of a Girl Scout leader giving a pep talk to the girls at the beginning of the annual cookie drive."[32]

The views of Republicans were just as predictable. Peggy Noonan, the bestselling author and onetime speechwriter for Reagan and Bush, said that "Whitman was so brisk, so disciplined.

Clinton was so undisciplined, so verbose and you might even say self-indulgent."³³

"It showed that she has a real core, a sense of direction and a sense of what the real needs of the people are," Steve Forbes said on the assembly floor. (He went unrecognized by many reporters as he stood quietly, watching the chaos. One even pushed him out of the way, brusquely complaining he was clogging the aisle.) In an *Asbury Park Press* interview, Forbes conceded that Whitman had seemed nervous but noted "you wouldn't be human if you weren't nervous when you're making your first speech to the nation. But I think she handled herself extremely well, as though she's done it before. And some of us hope that she will do it again."³⁴

Editorial reviews were mixed, with most at least praising Whitman's brevity. "Although her speech was not a memorable one, she [sent] the message that almost anything the federal government can do, the states can do better. . . . She's a GOP leader who has kept her promises to middle-income taxpayers, and she stands in contrast to the perception that President Clinton hasn't kept his," wrote the *Atlanta Journal and Constitution*.³⁵

The commotion over Whitman's national rise might have ordinarily subsided in a few days, but her political luck and timing—to the dismay of many Democrats—once more kept her in the spotlight. The annual National Governors Association conference began in Washington just four days after the State of the Union response, giving many top political reporters and network correspondents a five-day window to talk with Whitman. Anyone wandering around the NGA meeting site in Washington's J. W. Marriott hotel could easily spot Whitman and her entourage by simply looking for the glaring klieg lights: besides the myriad of camera crews trying to get a Whitman comment for daily newscasts, a crew from NBC's *Today* show trailed her everywhere, shooting footage for a profile scheduled for the following month. The three major weekly newsmagazines, *Time, Newsweek,* and *U.S. News and World Report,* published reports about her State of the Union speech on the conference's third day. The *U.S. News* story also carried a two-page picture of Whitman at the assembly po-

215

dium; a small insert showed Clinton in the House of Representatives chamber.

While most governors publicly complimented Whitman on her performance, staffers and even reporters from several states openly resented her celebrity status. Ohio's delegation, for example, wanted to know why Whitman omitted Governor George Voinovich from her list of tax-cutting chief executives.

"She's a star, and everyone wants to be a star," said Mike Murphy, watching the parade of governors wandering through the J. W. Marriott lobby. "At the staff level, sometimes there are jealousies because staffs promote their governors and there are governors who are actively running for vice president and are probably jealous that Christie Whitman gets as much attention as she does."[36]

Much of the publicity was fortuitous. Whitman and Colin Powell sparked a furor when they found themselves seated together at a posh Republican dinner. The *Washington Post* published a picture of the governor and her husband gliding across the East Room floor at a White House dinner. At the J. W. Marriott, cameras frequently focused on Whitman, the sole woman in the long rows of white men at the full-scale governors' meetings. "When you look at that table, it's easy to tell which one is Christie Whitman. It's hard to tell which is, say, Tommy Thompson. You can say he's the one in the gray suit, but on any given day, there may be thirty guys in a gray suit," Judy Shaw said.[37]

Whitman discouraged any overt publicity efforts. There were no copies of her State of the Union response for reporters in their NGA newsroom, next to clipping portfolios of Pete Wilson, free videos of Pennsylvania governor Tom Ridge's inaugural address, or the welfare reform plans being pushed by a half-dozen governors. She publicly chastised John for joking at a White House dinner that he had brought a measuring tape to size up the place for their eventual move there, turning red at the comment and dragging him away from reporters.

Not all of the coverage was entirely complimentary. In another coincidence of timing, the *New Republic* magazine published a cover story portraying Whitman as a liberal—a naughty word to millions of GOP voters—whose future rested on whether conservatives were willing to nominate someone whose views on social issues were so far afield from their own. The cover story by John B. Judis depicted Trenton as a gang-dominated, drug-infested wasteland where "you can sit in state offices and hear gunshots from nearby crack houses." While Trenton is hardly a crime-free region, even Whitman's critics thought the description was excessive. Judis's review of Whitman's strengths and weaknesses, however, was considered fair by many supporters and critics alike.

"One New Jersey Republican political consultant, asked to grade Whitman's performance during her first year, gives her an 'A plus' in public relations, a 'B' in policy and a 'C' in addressing long-term problems. That strikes me as accurate," Judis wrote. "While displaying great skill as a politician, Whitman has been less impressive as a policymaker. She has convinced voters of the need for her tax cuts, but not the state's economists—not even some that she herself appointed. For good reason: her numbers still don't add up," he noted.[38]

This criticism, though, paled in contrast to the nationwide outcry at Whitman's renewal of her on-air relationship with Howard Stern, the radio shock-jock. During the campaign, she had half-jokingly promised to honor Stern by naming a highway rest stop after him if she won. A year later, Volk and Keith Nahigian recalled the pledge and suggested Whitman follow through.

The governor surprised Stern at his New York studio two days after the State of the Union response, telling him on-the-air about his honor. The cast-aluminum plaque bearing his name would be mounted on a bathroom wall at an obscure rest stop along Route 295 in Burlington County. The plaque was designed by a state employee on his own time, and the Republican state committee paid its $1,000 cost. To Whitman, it was an amusing way to call attention to her insistence on fulfilling campaign promises.

"I've always dreamt of a rest stop that I could drive by with my family, and people could relieve themselves while they speak my name. . . . You are a governor who keeps her word," Stern told Whitman on the air.[39]

No one around Whitman expected the anger generated by her prank. Democrats, Republicans, men, women, supporters, critics— the outrage was widespread, cutting across all categories. Rest stops along the Garden State Parkway and New Jersey Turnpike were named after great Americans who came from New Jersey, including Woodrow Wilson, Grover Cleveland, Thomas Edison, and Molly Pitcher. Where did Howard Stern fit in that list?

"It simply amazes me that the governor would take part in a cheap publicity stunt like this, after putting our state in the national spotlight with her State of the Union rebuttal. Here we had a chance to dispel our Jersey joke image and then she names a toilet facility after Howard Stern," complained Assemblyman Joe Roberts, the Democratic budget officer.[40]

"To Howard Stern, women are sex objects for his own amusement," said Myra Terry, state president of the National Organization for Women and a staunch Whitman supporter. "He promulgates stereotypes that label women as whores, lesbians, or bitches. As we approach the twenty-first century, it's high time for women to be respected as equal human beings and not in terms of their sexual value."[41]

Whitman claimed she was making a joke, not endorsing Stern's philosophy. She became openly exasperated when reporters continued to ask her about the episode. "Let's not get ridiculous about this," she said.[42]

Yet even the Stern fiasco—perhaps the most embarrassing blunder of her career—produced a political bonus. Stern's show was nationally syndicated and, unlike more conservative, issue-oriented talk shows such as Rush Limbaugh's program, reached a largely apolitical audience. For days Stern praised Whitman and provided updates on what he called "the Great Rest Stop Controversy."[43] As a result she gained an entire new legion of fans.

"Christie Whitman? Yeah, I know who she is," a teenager in Los Angeles said a few months later, while Whitman was in southern California for speeches at the Richard Nixon and Ronald Reagan presidential libraries. "She's the one who Howard Stern likes so much, who gave him that bathroom in New Jersey. She's pretty cool."[44]

12

Reality Check

> She's an intelligent, imaginative and hardworking executive who could be vice president or even president someday. Nonetheless, she made a crucial mistake. . . . She promised to give the voters what they really want: lower taxes, better services and no sacrifices. No one can deliver on that, including her.
>
> —*Money,* May 1995

FOR MOST POLITICIANS, A MONTH LIKE WHITMAN ENJOYED IN JANUARY 1995 comes infrequently. She had reached heights that few ever achieve, but for a while there would be no more State of the Union responses, no more nationwide addresses broadcast on all networks. No more celebrity magazine year-end roundups, upbeat State of the State speeches, or new tax cuts for the rest of 1995.

In Trenton, Whitman and her staff knew they had to set aside their national emphasis and focus on the state's business, particularly on the budget proposal. Reporters did the same. During the hectic weeks of three major speeches, the NGA conference and the rest-stop dedication, few had scrutinized the budget's specifics. By early February, when the New Jersey Treasury Department released detailed explanations of her spending proposals, they were ready to take a close look, especially at components that were already drawing complaints from lawmakers.

Much of the criticism echoed Democratic themes from the 1994 budget debate. Property taxes were climbing in most communities, with Whitman, mayors, and Democratic leaders arguing over responsibility for the increases. The new budget maintained the administration's widely criticized dependence on reducing contributions to employee pensions to pay for the income-tax cuts. The cuts, in their final form, would give the largest percentage savings to low- and moderate-income residents, but the one-sixth of the population with the highest incomes and steepest tax bills would keep half of the actual dollars saved, Democrats complained.

In addition, legislators on both sides of the aisle believed several of Whitman's new proposals to enhance revenues or lower costs to be politically foolhardy. The planned five-dollar surcharge for in-person transactions at motor vehicle offices could disproportionately hit poorer residents, who often preferred to conduct their business at the agencies rather than by mail. Proposals to charge sales tax on any money saved through the use of store coupons and to increase senior citizens' co-payment on their state-subsidized prescription drug program prompted charges that the governor was making the poor and elderly pay for her politically popular tax cuts.

"This budget document lashes out with higher taxes today for senior citizens who cut supermarket coupons, while it puts the squeeze on the taxpayers of tomorrow who will have to pay off the governor's debt," said Bernard Kenny, the Democratic senate budget officer.[1]

Many of the maligned proposals would yield relatively little revenue in a budget of nearly $16 billion. The new sales taxes on coupons, for example, would reap about $15 million per year, and the walk-in fee could bring in another $15 million. By contrast, Whitman forecast a $500 million surplus, more than enough to take care of the politically pesky plans. Although some Democrats believed that Whitman purposely included the proposals to give GOP legislators unpopular programs they could defeat—and thus gain credit with voters in the fall elections—others contended that her staff was not politically creative enough to concoct such a scheme.

While Whitman was hailed as brilliant with voters, her administration's lack of political savvy still haunted her legislative program. With a few exceptions, no one in Whitman's inner circle focused regularly on statehouse politics or worried about the public ramifications of her budgetary proposals. She seldom included the chairwoman of the Republican state committee, Virginia Littell, in planning or strategy sessions and rarely used the party apparatus for major outreach efforts.

Just as in 1994, Whitman could not afford a major defeat on her tax-cut proposals or the basic elements of her spending plans. As her national profile rose, expectations grew that Whitman's fiscal policies would be easily ratified by the GOP-controlled legislature. Republican lawmakers, however, vowed it would not be so easy this time; they had given Whitman the benefit of the doubt in 1994, but they were not going to surrender without a fight in 1995.

By March, it appeared that the greatest threat to the tax cut and other budget proposals would come from several Republican members of the state senate budget committee. The two Democrats on the seven-member panel would clearly oppose most of Whitman's plans; if two of the five Republicans sided with the Democrats in committee votes, they could block the governor's initiatives indefinitely, and three of them seemed poised to do just that.

Republican senators Richard LaRossa and Peter Inverso had the most to lose by siding with Whitman. Tens of thousands of state employees lived in their districts. Many were politically active, aware of their legislators' votes on specific issues—and vehemently against Whitman's proposals. The state workers worried less about budget problems bandied about by Democrats, such as property taxes, and more about issues that could immediately affect their jobs and families: layoffs, privatization of state operations, and Whitman's insistence that the next round of union contracts require employees to pay part of their health-care costs or enroll in less expensive managed-care plans. Even with the budget votes months away, LaRossa and Inverso warned that they might have to oppose Whitman, potentially derailing her entire fiscal program.

"I don't go out of my way to look for things to be against. . . . I've got to be given a reason for something, and so far this administration hasn't been providing me with those answers," LaRossa said. "All I'm getting is a pat on the head and I'm being told, 'It'll be fine.' I deserve more answers so I can give answers to the people I represent."[2]

As lawmakers prepared for the spring budget hearings, Whitman knew the other potential Republican "no" vote could come from Robert Littell, the senate budget committee chairman. Littell's public statements focused on suggestions that the tax-cut votes be delayed until the fall, when lawmakers would know the amount of federal aid that could be expected in the coming year. Underlying that policy concern, though, was a personal motive: in March, Whitman had asked Virginia Littell, his wife, to step down as party chairwoman when her current term ended in June. Whitman had no official authority to replace her, though governors traditionally controlled their party's state apparatus. While many Republicans believed that Chuck Haytaian, the heir apparent as chairman, would more aggressively promote the GOP's party line, most recent GOP gains had come under Virginia Littell's reign— and she didn't plan to fade away without a fight that threatened to stretch through the spring.

Whitman would have to face both threats—Virginia Littell's hopes of saving her job and the potential rebellion by Bob Littell, LaRossa, and Inverso—with a juggled staff alignment. Judy Shaw, worn down by the around-the-clock demands of the chief of staff position and by the need to separate her duties from her friend-

223

ships with Hazel Gluck and other former lobbying partners, had stepped down several weeks after the State of the Union address. The new team would be led by Peter Verniero; Margaret Foti, a Bergen County attorney and former FBI agent who had worked with Whitman at the Board of Public Utilities, replaced Verniero as chief counsel. Carl Golden became more of a factor in policy deliberations, and several second-tier staffers were transferred from the governor's office to cabinet departments.

For Republican legislators, the changes offered little hope that the administration's habit of ignoring their political needs would soon improve. Foti had never worked in the statehouse, and Verniero's lawyerly approach to his job was well known. Additionally, Whitman maintained the often-confusing structure of three coequal chiefs, though she also ensured that everyone understood Verniero was in charge. But Whitman didn't overly worry about the threats from the GOP lawmakers. She felt more comfortable as governor in her second year, more secure in making changes, more at ease with the job's demands and responsibilities. Still, every aspect of her life had been altered, and not always for the better—for instance, there was the lack of time to spend with her family and friends.

"What really took me the longest is identifying myself on the phone. I'd call the office and say, 'It's Christie,' and everyone would go, 'huh?' And it took a long time for me to talk about myself in the third person, which I don't always do anyway. Another way I get around it is say, 'Hi, it's me,' if I'm calling the office and hope they figure out my voice by now."[3]

Still rankling her too were the constant need for security and the never-ending scrutiny of reporters and camera crews. For someone so comfortable with voters, Whitman also had surprising difficulty adjusting to the public's new view of her. Drugstore clerks usually needed five or ten minutes to calm down when she walked in for a soda or a newspaper, waiters and waitresses tended to fawn, and she all but gave up shopping in local malls because of admiring crowds. She was all for support and encouragement, but watching teenagers behind a cash register suddenly become too nervous to speak, or drop everything they were holding, was more embarrassing than flattering.

John and the children also had to endure her celebrity status. Kate turned down her acceptance to Princeton University, Web Todd's alma mater, partially because of the school's proximity to Drumthwacket and Trenton and the pressures of attending college in a state where Mom was the governor. She enrolled instead at Connecticut's highly regarded Wesleyan University, where she defended moderate Republican positions in political science classes and debated liberal Democratic classmates. At Deerfield Academy in Massachusetts, Taylor's friends took his mother's job in stride—especially after George Pataki's daughter enrolled in his class.

John Whitman was accustomed to his wife's public career, after her decade as a freeholder, cabinet member, and gubernatorial and Senate candidate. Although he limited his active participation in public causes to a few selected favorites, such as a breast cancer awareness campaign and creation of the state's Vietnam Veterans Memorial, the demands of serving as First Spouse often took time from his business ventures. Sometimes they even took precedence over hockey, but during the New Jersey Devils' 1995 championship playoffs, the governor went alone to an annual political dinner while John—who had a dinner place set for him—went instead to the hockey game at the Meadowlands Arena.

"I think it's a lot of fun [being a governor's husband]. I'm not forced to do anything. Someone asked me, 'What do you absolutely have to do?' I sort of thought about it and said, 'Well, I have to go to the State of the State message, and I probably have to go to the budget, and I probably have to go to one or two Republican things, like the governor's gala. But there's nothing else I have to do, and from that point of view, I get to choose," John said. "I almost can't remember when she wasn't governor, even though it was only two years ago. It's all pervasive in your life," he added.[4]

Kate and Taylor were also accustomed to her hectic schedule—she first ran for office when they were five and three—and presumed it was "part of her life forever," Whitman said. As a family, they seldom discussed Whitman's political future, except in jest.

No one was anxious for more lifestyle changes, new demands, and increased security protection. "[Even] now I think I get isolated if I don't work hard. . . . because I have troopers around me. Secret Service would be ten times worse in terms of being closeted in. . . . It just isn't a very pleasant prospect. You've got to really want to put up with what you have to put up with for the kids and for John," Whitman said.[5]

She still deflected talk about running for vice president or president, prompting statehouse reporters to hunt for new and creative ways to ask the question in a manner that would produce an answer. On almost any other topic, Whitman was still surprisingly candid. Occasionally, she would respond to a question cautiously if it dealt with a sensitive issue such as union contract negotiations. Usually, though, Whitman said whatever she thought. When a reporter asked her, during an outer-office press conference, about a potentially explosive remark she had made about racial issues to a London newspaper, Whitman admitted she knew it would cause trouble as soon as she said it.

Golden and Verniero, standing on the side, looked at each other in surprise. "I can't imagine any other politician, and I don't care whether it's Jim Florio, Tom Kean, or whoever, responding to a question by saying, 'I knew the minute I said it I was going to be in trouble,' " Golden said.[6]

Whitman had made the remark to a reporter from the *Independent,* a London weekly doing a profile in advance of her six-day trade mission to England that would take place in April. Their conversation had turned to Newt Gingrich's Contract With America and its call for ending welfare payments to unwed teenage mothers. Whitman explained that many cultural problems, such as teenage pregnancy, "cannot be legislated away. If you could it would be wonderful, but you can't. . . . And as regards the unwed mothers, there's a game called 'jewels in the crown' that young black males have, and it's how many children you can sire outside of wedlock. You can't legislate against that."[7]

The London reporter thought the comment was unimportant and buried it deep in his story. Four days later, the staff of Demo-

Whitman and former president George Bush on the stump for Chuck Haytaian in 1994. Despite the support, Haytaian failed to unseat Sen. Frank Lautenberg.

Whitman waited eighty-one minutes for President Clinton to complete his 1995 State of the Union Address before she could make the official Republican response.

Whitman hosted *Larry King Live* on CNN on August 6, 1995, appearing with political analysts Leslie Stahl and Jeff Greenfield.

President Clinton and New Jersey Devils team captain Scott Stevens hoist the Stanley Cup at a White House ceremony honoring New Jersey's hockey team in July 1995. The team's owner had bedeviled Whitman with threats to move the franchise to Nashville.

With chief of staff Peter Verniero

Whitman's moderate positions on social issues have kept her at arm's length from many conservative Republicans. (Courtesy Steve Breen)

With House Speaker Newt Gingrich at a fund-raising event

Despite her lifelong friendship with presidential hopeful Steve Forbes, Whitman announced her endorsement of Senate Majority Leader Bob Dole on December 11, 1995.

Whitman and an exhausted entourage complete a cross-state bike ride in
Point Pleasant Beach in August 1995.

Whitman's ability to have fun and laugh at herself has endeared her to both Democrats and Republicans across the country. (Noah K. Murray, *Asbury Park Press*)

cratic state senator Wayne Bryant, who had sponsored the New Jersey law that stopped additional payments to mothers who give birth after going on welfare, alerted him to the remark. He attacked it as "personally offensive, racially divisive, and totally inappropriate" and stressed that Whitman was "bright enough" to understand the consequences of her statement.[8]

"A comment of this venomous character would not be unexpected from shock-radio disc jockeys or hate-inspired talk-show hosts. But it is beneath the dignity of the person holding the office of Governor of the State of New Jersey," Bryant said.[9]

In a statehouse press conference, Whitman apologized for singling out a specific racial group but defended talking about the overall problem of teenage out-of-wedlock pregnancies. Whitman had heard about "jewels in the crown" in a conversation at a Newark AIDS clinic, she said. "The game 'jewels in the crown' is real. I'm not going to apologize for bringing it up because I think we've got to face these problems. . . . We can't pretend that everything is rosy and we don't have some very serious social problems," Whitman said.[10]

Although some African-American leaders denied that such a game existed, none disputed statistics showing that the percentage of out-of-wedlock births was higher among African-American teenagers than among white teenagers. To them, that was not the point at issue. Rather, it was Whitman's decision once again to single out their specific group in a negative context. They saw her continued involvement in racially sensitive controversies as a pattern: witness the Larry McCarthy, Ed Rollins, Khalid Muhammad, and Bob Grant episodes. Only seven weeks earlier, she had decided against calling for the resignation of Rutgers University president Francis Lawrence for linking low test scores among minority students to their "genetic hereditary background"; Lawrence later apologized for what he called a misstatement. Now, the "jewels in the crown" comment.

"When people keep having to apologize, it makes me wonder if this is what they believe to be the truth," said Trenton mayor Douglas Palmer.[11]

In a *Star-Ledger* column, David Wald wrote that "Whitman is not a red-necked yahoo conservative. She is reasoned, moderate, and painfully aware that her cherished Republican party has trouble succeeding because it includes too many intolerant conservatives. . . . But there have been occasions when she has been perceived as being insensitive to racial politics in this state, behavior which reinforces another stereotype: Whitman is too blue-blooded ever to approach an understanding of urban and black America."[12]

Trying to end the controversy, Whitman started forums on teenage pregnancies and welfare reform, stressing that "it's time to stop playing politics with this issue."[13] But snuffing out doubts about her relationship with the state's African-American communities would take time, certainly more than the two weeks she would be in London for a trade mission and in California for appearances at the Nixon and Reagan presidential libraries. On both trips, reporters wanted to know about her vice-presidential prospects, the impact of her tax cuts on property taxes—and why she could not shake her problems with racial issues.

"How do you counter the perception of racism, which is there whether you like it or not?" a California political writer asked at a breakfast with reporters. Appearing annoyed, Whitman tried her standard retort: the complaints about problems with the African-American community were political rhetoric, she had a fine record of appointing minority New Jerseyans to her administration, 150 languages are spoken in the state, a host of initiatives were helping the urban poor, and so on. Whitman also became angry at a reporter's suggestion that her problems with the African-American community began with Ed Rollins's allegations eighteen months before. "I take exception with that. I keep getting hammered with something that never happened," she insisted.[14]

Rollins's lasting effect, though, was a reality she had to live with, as she had feared from the start. "Nationally, when you've had an incident like that, it's always mentioned in the first three paragraphs," said Larry Sabato of the University of Virginia.[15]

She faced the same questions—asked more politely, in less accusatory tones—in London. John Carlin, the *Independent* reporter who published the original "jewels" comment, compared the racial controversy surrounding Whitman to racial divisions in South Africa. (Not all of the London reporters fully understood American government, or Whitman's position in it; a *Daily Mail* story described Whitman as an official with "a high profile in Speaker Newt Gingrich's administration.")[16]

For most of the London trip, Whitman focused on economic concerns and her hopes that she and Gil Medina, her commerce commissioner, could persuade overseas firms to invest in the state. She met dozens of corporate executives, English noblemen, top British government officials, diplomats, Americans living abroad, reporters, and curious Londoners. Medina had her constantly on display, shaking hands and making small talk each day from dawn to late in the evening. There were also numerous interviews, including appearances on the BBC and Skyview Television, which reached throughout the United Kingdom and much of Europe. A profile in the *Guardian*, a London newspaper, carried the headline MADE FOR THE WHITE HOUSE.[17]

"Her reputation is spreading almost worldwide. We certainly know of her, and I think she's done a grand job," said Sir John Quinton, chairman of an English firm that owned quarries in New Jersey.[18]

Medina found her to be "the best marketing person I've ever seen. She is the Michael Jordan of promotion. It's astounding to see her in front of a crowd of people."[19]

England was an ideal choice for Whitman's first overseas mission. She and John had lived in London for two years in the 1970s, and Kate had been born there. Now John flew to London to join his wife, after a personal business excursion to the Middle East. The frantic pace of speeches, interviews, appearances, and business meetings left both exhausted. With Whitman's time in London so limited, Medina and Keith Nahigian squeezed more than two dozen events into a seventy-two-hour span.

Keeping up with Whitman at any time was a formidable task, but reporters traveling with her on out-of-town trips found the schedule almost too fast-paced to bear. New Jersey Network reporter Michael Aron, following Whitman in London, found that "my feet were so sore that I couldn't put shoes on. I had to wear sneakers and walk into the House of Lords with dirty white Reeboks on my feet. I got a sneer from so many people."[20]

The trip's highlight was a private one-hour meeting with Margaret Thatcher, the former prime minister who was revered by conservatives in the United States and around the world. As prime minister, Thatcher had privatized numerous government operations, including British Airways, much as Whitman hoped to do with many state services. An opportunity to be evaluated—and hopefully praised—by Thatcher was too tempting for Whitman promoters to resist. Even before their meeting, planners announced a joint public appearance, on the steps of Thatcher's office. They needn't have worried: although neither would reveal the details of their discussion, the former prime minister was highly complimentary of Whitman. "When you get into government, just exactly as the governor did, what she said she would do, she did, and that's terrific, and it works and it augers very well for her whole future," Thatcher said.[21]

Whitman's supporters hoped that Thatcher's praise would enhance Whitman's reception in California, where she planned to emphasize the need to look at more than social issues as criteria for candidates on the 1996 ticket. If political trips were football plays, Whitman might have called the three-day foray to southern California "54 Right."[22] Fifty-four was the number of electoral votes the state controlled in the 1996 presidential election, more than New Jersey and New York combined; right was the political direction that many California Republicans clearly preferred—and that Whitman had to face if she hoped to make any headway. More than a year before the 1996 convention, Whitman's supporters knew it was premature to label the trip as crucial to her potential future as a national figure. Yet political experts insisted it could be a key indicator of whether she would someday be accepted by social conservatives as either a party leader or a national candidate.

The trip was built around an invitation from Tricia Cox Nixon,

a onetime classmate of Whitman's, to speak at ceremonies commemorating the first anniversary of her father's death; in addition,
Whitman would speak at the Reagan library. Most of her southern
California audiences, she knew, would not share her moderate social philosophy. The Nixon library was located in Orange County,
one of the nation's most conservative regions. The Reagan library
address would be the first in a new "Ronald Reagan Lecture Series"—hardly a forum where Whitman might find a pro-choice
audience.

"We were looking for a conservative thinker who's on the cutting edge of conservative philosophy. We felt there was a unique fit
with Ronald Reagan's philosophy, which was formed at the statehouse level as a tax cutter" when Reagan was California's governor, said Lynda Schuler, deputy director of the Ronald Reagan
Center for Public Affairs. She admitted that the term "conservative" did not apply to all of Whitman's beliefs, noting, "In this
sense, I'm applying it to Governor Whitman as a fiscal conservative
who is close to the people. . . . There's a legitimate semantic debate going on in the Republican party on what you call a conservative."[23]

Whitman's initial appearance, a breakfast talk in the Nixon library lobby to the powerful Orange County Lincoln Club, reminded a few California political writers of a sacrificial ritual.
George Bush received his largest plurality of any county in the
nation from Orange County in 1988. Orange County also was
home to conservative congressman Robert Dornan, the 1996
GOP presidential candidate who was a frequent substitute host on
Rush Limbaugh's television show. Pro-life demonstrators protested her appearance, insisting that Whitman was a traitor to Republican values.

Still, the Lincoln Club, comprised largely of leaders of southern California's business and financial communities, was anxious to
hear Whitman's conservative fiscal message. A few months before,
Orange County's government had declared bankruptcy after years
of reckless investing—and Whitman focused on her tax cuts and

231

job-creation program in her off-the-cuff remarks, carefully avoiding any mention of the abortion issue.

"We talk about her every chance we get. We even tell Pete Wilson that she's doing some of the things that he ought to," said Doy Henley, an aerospace executive who was the Lincoln Club president.[24]

Tom Fuentes, the county's Republican chairman, praised Whitman's message of smaller government and stressed that "we want to be big-tent oriented." However, he went on, "on the other hand, much that motivates the grass roots of our party are conservative activists who are very convinced of the necessity to sustain the values and traditions of our party. That includes a pro-life statement."[25]

While her Nixon library speech also avoided a direct discussion of abortion, Whitman sounded an obvious call for party unity—and admitted that she disagreed with parts of the GOP's Contract With America.

"The months ahead will produce many distractions for all of us," she said. "During the battle for the presidential nomination, many will try to divide our country. Rather than responding to their efforts, we must remain fixed on our own determination to build and to hope. . . . A little more than a year from now, Republicans will have a candidate for the presidency—and for the vice presidency. Those persons, whoever they may be, must have the confidence and support of the entire party."[26]

The reception was warm and supportive, even if many Orange County residents still focused on Whitman's pro-choice position. "I doubt that everyone who was clapping was where I am on the issue of choice itself. But they were certainly supportive of the idea that it's not a litmus test," Whitman told California's top political reporters.[27]

She constantly resisted questions about whether she would endorse Wilson for the presidential nomination, explaining that she wanted to defer any decision, and denying any interest in the second spot "for the sixty billionth time."[28] At the Reagan library, standing near the presidential desk in a full-scale replica of the

White House Oval Office, she jokingly told reporters, "That's the closest you're ever going to see me to it."[29]

The pressures to throw her support—and New Jersey's considerable fund-raising base—behind one of the growing field of Republican presidential contenders grew almost daily. Whitman's policy differences with Dornan, Alan Keyes, Phil Gramm, and Pat Buchanan made an endorsement of their campaigns unlikely. She shared more with the leading moderate contenders—Pete Wilson, Bob Dole, and Lamar Alexander—in terms of both philosophy and mutual supporters. Lewis Eisenberg, her choice to chair the Port Authority in 1995, was a Dole national finance cochairman, Tom Kean and Mike Murphy were backing Alexander, and Hazel Gluck signed on with Wilson.

With the field still murky and Colin Powell's status uncertain, Whitman insisted that rank-and-file Republicans should be able to take their time in choosing a candidate and refused to move the state's last-in-the-nation primary to an earlier date. Her insistence on neutrality annoyed many Republican legislators who wanted to sign on with a candidate, and a few of the contenders themselves. Dole's supporters were particularly peeved—he was, after all, the Senate majority leader—and vented their irritation to national reporters, such as Robert Novak.

"Some of her top people are going into Pete Wilson's campaign," Novak said on CNN's *Inside Politics*. "They are both pro-choice on abortion—that is, Whitman and Wilson. There's no chance that the Republicans will nominate two pro-choice candidates. Her chance to be on a ticket as vice president is with the anti-abortion Senator Dole. So, I would say that this is not a good sign for her getting in good with Senator Dole."[30]

She nevertheless stuck to her neutrality pledge, ignoring the complaints and the media stars who prattled about them. Democrats, united behind President Clinton, enjoyed watching the state GOP's intraparty squabbles. Whitman's budget difficulties and her out-of-town trips—especially her decision to charge the state for the $9,500 cost of the California excursion—also made convenient targets for Democratic salvos. Whitman's claim that the trip qualified as official business because of the invitations from the presidential libraries was undercut by the Nixon library's decision to market her speech as a video titled "Victory in '96: The Republican Opportunity."[31]

"While New Jersey residents are trying to make ends meet after paying their tax bills, they shouldn't have to be insulted by being forced to pay thousands of dollars so the governor can wine and dine with California Republicans. Republicans should have the grace to pay political bills from the substantial political war chests," Democrat John Lynch, the senate minority leader, said. "It doesn't sound like there's anything there for New Jersey taxpayers back home. . . . The governor and her political supporters have every right to fuel speculation about her national ticket ambitions, but New Jersey taxpayers shouldn't have to pay for it," Lynch added.[32]

For Democrats, the upcoming budget debates offered the last opportunity to block—or at least postpone—her income-tax cuts. The timing, they calculated, might never be better. Unions representing tens of thousands of state workers threatened job actions that could shut down toll roads and many other facilities if they did not have new contracts when their current pacts expired June 30. Union leaders depicted Whitman as a blue-blooded heiress who had never struggled for money and who hoped to improve her national political image with tax cuts financed through reduced health benefits for hourly state employees.

The union opposition created more pressure on wavering Republican lawmakers. In the senate, Bob Littell's support appeared even more questionable after Whitman followed through on replacing Virginia Littell with Chuck Haytaian. Republican conservatives were also annoyed by Whitman's conditional veto of the "three strikes and you're in" bill that required a mandatory life term without parole upon conviction for a third felony; she feared that the bill's broad parameters would overcrowd prisons and unfairly penalize those convicted of repeated nonviolent or comparatively minor crimes.

The budget's mathematics also seemed questionable because

of a slowing economy and federal aid cutbacks. The state's nonpartisan legislative services staff estimated that Brian Clymer's projections for the cost of the tax cuts and revenues from motor vehicle surcharges were too optimistic, even discounting any economic turndown.

Suddenly there were indications that voters might finally have started to turn against Whitman. While a *Record* poll found that they still approved of her job performance by a margin of more than two to one, an *Asbury Park Press* survey showed strong opposition to her plan to privatize motor vehicle agencies. Local governments and school boards began approving their annual budgets, reminding voters of still another round of property-tax increases ahead and giving new ammunition to Democratic lawmakers. Another headache came from an unlikely source: the New Jersey Devils, Whitman's favorite sports team and the 1995 National Hockey League champions.

The battle between the state and John McMullen, the Devils' irascible owner, had been brewing for years. He had moved the team from Colorado to the state-owned Meadowlands arena in 1982, signing a thirty-year lease that was renegotiated—in the Devils' favor—in 1986 and 1991. Still, after more than a decade in the Meadowlands, McMullen's team consistently finished each year behind the New York Rangers in both ticket sales and media attention. Sports franchises, especially championship teams, were valuable commodities for cities, producing tens of millions of dollars each year in local revenue. Municipal leaders in Nashville, Tennessee—which had no major league team in any sport—badly wanted a franchise and were dangling a multimillion-dollar windfall to any owner willing to relocate.

For the right price, McMullen was willing to listen—and to abandon the Meadowlands. Looking for a way out of his lease, he claimed in late April 1995 that the state had violated it. Whitman soon asked her husband to coax the two sides into negotiations: John Whitman knew McMullen from years of attending games, and he had worked with the Sports Authority executives a year earlier as cochairman of the host committee for World Cup soccer matches played at Giants Stadium. Abandoning his policy of staying out of government business, he agreed.

For Whitman, the Devils' departure could be politically devastating. No major league team had ever moved immediately after winning its league's championship, and no team had left the New York metropolitan area since baseball's Brooklyn Dodgers and New York Giants relocated to California nearly four decades earlier. Losing the Devils to Nashville—a far smaller market—could destroy Whitman's success in portraying New Jersey as a business-friendly, economically robust state.

Democrats gleefully congratulated each other for finally stumbling on a political puzzle that Whitman apparently couldn't solve. If her husband and the Sports Authority negotiators convinced McMullen to stay, Democrats could probably charge her with squandering taxpayer money to keep hockey fans happy. If the Devils left for Tennessee, they could refute her claim that New Jersey was "open for business." A thirty-second commercial combining film clips of Whitman cheering at a Devils game with shots of the team in Nashville, Democrats calculated, could hurt Whitman's popularity and reputation by reminding voters of the loss.

Whitman made efforts to separate herself from the sputtering closed-door talks and to lower expectations with gloomy predictions that the Devils would probably move. Both fared poorly. She had made no secret of her love for hockey or her ties to the team and openly rooted for the Devils throughout the Stanley Cup playoffs. John's involvement, and Hazel Gluck's representation of McMullen in the negotiations, added to her political stake in the outcome. At the team's Stanley Cup celebration in the Meadowlands parking lot on June 28, fans booed Whitman and held signs proclaiming NO DEVILS, NO WHITMAN.

"Governor Whitman's dire predictions didn't stop her from attempting to use the event last night as her own little photo opportunity. But Devils fans showed her what they think of her handling of this situation by booing her right off the stage," said Democratic Assemblyman Anthony Impreveduto. "It's bad enough that New Jersey jobs are being lost to Sunbelt states, but now our hockey team is moving there too," he said.[33]

By now, to the Democrats' delight, Whitman faced challenges on half a dozen fronts. Politically, compromise was the safest route in several areas. She could simultaneously avoid messy job actions and secure enough votes for the income-tax cuts by giving in to a few union demands and alleviating the concerns of senate Republicans such as Inverso and LaRossa. Spending part of the budget's half-billion-dollar surplus might prompt Wall Street analysts to reduce the state's bond rating—a story that many readers would ignore—but would also provide enough revenue to satisfy McMullen's demands and throw a few tidbits to Democratic mayors complaining about property-tax bills.

But those who predicted that Whitman would compromise still underestimated her determination. Tom Martello, the Associated Press's Trenton bureau chief, succinctly summarized "the reality of state politics in New Jersey: it is Whitman's way, or no way at all. . . . The Republican governor knows how to use her considerable powers and popularity. She knows how to streamroll lawmakers in negotiations. And she certainly knows how to enhance her national image as a tax cutter—even when members of her own party are worried about where the money will come from."[34]

Over a crucial three-week period in late June and early July, Whitman repeatedly refused to back down in a series of confrontations. She took McMullen and the Devils to court for trying to break their lease, producing a temporary agreement that eventually led to a new long-term lease at a minimal cost to the state. Most of the Sports Authority's concessions would be paid for by initiatives such as new luxury boxes and renaming the arena—called the Brendan Byrne Arena for more than a decade—for the corporate sponsor submitting the highest bid. There were minor concessions on the budget, but Whitman refused Inverso's request to postpone the privatization of motor vehicle agencies, which would eliminate the jobs of three hundred state workers who lived in his district. With his eyes brimming, Inverso walked from Whitman's office to the senate floor, where he loyally cast the vote that passed the budget. On the tax-cut votes, Democrats went in different directions, ultimately powerless to stop Whitman's plans.

"Some of my members believe that any tax cut is better than none at all. They will vote yes. Others oppose this concept, but they know the realities of big-money politics in the media age. They will vote yes because they know [they] could be unfairly branded [anti-tax] in an upcoming election," said Democratic assemblywoman Loretta Weinberg. "Others are abstaining. They also might fear the brand of being caught between the proverbial rock and a hard place on a volatile issue. Finally, there are those—like myself—who will vote no. We are thoroughly convinced that this tax cut lays the groundwork for a fiscal disaster of higher property taxes and poor economic performance."[35]

Whitman signed the tax cut at a stage-managed Fourth of July picnic, in front of a dozen television camera crews anxious to cover anything resembling a news story on the holiday. Planners provided everything necessary for a star-spangled media event, most of it donated by private firms: five thousand hot dogs, fifty kegs of beer, hundreds of gallons of root beer, several thousand small American flags. They also rounded up hundreds of playful children and a character dressed as Uncle Sam.

It was the first time in nearly a decade that she had skipped reading the Declaration of Independence aloud as part of an annual Somerset County commemoration at a Revolutionary War battlefield. Instead, she invoked the Spirit of '76 to a far larger audience. "If you look back in 1776, our forefathers were saying, 'No taxation without representation, enough on taxation.' I agree with them, enough on taxation, so what we're doing here in New Jersey is providing a little extra on our Fourth of July that says enough with taxation." Reporters noted it was the second time she had invoked the American Revolution while signing a tax-cut bill, but she plowed ahead, proclaiming, "Let's make a little history here."[36]

She signed several other bills in ceremonies that produced widespread media coverage. The "three strikes" bill, revised to apply only to violent crimes, was signed in front of two dozen uniformed state troopers in a state prison yard surrounded by barbed wire. Another measure set a national precedent by forcing insurance companies to pay for mothers to stay in hospitals for forty-eight hours after giving birth. The bill, which Whitman strongly supported, became law in a ceremony at a Bergen County hospital, where she visited with mothers and their babies under the scrutiny of network television cameras.

She also won a major victory in a direct confrontation with the state's employee unions. With several contracts expiring at the end of the fiscal year on June 30, workers threatened to walk off their jobs, potentially shutting down state highways, facilities for the aged and disabled, and many other essential operations. Whitman appealed directly to voters, pointing out that state workers received health care and other benefits that were far more generous than those traditionally provided by private businesses, and vowed to fire any employee who stayed out for more than four days, as permitted by state law.

The biggest battle came over the Fourth of July weekend, when toll collectors tried to disrupt holiday travel and walked off the job for a day. Whitman replaced them with managers and temporary workers, quickly ending the threat and prompting many comparisons to Ronald Reagan's refusal to give in to air-traffic controllers in 1981, when they called a strike to protest proposed benefit cuts. Contracts with the various unions, signed in the following weeks and months, contained many worker concessions in health care and other areas.

"At first I thought that going after state workers' health benefits would show a kind of callousness and a misreading of public cynicism about state workers. . . . But now looking back at how this has unfolded, most folks have said, 'Yeah, she stood up to the union,'" said David Rebovich, the Rider University political science professor.[37]

Not all aspects of her budget and legislative program ended as easily. The transfer of the state's motor vehicle agencies to private control in early July was handled abysmally, with the contracts to run several offices given to Republican politicians with little or no experience in managing such operations. Rather than postpone the changeover, as many legislators and union leaders recommended, Whitman insisted on adhering to the original schedule, producing chaos at offices that were initially badly understaffed. Lines of angry motorists, many waiting for several hours to perform routine transactions, stretched through motor vehicle offices for days, until more workers could be hired and trained in their new duties.

For New Jerseyans, renewing car registrations or drivers' licenses was one of the few required annual contacts with the state, besides filing income taxes. For many, it was also the first taste of Whitman's changes in the operation of state government, and standing in long lines didn't leave a good impression. The total savings of the switchover was $4 million, hardly enough to warrant the statewide chaos, Democrats insisted.

But the motor vehicle privatization was the only major blunder in what could have been a disastrous series of events for Whitman in late June and early July. The highways stayed open, state workers were—unhappily—at their jobs, the 30 percent tax cut became a reality, and the Devils would be staying at the Meadowlands. Even her opponents conceded that Whitman's display of gritty determination played well with most voters—especially when the other side backed down.

"She now has a reputation for 'out-toughing' everyone," said Democratic assemblyman Robert Smith. "It's good theater. It's clear to me that kind of conflict is great for getting headlines and media attention, but the ultimate question is what is in the best interest of the citizens of the state."[38]

John Whitman noted that "it was asked during the Bradley campaign, it was asked during the Florio campaign, it was asked after she was governor, 'Is she tough enough to do this job?' I think we're just getting to the point where nobody asks that question anymore."[39]

Media adviser Mike Murphy, who came from Washington to watch Whitman sign the tax-cut bill, explained that "people like a governor as a tough executive who puts the state ahead of special interests and doesn't kowtow when somebody tries to push her around. . . . Somebody's got to make the tough calls, and she's going to make a lot of points for doing it."[40]

Around the country, Whitman's victories attracted notice. The Devils' proposed move and the tax-cut adoption had been well covered; additionally, the toll-taker's walkout over the holiday weekend provided the television networks lots of easy footage—near their New York headquarters—during a quiet news week.

"Governor Whitman turned what could have been a public relations catastrophe into a political coup, and this week's play of the week. She also boosted her chances of getting on the Republican ticket next year," said William Schneider on CNN's *Inside Politics*.

"Taking on public employee unions is a pretty good way to burnish your conservative credentials," he added.[40]

13

The Sweep of History

New York Times columnist William Safire always ends one
year with a flurry of predictions for the next. So can we.
. . . Dole will pick New Jersey governor Christine Whitman as his running mate, angering conservatives but winning over a lot of people who usually vote Democratic.

—CNN correspondent Bruce Morton, December 31,
1995

SINCE ROSS PEROT CHOSE CNN's *LARRY KING LIVE* TO LAUNCH HIS
1992 presidential bid, the show had been a showcase for such
guests as Bill Clinton, Al Gore, and other prominent people. It
reached more than two hundred countries and territories, as well as
millions of American homes. A call to Whitman from King's pro-
ducers in late June 1995, though, conveyed more than an invitation for a fifteen-minute interview slot: CNN wanted her to host
an entire program while King was on vacation in early July.

"This really launches her. It makes her a real national figure. She's been seen before, but this is a chance for people around the country to get a good look at her," said Thomas Hartmann, a Rutgers University media professor. "You're not really legitimate unless you're seen on television. Nobody thinks you're a real player until you can afford to buy TV time, and if you get it for free for an hour, it's a godsend."[1]

The hour-long program, which aired on July 6, featured Whitman moderating a discussion among three network news correspondents, ABC's Jeff Greenfield, NBC's Lisa Meyers, and CBS's Lesley Stahl. It focused largely on how the journalists covered political news.

A woman caller from Toms River, New Jersey, asked Stahl, "Lesley, would you please ask the governor what the unemployment rate is in the state of New Jersey, and what she's doing sitting in as host of the Larry King show, when she should be sitting in Trenton."

"Well, there is nothing happening in Trenton tonight," Whitman retorted, after CNN staffers cut off the caller. "But the unemployment rate of the state of New Jersey, I'll just answer that quickly, is slightly above the national average now, 6.1, but below where we were before. We created more jobs in 1994 than we have since 1988. And, in fact, since the first set of tax cuts went through, 90,000 new jobs have been created in the state of New Jersey. So we're doing well."

"Let it be pointed out," Greenfield stressed, "that the first hostile question to you came from a listener and not a journalist."[2]

Whitman's growing celebrity status led to more media coverage, in a never-ending cycle. Each new national magazine profile, any major newspaper story suggesting Whitman could be the 1996 vice-presidential nominee, generated another one, or two, or six. In the summer of 1994, Whitman rode her bike across the state accompanied by only Jason Volk, John, Taylor, and a trooper. A year later, her fellow bike riders included numerous newspaper reporters and a WCBS news-radio anchorwoman who broadcast live reports along the sixty-mile route; television camera crews also met

243

the entourage at the various scheduled stops. One New York television reporter, joining the troupe at the thirty-one-mile mark, lasted for less than three quarters of a mile before being rescued by her cameraman in a van.

For reporters, the trek offered glimpses into the mesh of Whitman's public and private personas. She could have made the trip without the media, ordering aides to keep quiet about her plans, but inviting the press guaranteed widespread coverage during one of the year's slowest news weeks. At each stop, her political drive clearly came through, as she shook dozens of hands and chatted with local officials while reporters and aides collapsed on the side, gulping Gatorade and stretching aching muscles. At the same time, the event provided glimpses at her personal side. Twice she yelled at Taylor for hanging on to the side of a state police car that was slowly leading the way, and she furtively iced a sore shoulder with cold packs provided by troopers. Aides said that the shoulder, injured a year before, would eventually need surgery, but Whitman had no intention of displaying even a hint of pain to the public.

The celebrity moments popped up again and again through the late summer and early fall, some coincidental to her national rise and others directly generated by it. As the host state governor, she greeted Pope John Paul II on October 4 when he arrived at Newark airport for a four-day visit to New Jersey, New York, and Maryland. She celebrated with Clinton and the Devils players in a Stanley Cup ceremony in the White House East Room, toured three Canadian cities in the year's second foreign trade mission, and helped the state GOP raise $4 million at the annual gubernatorial ball, setting a national record for a single-night state fundraising event. More than 3,500 people paid $1,000 each to eat filet of beef in an exposition hall resembling an airplane hangar; hundreds of guests paid an extra $500 for a private picture with Whitman.

With the first legislative elections since her inauguration just a few months away, she knew that the fund-raiser would help Republican candidates remind voters about their tax-cutting record by financing television ads in the fall campaign. "You need to raise money to be able to get your message out, so something like this is important. . . . You have to buy television in New York, the most expensive market, and in Philadelphia, the third most expensive market," she said.[3]

All eighty seats in the assembly were on the November 1995 ballot, with the GOP hoping to maintain its 53–27 margin. Midterm gains for the out-of-power party were common, and Democrats targeted several urban districts they had lost in the 1991 anti-Florio landslide. Whitman knew a substantial Democratic rebound in an off-year election could have national political reverberations.

"I think Democratic loyalty is a little stronger this year, and she's starting to wear out her welcome," said Steve DeMicco, a Democratic consultant. "It's simply that she's an incumbent executive office-holder in this day and age. As political figures go, she's about as popular as they come. But people just don't give them much slack anymore."[4]

Even so, Democrats knew that attacking Whitman or her tax cuts would be ineffective. Their assembly candidates would fare better, party leaders calculated, by instead focusing on the Contract With America—and voters' fears that the federal spending cuts being pushed by Newt Gingrich's Republican Congress could produce drastic reductions in such programs as Medicare and Medicaid.

For New Jersey residents, those cuts could be devastating. The state's elderly population was among the nation's largest; any Medicare service reduction could reduce the quality of health care for hundreds of thousands of New Jersey senior citizens. Gingrich's formula for reallocating Medicaid funding would penalize northeastern states in favor of the Sunbelt, forcing New Jersey either to find new revenues—most probably, taxes—or to reduce benefits for 700,000 Medicaid clients.

"We need to put New Jersey on record declaring that we won't stand for this assault on our senior citizens, college students, and children. . . . We won't let New Jersey be 'Newtered,' " Joe Doria, the Assembly Democratic leader, declared.[5]

245

Whitman's national standing enabled her to negotiate on the state's behalf with Gingrich, Dole, and other congressional leaders, prompting Democrats to link her—and, by extension, the Republican assembly candidates—to the GOP plans. Lobbying for a better Medicaid allocation, Whitman became a frequent commuter to Capitol Hill, often flying on a private plane from a local airport with Volk and state troopers. She also spoke regularly with Republican leaders.

"I can call the Speaker and he will pick up the phone and respond to the call. That makes a big difference for us in this state. We have a lot of allies. There is obviously always the concern that when you divide up real dollars, everybody wants to make sure their state is treated equitably, every governor, every congressperson," Whitman said.[6]

Whitman differed with Gingrich on a broad range of social issues. She strongly supported affirmative action; Gingrich backed Pete Wilson's plan to end all programs giving preference based on race. She was one of her party's most prominent abortion rights spokeswomen; he was vehemently anti-abortion. Yet despite their differences, Whitman and Gingrich had a comfortable working relationship. He had campaigned for Whitman on network television during the 1990 Senate race against Bradley and picked her to deliver the State of the Union response. In mid-October, Gingrich flew to Princeton to star at a $1,000-per-person fund-raiser for the state's Republican candidates, proclaiming that "we think of Clinton as a more pleasant Florio."[7] Whitman returned the favor two weeks later, flying to Atlanta—in the midst of the city's World Series frenzy—to be the main attraction at his congressional reelection campaign fund-raiser.

For Whitman, the whirlwind overnight trip—which included choice seats at the final game of the Series—offered both opportunities and risks. Appearing with Gingrich, especially at his request, could reduce tensions between her and the party's conservative leaders. Indeed, the governor received a standing ovation from the crowd of over four hundred Georgians, while another speaker, North Carolina Republican congresswoman Sue Myrick, was given a lukewarm reception. Yet openly supporting Gingrich brought Whitman more problems at home. An *Asbury Park Press* poll had recently found that many New Jerseyans disapproved of Gingrich, and state Democratic leaders were almost gleeful over their potential boost from the governor's trip.

"You've got to get along with people, but that doesn't mean that you have to praise Gingrich's extremist agenda. People are starting to figure out that Republicans are two-faced on a number of issues, like Christie's been with Newt," said Tom Byrne, the state Democratic chairman.[8]

Whitman explained in Atlanta that "I just don't campaign for moderates, I campaign for Republicans. . . . This label of conservative, moderate, liberal is nothing I can quantify. You ask me what I am, you tell me the issue, and I'll decide."[9]

With a big grin, Gingrich conceded that his invitation to Whitman was a blatant attempt to reach out to GOP moderates. At his request, party officials produced a flattering video political portrait of Whitman, which he used to introduce her. "I'm being pretty open about it," he said, calling Whitman "absolutely one of the stars of the Republican party."[10]

One week later, voters gave Democrats a net gain of three seats in the Assembly primarily from victories in traditional strongholds that had been swept by the GOP four years earlier. Leaders of both parties claimed an advantage.

"It shows the Democratic party is alive and well and a vital force in New Jersey politics and well positioned to keep winning in 1996 and 1997. A message was sent to Trenton that voters are uneasy with fiscal policies that mortgage our future," Byrne said.[11]

"If Tom Byrne's happy with 38 percent of the assembly, I'm happy to keep him happy. . . . To end up with a party that controls the assembly fifty [seats] to thirty is pretty decisive," Whitman retorted.[12]

With the legislative elections behind them, the state's political community focused on the upcoming presidential primaries—and Whitman's continuing insistence on remaining neutral among the Republican contenders. Many party leaders assumed Whitman would endorse Pete Wilson, until he dropped out of the race in late September. On the day of Wilson's withdrawal, Whitman met with Bob Dole, the Republican front-runner, in his Capitol Hill office, just a few yards from the Senate chamber, as part of her Medicaid lobbying campaign.

Much of their hour-long discussion dealt with the ongoing budget deadlock. She offered no endorsement, and Dole did not request one. He did appear perplexed, though, at Whitman's delay in making a choice. "I know she wants to wait until after . . . sometime later," he told reporters, obviously hesitating as he groped to explain her neutrality.[13]

A few minutes later, Whitman told the reporters that Dole was the clear front-runner in New Jersey, while refusing to say he could win the party's nomination. "I am not at all sure this convention won't be a brokered convention. . . . There are a number of candidates with whom I'm impressed."[14]

To Dole's supporters—if not to Dole himself—Whitman's prognostication, made right outside his office, was an insult to his candidacy. In clear terms, they told Whitman's staff she had to publicly clarify her statement—and unequivocally reaffirm his role as a party leader and the unquestioned front-runner. Taken aback at the heavy-handed reaction to what she considered a casual comment, Whitman issued the statement that Dole wanted, but she still refused to back his White House bid.

No one from Dole's camp directly asked Whitman for her endorsement, but his emissaries made their presence felt. New Hampshire governor Steve Merrill, who signed on with Dole, told Whitman that the majority leader would be happy to talk with her anytime she wanted. She replied that Dole could call at any time.

Much of the media speculated that Whitman's reluctance to make a decision came from Steve Forbes's late entry into the presidential race. Forbes debated joining the GOP field through much of the summer and fall, seeking advice from Whitman and her husband and from other New Jersey leaders. She did not volunteer to stand with him at his formal declaration at the National Press Club in the fall or at any of his early fund-raisers. Forbes's commercials, which played over and over again in early caucus and primary states such as Iowa, New Hampshire, Delaware, and Arizona, cited his relationship with Whitman and his role in plotting her 30 percent tax cut; one commercial even displayed an *Asbury Park Press* story about their relationship. While Whitman still hesitated in choosing a candidate—partially because of Colin Powell's indecision about running—she never considered endorsing Forbes.

Turning her back on a longtime friend, to whom she owed at least a small part of her success, wasn't easy. Besides his friendship and advice, Forbes unabashedly supported her policies in the column that he wrote in *Forbes* magazine. Yet despite Forbes's initial surge in the polls, Whitman did not believe he could win the Republican nomination. She also disagreed with Forbes on several issues, most notably his call for a flat income tax with no deductions for home mortgage interest, charitable contributions, and state income taxes. Whitman's top priority was electing a Republican and defeating Clinton in 1996. Powell's eventual decision to stay out of the race, Wilson's withdrawal, and Dole's air of inevitability, prompted her to turn to the majority leader. Before announcing her endorsement, however, she had to have a difficult conversation with Forbes. The hardest part, she admitted, was "looking my good friend in the eye who is doing this huge gamble."

Whitman reflected, "Steve Forbes was someone I grew up with and who has been a wonderful supporter of mine and, I happen to think, very bright and very capable in the economic field. That was what was difficult. The decision to endorse Bob Dole for president was not a difficult one in that I really believe in his leadership strengths and capabilities. As much as I admire Steve and his intellect and his insight on economic matters and things in general, he hasn't been a part of the political process in a way that I believe will [make him] as effective as a leader as Bob Dole."[15]

Forbes had one request: in a recent interview, Whitman had given the impression that the 30 percent tax cut was created by a large group of people. Would she be willing, Forbes asked, to be open about his key role in developing her economic program?

"I'd indicated there were lots of people at the table, which there were. But he and Larry Kudlow were the two key architects of the 30 percent tax cut, no two ways about that. So I said I would," Whitman recalled. "He was fine about it. He was fine. And he called over Christmas just to say, 'Merry Christmas, Happy New Year,' and let me know we're still friends."[16]

Keith Nahigian orchestrated the Dole endorsement, picking a recently opened shoe warehouse to demonstrate the job-creation theme that Whitman and Dole both hoped to emphasize. On December 11, 1995, more than a dozen television cameras, from local stations and national networks, recorded the event. Ironically, a few weeks later Nahigian left Whitman's staff to handle event planning for the Forbes campaign.

While pro-choice advocates feared Whitman's endorsement meant she was softening her stance on abortion, most pundits believed her decision reflected the concerns of GOP moderates that nominating a conservative like Pat Buchanan would lead to Clinton's reelection. "Certainly poll results in New Jersey and in many parts of the country show some people are worried about the harshness or ruthlessness of the GOP revolution. Maybe Whitman feels it's time for her to put her two cents in to endorse, what would one say . . . a more moderate mainstream Republican who is not likely to cause budgetary upheaval," David Rebovich, the Rider University professor, said.[17]

Dole denied suggestions that the endorsement made Whitman his leading choice for the vice-presidential nomination at the party's August convention in San Diego. Whitman stuck to her standard line about being happy as governor, with a new wrinkle: "One of the things that I'm looking forward to is the last day of the convention, because then it will be abundantly clear that I'm not [the] vice-presidential candidate."[18]

She still kept her options open, initially refusing to state that she would not accept the ticket's second spot in 1996 or later, or denying interest in someday even running for president. There were also different contingencies to address: what if Dole called with an offer? Could she actually turn it down? If she ran and lost, what would happen to her prospects for reelection as governor in 1997? And did she really want to be vice president? Since World War II, four vice presidents—Richard Nixon, Lyndon Johnson, Gerald Ford, and George Bush—had moved into the White House. But three governors—Clinton, Carter, and Reagan—made the same move without serving in the position described by John Nance Garner, Franklin Roosevelt's first vice president, as not worth a "pitcher of warm spit."

"People around me say, 'No, you can't say no. What would you do if the party really called? If they said it's the only way that the Republicans can win, and it's key to have a Republican president?' First of all, the vice president has never been that important. Maybe with Dole, simply because he indicated so early that he would probably be a one-term president, it would take on more significance. . . . I cannot imagine any kind of arguments that they could make that would be convincing.[19]

Whitman's inner circle was torn about whether she should push herself among GOP leaders for the vice-presidential nomination in 1996—if that was even possible—or wait for better opportunities in 2000, 2004, or later. If Clinton was reelected—and polls through the first months of 1996 showed him comfortably ahead of all leading Republican contenders, including Dole—there would be no incumbent in the first election of the twenty-first century. Waiting beyond 1996 would also give Whitman a chance for a second term as governor, as well as several more years to build her reputation and collect IOUs from GOP leaders. But if a Republican won without Whitman on the ticket, she would lose the opportunity to become an unquestioned front-runner to succeed him in the White House.

"I would want her to be governor for two terms and run for president at the end of that," former chief of staff Judy Shaw said. "At the end of eight years, she will absolutely be the best of the best. But you only learn some of that through trial and error, and wins and losses."[20]

Lonna Hooks worried that "we have to have her in New Jersey for two terms. If she leaves, the programs are at a fragile point, a very delicate precipice . . . and then her legacy will be Ed Rollins."[21]

But to Don DiFrancesco, it "would be terrific for New Jersey if they actually picked Christie to be vice president as a candidate, and they actually won. She has a shot at that, I think." DiFrancesco openly admitted that he would benefit from Whitman's election as vice president: as state senate president, he would become governor until the next scheduled election, in 1997. He saw no disadvantage, however, to a vice-presidential bid in 1996. If she lost in November, he reasoned, "she would be the leading candidate in the country for the year 2000. She can only serve two terms in New Jersey anyway. And so I think it's a positive thing no matter what. She would benefit the ticket."[22]

Many Republicans, especially in New Jersey, shared DiFrancesco's sentiments. Whitman knew, though, that any national bid would prompt a mixed reaction from New Jersey voters and detract from any future programmatic efforts. Possibly, it would also damage her credibility. "Some people would say, 'Well, that's what she always wanted to do, and that proves that anything she's done in this state hasn't been real.' And there would be others that would say, 'Great,' and another group [would say], 'Hey, we elected you for this, you're supposed to serve your term,' " she said.[23]

Democrats had mixed feelings. Barring an unexpected economic downturn, no Democrat was favored to defeat Whitman in a 1997 reelection bid. By any measure, DiFrancesco or any other Republican would be a far easier opponent if she left Trenton before then. Yet the prospect that Whitman could be a national candidate provided Democrats with a convenient target: any major Whitman proposal that received favorable coverage, such as the welfare reforms she proposed in her 1996 budget address, was inevitably followed by Democratic claims that she was motivated by a desire for more national publicity.

"Her potential running for office as a vice-presidential candidate helps her and hurts her. In the beginning, it helped her, it added to the luster of her already very bright image. Now, it's a

252

mixed bag. It gives the people in the legislature the idea that she's not hands on, that she's not interested in governing because she's got her eyes on the national scene," said Bernard Kenny.[24]

Meanwhile, Dole's delegate lead soared through the New York, Junior Tuesday, and Super Tuesday primaries in March, prompting even more questions about Whitman's vice-presidential aspirations. She campaigned for Dole in New England and New York, and publicly called on Forbes to abandon his campaign, leading to inevitable speculation that she was attempting to win favor with the Senate majority leader. Much of the media speculated that Powell and Whitman were the only pro-choice possibilities for the ticket's second spot, and Powell had already firmly stated he did not want to run for office.

The biggest obstacle to her selection still appeared to be Pat Buchanan and the party's conservative wing. No one knew how Dole would react to the increasing pressure from the right for a completely pro-life ticket. Buchanan threatened to mount a third-party candidacy if either Powell or Whitman was selected; Gary Bauer, president of the Family Research Council, warned that Whitman's selection could split the party. "The message you send to voters [with a pro-choice candidate] is they're really not serious about the abortion issue. So I think for every moderate, suburban Republican woman that you might keep loyal to your party, you end up losing a traditional voter who will be angry," Bauer explained.[25]

The California primary at the end of March gave Dole the delegates he needed to guarantee victory, and provided an opportunity for a congratulatory call. In their brief conversation, Whitman took herself off of the list that the national media had put her on nearly two years before.

"I said it was no way a reflection on him," Whitman told reporters the next day. "I hope that I could do as much as possible in the campaign. I am certainly willing to go anywhere and speak anywhere."[26]

Not surprisingly, reporters and pundits didn't automatically accept Whitman's claim that her primary motivation was to end the speculation, which had clearly become a distraction. "Either she didn't think it was going to happen or didn't want it happen, so why go through the speculation to come in second?" asked Bill Palatucci, the GOP strategist.[27]

In a *New York Times* column, Trenton bureau chief Jennifer Preston noted that "a Dole-Whitman ticket would have been unlikely. It would have required a bold move Mr. Dole probably could not have made, given political reality." Preston added, though, that "let's say that Mr. Dole was seriously considering Mrs. Whitman for the job. Right now, President Clinton is way ahead in the polls. Is this really the presidential campaign that Mrs. Whitman wants to get involved with? A possible losing effort? A Republican Party that is being torn apart from within?"

"Maybe the presidential campaign that she has her eye on is really four years off. And that year, perhaps, she intends to be at the top of the ticket," Preston concluded.[28]

Whitman openly admitted she wanted a larger role in the national debate on a broad number of topics, ranging from welfare reform and the need for privatization to the controversial social topics that angered the GOP's conservative wing. Her selection by Dole and Haley Barbour in late April as a convention cochairwoman, along with Texas governor George W. Bush, ensured she would be a prominent player in San Diego, with extensive television exposure and media attention. Pro-choice activists were disappointed: they had hoped Whitman might instead chair the platform committee, an ideal position to mold the abortion plank. While any effort at the convention to soften the party's traditional anti-abortion language would likely feature Whitman in a major role, many doubted she would lead a floor fight that could damage Dole's prospects to defeat Clinton. Instead she preferred to deal with the abortion dilemma by fighting problems like unwanted teenage pregnancies—and by working within the party.

With Lew Eisenberg, a longtime supporter and a Dole finance co-chairman, she built the Committee for Responsible Government, a political action committee that supported GOP moderates like Bill Weld and Connecticut governor John Rowland. Critics contended that the committee's main purpose—like that of the PAC that Whitman ran before her gubernatorial campaign—was to push Whitman for national office. Even Hazel Gluck conceded that "she's not going to be a candidate for national office [in 1996], but if she wants to be in the future, this would be a good way to promote herself."[29]

Peter Verniero noted that "governors have to address national issues. You can't be an effective governor and chief executive of any state unless you address national issues which affect your state. And she's not going to be intimidated by that because there's a risk that her opponents or cynics will read too much into it. She'll do her job, she'll speak out on national issues. She'll wear her hat as the titular head of the [state] Republican party and as a Republican leader. And we can't be responsible for people reading too much into things. That's their problem."[30]

She still faced problems in New Jersey. With Whitman preparing to push her third state budget through the legislature in spring 1996, many Democratic leaders believed she would finally have to begin working with lawmakers on her proposals rather than sitting back and waiting for automatic approval. Her first major legislative blow had come when both parties combined to defeat her proposal to pay for hospital care of indigent patients with a twenty-five-cent hike in the state's cigarette tax. The former system, which expired at the start of 1996, diverted unemployment insurance funds to finance the program. Raising cigarette taxes to pay for health care seemed a reasonable policy alternative. Whitman waited until just before the deadline to publicly unveil her plan, too late for a formidable lobbying effort with undecided legislators.

"The real question to me, putting aside this national stuff, is can and will she govern now that things are being brought back into balance and the legislature is starting to closely examine issues. Everything is going through the grinder in the four [legislative] caucuses, and that did not happen in the first two years. It remains to be seen in the next two years whether she can govern in that atmosphere," Bernard Kenny said.[31]

Whitman's new budget lacked the dramatic tax cuts of the two previous years, robbing Democrats of their cherished claims that her spending plan would again force property taxes to rise. Several budget proposals, such as combining the banking and insurance departments and creating a new cabinet-level department dedicated to the needs of the elderly, were expected to be approved easily. Her welfare reform plans, which called for a five-year cap on benefits, would probably face more strident opposition. The year's trickiest issue, though, would almost certainly be the ongoing education battle between the Supreme Court, the legislature, and the executive branch. "The goal is not to win, The goal is a consensus between three branches of government," stressed Leo Klagholz, the state education commissioner.[32]

Democrats and much of the media would also continue to charge that Whitman's budget practices jeopardized the state's long-term fiscal health. Her new budget proposal did not include hundreds of millions of dollars needed to pay for indigent hospital care and to match federal grants for AIDS and tuberculosis programs. The state's bonded debt was growing steadily. Wage increases from the four-year union contracts finalized in the fall of 1995 would not hit until 1998.

Most voters, though, still seemed unaware of either the Democratic concerns or many of Whitman's policy initiatives, such as tort reforms that could unclog the court system and the start of a charter school program. After undergoing well-publicized laparoscopic surgery in November 1995 to remove a benign ovarian mass, Whitman told reporters that voters could recite three things about her two years in office: the income-tax cuts, Ed Rollins's allegations, and her surgery.[33]

"Clearly, I want to be known for something more than that," Whitman said later. "I saw a couple of articles or op-eds or analysis pieces over the last week that said this was kind of an inactive governorship. I was sitting there saying, 'You know, I just think they keep raising the damn bar up higher.' When I first proposed the income tax cut, they said, 'Oh, no, it's never going to get done.' When we got the first part, well, you'll never get the second part . . . We finally got it done and now, (people say) 'that was easy.' "[34]

Yet many political experts believed she owed much of her national rise to the intense focus on the tax cuts, to the near exclusion of all else. She was identified in the campaign with one major pledge—reducing income taxes by 30 percent—and she kept it, even beating her own deadline. "She promised that she would cut taxes, and nothing else, and she kept both those promises," Steve Salmore quipped.[35] John Engler asserted, "Her rise, her rapid rise, is directly the result of Governor Whitman's strict adherence to keeping her word, doing exactly what she said she would do. She said she'd cut taxes and she did cut taxes. She delivered."[36]

Her credibility contrasted sharply with the widespread distrust of Jim Florio. Any successor, pundits said, would have benefited from the comparison. But Whitman's two biggest assets—the trust she built by fulfilling the tax-cut pledge and her easygoing manner with voters—were perfect opposites of Florio's two biggest handicaps, his seemingly aloof manner and the belief that he lied to voters in his 1989 campaign.

Still, her popularity among New Jersey voters was only one part of Whitman's rise to stardom. New Jersey's off-year election cycle and the state's proximity to the massive New York and Philadelphia media centers gave her exposure to national pundits and decision makers that other accomplished Republicans could only dream about. As the only woman governor, she enjoyed a unique status. Magazines like *Elle* and *Working Woman,* which both profiled Whitman in November 1995, had no plans for similar stories on Phil Gramm or Pete Wilson. And in spring 1996, more profiles ran in national publications, including a cover story in the *New York Times Magazine* in early May.

She also enjoyed luck usually reserved for lottery winners and the 1969 Mets. Her tax cuts coincided with the national recovery from the prolonged recession of the early 1990's; the World Cup, the pope, and the 1996 NCAA Final Four championship came to New Jersey during her first years in office; and the state remained relatively free of natural disasters and political scandals.

"Timing and luck is everything," Harold Hodes said. "I don't know if you make your own luck, but you've got to be lucky."[37]

Whitman's critics conceded that she was intelligent, talented, and politically astute; her supporters admitted that her celebrity and her twenty-first-century presidential prospects came as much from her good fortune as from her ability. Just as professional athletic teams need both skill and luck to survive long enough to win a league championship, government officials like Whitman cannot count on just one part of the equation if they hope to reach the final round of America's political playoffs.

Roy Romer, the Democratic governor of Colorado, understood the secret of Whitman's success, perhaps better than most. If Whitman's first name "were Christopher, she wouldn't have been able to do everything she's done," he said, relaxing in NBC's Washington studios after appearing with Whitman on *Meet the Press* in February 1996.

There were two other factors that he felt were even more important in making Whitman into a bona fide political celebrity— and, to many, possibly the nation's first female president.

"You have to be very able," Romer said. "And she got caught in a sweep of history."[38]

Notes

Chapter 1 A Bold Move

1. Christine Todd Whitman, interview with author, 4 December 1995.
2. Whitman campaign release, 21 September 1993.
3. *The Campaign Inside*, aired on New Jersey Network, 18 January 1994, 9:00 P.M.
4. *The Campaign Inside*, aired on New Jersey Network, 18 January 1994, 9:00 P.M.
5. Whitman campaign release, 21 September 1993.
6. John Whitman, interview with author, 22 December 1995.
7. "Whitman Tax Data Challenged," *Asbury Park Press*, 22 September 1993.
8. Michael Aron, interview with author, 29 December 1995.
9. "Whitman Indicates Economic Leanings," *Asbury Park Press*, 15 July 1993.
10. C. Whitman interview, 4 December 1995.
11. "Magnate Force," *Asbury Park Press*, 29 January 1995.
12. "Supply-Side Economics Play New Jersey," *New York Times*, 3 October 1993.
13. J. Whitman interview, 22 December 1995.
14. C. Whitman interview, 4 December 1995.
15. J. Whitman interview, 22 December 1995.
16. Editorial, *Philadelphia Inquirer*, 24 September 1993.
17. C. Whitman interview, 4 December 1995.
18. Editorial, *Asbury Park Press*, 24 September 1993.
19. "Embracing Supply-Side Economics a Chore For Candidate," Robert Novak, *Chicago Sun Times*, 11 October 1993.
20. Donald DiFrancesco, interview with author, 29 December 1995.
21. Richard Reeves, "Jim Florio's Red-Hot, Ice-Cold Politics," *New York Times Magazine*, 17 October 1993.

22. "Florio Attacks Tax-Cut Plan By Whitman," *New York Times*, 23 September 1993.

23. Author's notes, 1993 gubernatorial campaign.

24. "Unpopular Governor Finds Himself in Unfamiliar Spot: Front-runner," Associated Press, 29 September 1993.

25. Carl Golden, interview with author, 23 November 1995.

26. C. Whitman interview, 4 December 1995.

Chapter 2   Republican Roots

1. *Charlie Rose*, Public Broadcasting System, aired 13 April 1994.

2. Pat Beard, "Leading Lady," *Town and Country*, March 1995.

3. Christine Todd Whitman, interview with author, 4 February 1996.

4. Ibid.

5. Eric Pooley, "The Liberation of Christie Whitman," *Vogue*, August 1994.

6. "Man at the Side of (Not Behind) Whitman," *New York Times* 17 January 1994.

7. Pooley, *Vogue*.

8. Whitman 1993 gubernatorial campaign commercial videocassette.

9. *The Campaign Inside*, aired on New Jersey Network, 18 January 1994, 9:00 P.M.

10. B. Thomas Byrne, interview with author, September 1994.

11. "They Sent a Strong Message—A Humbling Message," *Asbury Park Press*, 8 November 1990.

12. "Bradley, Whitman Tussle Over Taxes," *Asbury Park Press*, 8 October 1990.

13. Bill Bradley, *Time Present, Time Past.* New York: Alfred Knopf, 1996, 40–41.

14. "They Sent a Strong Message—A Humbling Message," *Asbury Park Press*, 8 November 1990.

15. *Nightline*, ABC News, aired 8 November 1990.

16. "Winner Whitman Avoids Nudge Toward State House," *Bergen Record*, 8 November 1990.

17. Ibid.

18. "Two Moderate Republicans With Much in Common," *Bergen Record*, 23 September 1992.

19. "A Nemesis of Bradley Eyes Florio," *New York Times*, 14 October 1991.

20. William Palatucci, interview with author, 28 December 1995.

21. "Whitman, Edwards Hired Illegals," *Asbury Park Press,* 23 January 1993.

22. Michael Aron, *Governor's Race.* New Brunswick, N.J.: Rutgers University Press 1994, 37.

23. Ibid.

24. Hazel Frank Gluck, interview with author, 19 January 1996.

25. "Whitman Pays Bigger Price in Illegal Alien Flap," *Asbury Park Press,* 26 January 1993.

26. Ibid.

27. Jim Ahearn, "The Front-Runner Stumbles," *Asbury Park Press,* 27 January 1993.

28. Adrian Heffern, "Illegal Aliens Jump-Start GOP Race," *Asbury Park Press,* 31 January 1993.

29. "GOP Hopefuls Should Stay in Race, Kean Says," *Asbury Park Press,* 31 January 1993.

30. "Whitman's School Vote Sorely Missed," *Asbury Park Press,* 1 May 1993.

31. Aron, *Governor's Race,* 83.

32. Golden interview, 23 November 1995.

33. Art Weissman, "It's the Campaign Stupid," *New Jersey Reporter,* March 1993.

34. "Consultant Takes Aim at Whitman," *Asbury Park Press,* 29 April 1993.

35. *Inside Politics,* Cable News Network, aired 17 August 1993.

36. "Poll Finds Florio's Tax Increase Winning Approval in Retrospect," *New York Times,* 28 September 1993.

37. C. Whitman interview, 4 December 1995.

38. Golden interview, 23 November 1995.

39. "Go Personal, Whitman Is Implored," *New York Times,* 29 September 1993.

Chapter 3 Florio Free

1. *The Campaign Inside,* aired on New Jersey Network, 18 January 1994, 9:00 P.M.

2. Ibid.

3. "Whitman Shakes Up Staff," *Asbury Park Press,* 30 September 1993.

4. *The Campaign Inside,* aired on New Jersey Network, 18 January 1994, 9:00 P.M.

5. Gluck interview, 19 January 1996.

6. Garabed "Chuck" Haytaian, interview with author, 4 December 1995.

7. "Go Personal, Whitman Is Implored," *New York Times*, 29 September, 1993.

8. *The Campaign Inside*, aired on New Jersey Network, 18 January 1994, 9:00 P.M.

9. C. Whitman interview, 4 December 1995.

10. "Top Ad Strategists Face Off in NJ Gubernatorial Race," *Asbury Park Press*, 5 October 1993.

11. Whitman 1993, gubernatorial campaign commercial.

12. "Excerpts From the Debates of the 2 New Jersey Gubernatorial Candidates," *New York Times*, 8 October 1993.

13. *The Campaign Inside*, aired on New Jersey Network, 18 January 1994, 9:00 P.M.

14. "Big-Name Backers," *Asbury Park Press*, 31 October 1993.

15. *Charlie Rose*, Public Broadcasting System, aired 13 April 1994.

16. "Whitman Still Supporting Rehabilitation of Criminals," *Asbury Park Press*, 14 October 1993.

17. "It's Whitman's Turn As Voters Oust Florio," *Asbury Park Press*, 3 November 1993.

18. Ralph Siegel, "At Fourth and Goal, Whitman Handed Ball to Undecided," *Burlington County Times*, 7 November 1993.

19. Keith Nahigian, interview with author, 21 November 1995.

20. C. Whitman interview, 4 December 1995.

21. Howard Stern, *Miss America*. New York: Regain Books, 1995, 450–51.

22. David Redneck, "Day of the Dittoed," *Washington Post*, 20 February 1994.

23. Steven Salmore, interview with author, 22 December 1995.

24. Anna Quindlen, "Public and Private; Gender Gaffe," *New York Times*, 24 October 1993.

25. Letter to the editor, *New York Times*, 30 October 1993.

26. Lonna Hooks, interview with author, 7 February 1996.

27. *The Campaign Inside*, aired on New Jersey Network, 18 January 1994, 9:00 P.M.

28. Whitman 1993 gubernatorial campaign commercial.

29. Ibid.

30. J. Whitman interview, 22 December 1995.

31. "Whitman Alters Ad Tactics to Fend Off Rivals' Claims," *Asbury Park Press*, 21 October 1993.

32. Golden interview, 23 November 1995.

33. J. Whitman interview, 22 December 1995.

34. C. Whitman interview, 4 December 1995.

35. Golden interview, 23 November 1995.

36. Ibid.

37. Christine Todd Whitman, interview with author, 19 December 1995.

38. "It's Whitman's Turn As Voters Oust Florio," *Asbury Park Press*, 3 November 1993.

39. *The Campaign Inside*, aired on New Jersey Network, 18 January 1994, 9:00 P.M.

40. News, domestic: "Incumbents Watch Out Seems to Be Voters' Message," Cable News Network, aired 4 November 1993, 3:48 A.M. EST.

41. News, domestic: "Clinton Views Democratic Losses as Local," Cable News Network, aired 3 November 1993, 12:08 p.m. et.

42. "Dinkins Concedes Mayoral Race to Giuliani" and *Inside Politics*, both aired on Cable News Network, 3 November 1993.

43. David Broder, interview with author, 4 February 1996.

44. Ralph Siegel, "At Fourth and Goal, Whitman Handed Ball to Undecideds," *Burlington County Times*, 7 November 1993.

45. "Residual Anger Was Too Great, Politicos Agree," *Asbury Park Press*, 4 November 1993.

46. "It's Whitman's Turn As Voters Oust Florio," *Asbury Park Press*, 3 November 1993.

47. "Whitman Triumphantly Pledges Income-Tax Cut by 1994 Budget," *New York Times*, 4 November 1993.

48. "Gone. Politically Dead. Stick a Fork in Her," *Philadelphia Inquirer*, 4 November 1993.

49. "Undecided Voters Threw Pollsters Off," *Home News*, 24 November 1993.

50. Jim Ahearn, "New Leader, New Era," *Asbury Park Press*, 7 November 1993.

51. C. Whitman interview, 4 December 1995.

52. Steve Giegerich, "Seasoned Advice Flavors a Dish of Crow," *Asbury Park Press*, 5 November 1993.

Chapter 4   Ed Rollins

1. C. Whitman interview, 4 December 1995.
2. Peter Verniero, interview with author, 21 November 1995.
3. Gluck interview, 19 January 1996.
4. "Regarding Allegations of Voter Suppression Raised by Edward J. Rollins Jr.". Michael Chertoff, George F. Kugler Jr., James R. Zazzali, released 12 January 1995.
5. "Transcript of Rollins' Remarks Explaining Game Plan for the Campaign," *Star-Ledger,* 11 November 1993.
6. "Regarding Allegations," Chertoff.
7. "Politicians and the Press, Once Over," *New York Times,* 10 January 1996.
8. *Larry King Live,* Cable News Network, aired 16 November 1993.
9. C. Whitman interview, 4 December 1995.
10. "Whitman Team Paid to Curtail Black Turnout," *New York Times,* 10 November 1993.
11. "Rollins: GOP Cash Suppressed Black Vote," *Washington Post,* 10 November 1993.
12. "GOP Paid Off Democrats," *Bergen Record,* 10 November 1993.
13. "Black Votes Bought Off?" *Asbury Park Press,* 10 November 1993.
14. Verniero interview, 21 November 1995.
15. C. Whitman interview, 4 December 1995.
16. Hooks interview, 7 February 1996.
17. "Regarding Allegations," Chertoff.
18. *The Campaign Inside,* aired on New Jersey Network, 18 January 1994, 9:00 P.M.
19. C. Whitman interview, 4 December 1995.
20. J. Whitman interview, 22 December 1995.
21. C. Whitman interview, 4 December 1995.
22. "Regarding Allegations," Chertoff.
23. "It Did Not Happen," *Home News,* aired 11 November 1993.
24. "Whitman Denies Campaign Report That Campaign Paid Off Blacks," *New York Times,* 11 November 1993.
25. "Outrage Reigns Among Black Leaders," *Asbury Park Press,* 11 November 1993.
26. "Democrats Calling for Investigation," *Asbury Park Press,* 11 November 1993.
27. Ibid.

28. "Whitman: Payoffs Didn't Happen," *Philadelphia Inquirer*, 11 November 1993.

29. "Whitman Denies Campaign Report That Campaign Paid Off Blacks," *New York Times*, 11 November 1993.

30. "It Did Not Happen," *Home News*, 11 November 1993.

31. "Judge OKs Democrats' Suit Steps," *Asbury Park Press*, 16 November 1993.

32. "Black Votes Bought Off?" *Asbury Park Press*, 10 November 1993.

33. "Whitman Welcomes Scrutiny," *Asbury Park Press*, 13 November 1993.

34. C. Whitman interview, 4 December 1995.

35. Verniero interview, 21 November 1995.

36. J. Whitman interview, 22 December 1995.

37. Gluck interview, 19 January 1996.

38. "Husband Learning to Choose Words," *Asbury Park Press*, 22 November 1993.

39. "GOP Declares Victory—Again," *Asbury Park Press*, 30 November 1993.

40. "Morning Edition," National Public Radio, aired 11 November 1993.

41. Daniel Weissman (no relation to author), interview with author, 26 December 1995.

42. Herb Jackson, interview with author, 14 December 1995.

43. Editorial, *Asbury Park Press*, 11 November 1993.

44. "Editorial Writers React to Rollins," *Trenton Times*, 12 November 1993.

45. Editorial, *Wall Street Journal*, 12 November 1993.

46. Jim Ahearn, "Grace Under Fire," *Bergen Record*, 17 November 1993.

47. Carl Rowan, "GOP Hostility Toward Blacks Revealed Anew," *Star-Ledger*, 21 November 1993.

48. "This Week With David Brinkley," ABC News, aired 14 November 1993.

49. *Inside Politics*, Cable News Network, aired 12 November 1993.

50. "Whitman in the Pews," *Asbury Park Press*, 15 November 1993.

51. "Rollins Mum on Testimony," *Asbury Park Press*, 19 November 1993.

52. Ed Rollins, "Ed Rollins: 'I Spun Myself Out of Control,'" *Washington Post*, 21 November 1993.

53. C. Whitman interview, 4 December 1995.

54. Verniero interview, 21 November 1995.
55. "Whitman Weary Of Media Queries," *Asbury Park Press*, 22 November 1993.
56. C. Whitman interview, 4 December 1995.
57. "Whitman Weary of Media Queries," *Asbury Park Press*, 22 November 1993.
58. C. Whitman interview, 4 December 1995.
59. "Democrats Drop Whitman Suit," *Bergen Record*, 30 November 1993.
60. "Whitman Calls Dispute Over," *Asbury Park Press*, 24 November 1993.
61. Verniero interview, 21 November 1995.
62. "Rollins Bruhaha Slows Transition," *Asbury Park Press*, 17 November 1993.
63. Haytaian interview, 4 December 1995.
64. Editorial, *Asbury Park Press*, 1 December 1993.
65. C. Whitman interview, 4 December 1995.
66. J. Whitman interview, 22 December 1995.

Chapter 5   Transition

1. Verniero interview, 21 November 1995.
2. "Whitman Adamant on Tax Cut in '94," *Asbury Park Press*, 23 November 1993.
3. Ibid.
4. Ibid.
5. Ibid.
6. "Florio Leaving Without Regrets," *Asbury Park Press*, 5 November 1993.
7. Richard Reeves, "Florio Was Punished for His Abruptness," *Asbury Park Press*, 8 November 1993.
8. "Leaders Say GOP Legislature Will Not Be Just a 'Rubber Stamp,'" *Asbury Park Press*, 3 November 1993.
9. Lee Seglem, *Asbury Park Press*, 16 December 1993.
10. "Whitman Adamant on Tax Cut in '94," *Asbury Park Press*, 23 November 1993.
11. J. Whitman interview, 22 December 1995.
12. C. Whitman interview, 4 December 1995.
13. Verniero interview, 21 November 1995.
14. Harold Hodes, interview with author, 11 December 1995.

15. "Whitman's Transition Office Opens," Associated Press, 9 November 1993.

16. Art Weissman, "Business As Usual," *New Jersey Reporter*, May/June 1994.

17. "Assuming Power: Access Is Everything for Lobbyist Gluck," *Asbury Park Press*, 16 January 1994.

18. Gluck interview, 19 January 1996.

19. Author's notes.

20. "Whitman's Right-Hand Woman in Trenton: Hazel F. Gluck, Friend and Political Pro, Has No Office but Plenty of Power," *New York Times*, 7 January 1994.

21. "Assuming Power: Access Is Everything for Lobbyist Gluck," *Asbury Park Press*, 16 January 1994.

22. C. Whitman interview, 19 December 1995.

23. Gluck interview, 19 January 1996.

24. C. Whitman interview, 19 December 1995.

25. Brian Clymer, interview with author, 17 January 1996.

26. Whitman inauguration coverage, New Jersey Network, aired 18 January 1994.

27. C. Whitman interview, 4 December 1995.

28. Gluck interview, 19 January 1996.

29. "Man at the Side of (Not Behind) Whitman," *New York Times*, 17 January 1994.

30. C. Whitman interview, 19 December 1995.

31. "Whitman Wants Extra Month to Develop State Budget," *Asbury Park Press*, 9 December 1993.

32. Mike Kelly, "Whitman At the Gate,"*Bergen Record*, 16 January 1994.

33. "Whitman Says Tax Reductions Will Hurt," *New York Times*, 6 January 1994.

34. "What Governor, Legislative Leaders Were Heard to Say," *Asbury Park Press*, 12 January 1994.

35. "Whitman 'Confident' of Fulfilling Tax Pledge," *Asbury Park Press*, 16 January 1994.

36. "A Call for Change," *Asbury Park Press*, 12 January 1994.

Chapter 6   Dogs and Taxes

1. C. Whitman, interview, 4 December 1995.

2. Keith Nahigian, interview with author, 18 December 1995.

3. C. Whitman interview, 19 December 1995.

4. Whitman inauguration speech text, 18 January 1994.

5. Haytaian interview, 4 December 1995.

6. Whitman inauguration speech text, 18 January 1994.

7. C. Whitman interview, 4 December 1995.

8. Whitman inauguration speech text, 18 January 1994.

9. Whitman inauguration coverage, New Jersey Network, aired 18 January 1994.

10. "Reporter's Notebook: Little Warning Given of Tax Cut in Whitman Speech," and "New Jersey's New Governor; Inaugural Surprise: Whitman Wants Tax Cut Now," both *New York Times*, 19 January 1994.

11. New Jersey State Assembly Democratic release, 18 January 1994.

12. C. Whitman interview, 4 December 1995.

13. "Grand Old Party's Grand Party," *Asbury Park Press*, 19 January 1994.

14. "A Very Republican Party Celebrates Return to Power," *Bergen Record*, 19 January 1994.

15. Editorial, *Washington Post*, 21 January 1994.

16. Editorial, *Philadelphia Inquirer*, 19 January 1994.

17. Editorial, *Christian Science Monitor*, 27 January 1994.

18. *The Campaign Inside*, New Jersey Network, aired 18 January 1994, 9:00 P.M.

19. Salmore interview, 22 December 1995.

20. "New Jersey's New Governor: On Her Own Course," *New York Times*, 19 January 1994.

21. Hodes interview, 11 December 1995.

22. J. Whitman interview, 22 December 1995.

23. "Whitman Cleans House at Sports Authority, Replaces Byrne, 2 Other Members," *Bergen Record*, 21 January 1994.

24. "Whitman Debating Sale of the Sports Authority," *New York Times*, 21 January 1994.

25. D. Weissman interview, 26 December 1995.

26. Carl Golden, interview with author, 11 December 1995.

27. *Charlie Rose*, Public Broadcasting System, aired 13 April 1994.

28. "Whitman Concedes Chance of Higher Property Taxes," *New York Times*, 22 January 1994.

29. "State's Mayors Urged to Be Frugal," *Asbury Park Press*, 27 January 1994.

30. Editorial, *Morris County Daily Record*, 28 January 1994.

31. Golden interview, 11 December 1995.

32. "Whitman at Center Stage in Washington, Trenton," *Bergen Record*, 29 January 1994.

33. "Governor Swings On," *Asbury Park Press*, 31 January 1994.

34. *MacNeil/Lehrer News Hour*, Public Broadcasting System, aired 31 January 1994.

35. "This Week With David Brinkley," ABC News, aired 30 January 1994.

36. "Whitman Enjoying the Honeymoon—While It Lasts," *Asbury Park Press*, 13 February 1994.

37. C. Whitman interview, 19 December 1995.

38. Ibid.

39. Ibid.

Chapter 7   One Family

1. "Whitman Fights Hate; 'List' Film to Be Shown 5 Times Free," *Asbury Park Press*, 18 February 1994.

2. Editorial, *Boston Globe*, 27 January 1994.

3. Editorial, *Newsday*, 26 January 1994.

4. Whitman inauguration speech text, 18 January 1994.

5. C. Whitman interview, 19 December 1995.

6. "Hooks in the Front Lines on Racial Issues," *Asbury Park Press*, 27 February 1994.

7. Hooks interview, 7 February 1996.

8. "Spielberg Cites New Jersey Program," *Asbury Park Press*, 19 July 1994.

9. "Whitman On Race: Hateful Ideas Must Be Challenged," *Asbury Park Press*, 18 February 1994.

10. "State Plots Assault on Hate, Whitman Calls for Tolerance," *Bergen Record*, 18 February 1994.

11. "A War on Hate or Business As Usual?" *Asbury Park Press*, 26 February 1994.

12. "Islamic Figure's Speech Takes Soft Tone," *New York Times*, 1 March 1994.

13. Hooks interview, 7 February 1996.

14. C. Whitman interview, 19 December 1995.

15. Ibid.

16. Palatucci interview, 28 December 1995.

17. Author's notes.

18. C. Whitman interview, 19 December 1995.

19. Ibid.

20. Ibid.

21. Golden interview, 11 December 1995.

22. "Battle Seen on Teacher Tenure," *Asbury Park Press*, 3 February 1994.

23. "Whitman in Risky Battle With NJEA," *Asbury Park Press*, 10 February 1994.

24. "The Republican Party's Party Train," *Asbury Park Press*, 4 February 1994.

25. Ibid.

26. C. Whitman interview, 4 February 1996.

27. "Hopes of Power and Safety for Women," *Asbury Park Press*, 10 March 1994.

28. "Whitman Mixes Substance and Style in Fast Start," *Asbury Park Press*, 25 April 1994.

29. "Christie Relishes Job," *New York Daily News*, 24 April 1994.

30. "All Outdoors; Whitman Feels at Home on Skis, Horses, Streams," *Star-Ledger*, 10 April 1994.

31. Jason Volk, interview with author, 26 February 1996.

32. "Whitman Mixes Substance and Style in Fast Start," *Asbury Park Press*, 25 April 1994.

33. C. Whitman interview, 4 February 1996.

34. John Whitman, Christine Todd Whitman, interview with author, 4 February 1996.

35. "Whitman Mixes Substance and Style in Fast Start," *Asbury Park Press*, 25 April 1994.

36. Golden interview, 11 December 1995.

37. Christine Todd Whitman, interview with author, 9 January 1996.

38. Ibid.

39. Ibid.

40. Nahigian interview, 18 December 1995.

41. "Whitman Succeeds at TV Appeal, but Draws Criticism for It," *Asbury Park Press*, 26 April 1994.

42. "Whitman Succeeds at TV Appeal, but Draws Criticism for It," *Asbury Park Press*, 26 April 1994.

43. "Environmental Research Funds to Stay Home in NJ," *Bergen Record*, 21 January 1994.

44. Steve Adubato, "Christie Learns to Listen," *Asbury Park Press*, 9 January 1994.

45. "Whitman and Cuomo Seek to Cut Different Taxes for Same Reason," *New York Times*, 20 January 1994.

46. "GOP Plans for Surpluses to Make Up For Tax Cuts," *New York Times*, 1 February 1994.

47. "Democrats Changing Tune on Taxes," *Asbury Park Press*, 3 March 1994.

48. "Triumphant Whitman Makes Tax Cut Official," *Trenton Times*, 8 March 1994.

49. "Tax Cut Will Go Down in History," *Asbury Park Press*, 8 March 1994.

50. "Whitman Starts to Make Good on Campaign's Income Tax Pledge," *Atlantic City Press*, 8 March 1994.

51. Jane Kenny, interview with author, 21 December 1995.

52. C. Whitman interview, 19 December 1995.

53. Ibid.

54. J. Whitman interview, 22 December 1995.

55. "Magnate Force," *Asbury Park Press*, 29 January 1995.

56. Clymer interview, 17 January 1995.

57. "Budget Still Shrouded in Secrecy," *Asbury Park Press*, 11 March 1994.

58. C. Whitman interview, 19 December 1995.

59. Ibid.

Chapter 8   Tax Cut II

1. Whitman budget address text, 15 March 1994.

2. "Income Taxes for '95 Would Be Cut 6–10%," *Asbury Park Press*, 16 March 1994.

3. Bernard Kenny, interview with author, 21 December 1994.

4. Ibid.

5. "Income Taxes for '95 Would Be Cut 6–10%," *Asbury Park Press*, 16 March 1994.

6. Editorial, *New York Times*, 17 March 1994.

7. "Big Cuts Missing in NJ Budget for the Most Part, Aid to Municipalities and School Districts Was Untouched," *Philadelphia Inquirer*, 15 March 1994.

8. Mary Caffrey, interview with author, 15 January 1994.

9. David Wald, "Governor Projects the Image of Winner 100 Days Into Her Term," *Star-Ledger*, 24 April 1994.

10. "Whitman Riding High After 100 Days," *Trenton Times*, 24 April 1994.

11. "For Whitman, Applause in the Early Acts," *New York Times*, 19 May 1994.

12. Jackson interview, 14 December 1994.

13. Salmore interview, 22 December 1995.

14. George Will, "National GOP Has Its Eye on Whitman," *Trenton Times*, 3 April 1994.

15. "Whitman, Kean Recall Nixon As Sage Advisor," *Asbury Park Press*, 23 April 1994.

16. William Safire, "Nixon on Nixon," *New York Times*, 12 May 1994.

17. "GOP Dreams of Powell & Whitman Ticket in '96" *New York Post*, 14 April 1994.

18. "Christine Scissorhands," *The Economist*, 23 April 1994.

19. "Whitman Button Sign of Rising Star," *Asbury Park Press*, 23 May 1994.

20. "Whitman Says She'll Stay in N.J." *Asbury Park Press*, 15 April 1994.

21. *Charlie Rose*, Public Broadcasting System, aired 13 April 1994.

22. "Powell and Whitman Scotch Nomination," *Star-Ledger*, 19 May 1994.

23. *Charlie Rose*, Public Broadcasting System, aired 13 April 1994.

24. Larry Sabato, interview with author, 26 December 1995.

25. J. Whitman interview, 22 December 1995.

26. Dan Todd, interview with author, 30 January 1996.

27. J. Kenny interview, 21 December 1995.

28. Sabato interview, 26 December 1995.

29. "Whitman's Riding Wave of Approval," *Asbury Park Press*, 15 May 1994.

30. Ibid.

31. Robert Torricelli, interview with author, May 1994.

32. "Whitman Points to Tax Cut As Highlight of First 100 days," *Star-Ledger*, 22 April 1994.

33. Golden interview, 11 December 1995.

34. John O. Bennett, interview with author, 7 February 1996.

35. Whitman inauguration coverage, aired on New Jersey Network, 18 January 1994.

36. DiFrancesco interview, 29 December 1995.

37. Ibid.

38. Not-for-attribution interview with author, November 1995.

39. DiFrancesco interview, 29 December 1995.
40. Haytaian interview, 4 December 1995.
41. Author's notes.
42. C. Whitman, interview, 19 December 1995.
43. Judy Shaw, interview with author, 22 January 1996.
44. Peter Verniero, interview with author, 19 December 1995.
45. DiFrancesco interview, 29 December 1995.

Chapter 9   Media Darling

1. "Higher Education Chancellor Vacating Office, but Not Happily," *Asbury Park Press*, 19 June 1994.
2. Adrian Heffern, "Whitman's Lesson Plan: Subtraction," *Asbury Park Press*, 12 June 1994.
3. Robert Braun, "Whitman's Plan Devoid of Any Hint of Vision," *Star-Ledger*, 6 May 1994.
4. Christine Todd Whitman, interview with author, 25 January 1996.
5. Golden interview, 11 December 1995.
6. C. Whitman interview, 19 December 1994.
7. J. Whitman interview, 22 December 1995.
8. Golden interview, 11 December 1995.
9. Shaw interview, 22 January 1996.
10. C. Whitman interview, 25 January 1996.
11. J. Whitman interview, 22 December 1995.
12. Carl Golden, interview with author, 23 January 1996.
13. C. Whitman interview, 25 January 1996.
14. Ibid.
15. Jim Goodman, interview with author, 29 December 1995.
16. Aron interview, 29 December 1995.
17. Nahigian interview, 18 December 1995.
18. D. Weissman interview, 26 December 1995.
19. "GOP Governors Push Big New Tax Revolt—At the State Level," *Wall Street Journal*, 2 May 1994.
20. "Victory Over the Doubters," *New York Times*, 1 July 1994.
21. "Reclaiming Tax Cuts for the GOP," *Boston Globe*, 9 July 1994.
22. "Whitman Won't Be Untested for Long," *Washington Times*, 27 June 1994.
23. "Christine Whitman, Born to Run," *Washington Post*, 24 January 1995.

24. CBS News, hourly newscast, WCBS New York, aired 7 February 1996.

25. Broder interview, 4 February 1996.

26. C. Whitman interview, 9 January 1996.

27. "Tax Cut II OK'd," *Asbury Park Press*, 1 July 1994.

28. "Whitman Pitches Cuts," *Asbury Park Press*, 2 June 1994.

29. Bennett interview, 7 February 1996.

30. "With Royal Flourish, Whitman Carves Income Tax 10%," *Asbury Park Press*, 7 July 1994.

31. Golden interview, 11 December 1995.

32. "NJ Gov. Urges GOP to Strip Anti-Abortion Plank," *Los Angeles Times*, 12 July 1994.

33. "Whitman Urges GOP to Reign in Right Wing," *Star-Ledger*, 12 July 1994.

34. "Rep. Smith Attacks Whitman View on Abortion," *Star-Ledger*, 20 July 1994.

35. Ray Kerrison, "Claim That GOP Right Wing Cost It '92 Won't Fly," *New York Post*, 15 July 1994.

36. "Whitman Fires at Abortion Stance," *Bergen Record*, 12 July 1994.

37. Author's notes

38. C. Whitman interview, 25 January 1996.

39. Golden interview, 23 January 1996.

40. George Will, "Women We Love," *Esquire*, August 1994.

41. Jim Hooker, "Governor Is a Media Happening," *Asbury Park Press*, 24 July 1994.

42. Golden interview, 23 January 1996.

43. Joseph Kyrillos, interview with author, 21 November 1995.

44. C. Whitman interview, 9 January 1996.

45. "Whitman Hailed As 'A Serious National Player,' " *Bergen Record*, 2 August 1994.

46. Ibid.

Chapter 10   Campaigning Coast to Coast

1. Nahigian interview, 18 December 1995.

2. Pete Wilson, interview with author, 6 February 1996.

3. "Whitman Starts Four-State Campaign for GOP," *New York Times*, 29 August 1994.

4. C. Whitman interview, 9 January 1996.

5. "Campaigns Helped By 2 Whitmans," *Asbury Park Press*, 1 September 1994.

6. Ibid.

7. C. Whitman interview, 9 January 1996.

8. "Getting Lessons From Texans," *Asbury Park Press*, 29 August 1994.

9. "GOP Eager to Grab Ride on Whitman's Rising Star," *Asbury Park Press*, 4 September 1994.

10. "Tuning In to Gov. Whitman," *Asbury Park Press*, 2 September 1994.

11. "GOP Eager to Grab Ride on Whitman's Rising Star," *Asbury Park Press*, 4 September 1994.

12. C. Whitman interview, 4 December 1995.

13. Ibid.

14. "Youth Corps Urged for New Jersey," *Asbury Park Press*, 3 September 1994.

15. "Potshots Aimed at Governor's Trips," *Asbury Park Press*, 21 September 1994.

16. "Wishing on Whitman's Star," *Washington Post*, 24 October 1994.

17. "Move Over, Rockefeller, GOP's Got a New Ideal," *New York Times*, 4 October 1994.

18. Howard Fineman, "Now the Volvo Republicans," *Newsweek*, 13 October 1994.

19. David Broder, "Stump Power, Whitman, Hillary Clinton Hit on the Hustings," *Asbury Park Press*, 19 October 1994.

20. C. Whitman interview, 9 January 1996.

21. "Potshots Aimed at Governor's Trips," *Asbury Park Press*, 21 September 1994.

22. C. Whitman interview, 9 January 1996.

23. Weissman, *New Jersey Reporter*, May/June 1994.

24. C. Whitman interview, 9 January 1996.

25. "Probe Urged of Whitman Aide's Action," *Asbury Park Press*, 5 August 1994.

26. Editorial, *Star-Ledger*, 11 August 1994.

27. D. Weissman interview, 26 December 1995.

28. Jim Goodman, "Lobbyists Call Shots on Welfare," *Trenton Times*, 14 August 1994.

29. "Megan's Law Now N.J. Law," *Asbury Park Press*, 1 November 1994.

30. Verniero interview, 19 December 1995.

31. "Copter Trip Haunts Whitman," *Asbury Park Press*, 22 September 1994.

32. Steve Adubato, "Whitman Hits 'the Zone,' " *Asbury Park Press*, 10 October 1994.

33. "Haytaian Offers Economic Plan," *Asbury Park Press*, 21 September 1994.

34. Golden interview, 23 January 1996.

35. Philip Gourevitch, "Dial Hate," *New York* magazine, 24 October 1994.

36. "Governor Distances Self From Commentator After Protest," *Asbury Park Press*, 22 October 1994.

37. "Whitman Asks Truce of Talk Host," *Asbury Park Press*, 25 October 1994.

38. "Governor Distances Self From Commentator After Protest," *Asbury Park Press*, 22 October 1994.

39. C. Whitman interview, 9 January 1996.

40. "GOP's Big Gains Challenge Whitman," *Asbury Park Press*, 13 November 1994.

41. Sabato interview, 26 December 1995.

42. "Whitman: A Natural in Helping the G.O.P.," *New York Times*, 17 November 1994.

43. "Whitman's Star Power on Display," *Trenton Times*, 22 November 1994.

44. "Whitman: A Natural in Helping the G.O.P.," *New York Times*, 17 November 1994.

Chapter 11   Whitman 1, Clinton 0

1. "Christine Todd Whitman," *People*, 26 December 1994.

2. Golden interview, 23 January 1996.

3. DiFrancesco interview, 29 December 1995.

4. C. Whitman interview, 9 January 1996.

5. Carroll Bogert, "On the Cutting Edge," *Newsweek*, 5 December 1994.

6. Peter Keating, "How to Keep Your State and Local Taxes Down," *Money*, January 1995.

7. Bob Herbert, "The Shell Game," *New York Times*, 1 February 1995.

8. Author's notes.

9. B. Kenny interview, 21 December 1995.

10. Sabato interview, 26 December 1995.

11. "Juvenile Justice Reforms Outlined," *Asbury Park Press*, 6 January 1995.

12. "Summit of Popularity," *Asbury Park Press*, 18 December 1994.

13. Ibid.

14. "Political Theater, Loud Applause, Rave Reviews," *Asbury Park Press*, 11 January 1995.

15. Whitman State of the State text, 10 January 1995.

16. "Political theater, Loud Applause, Rave Reviews," *Asbury Park Press*, 11 January 1995.

17. Ibid.

18. "Behind Tax Pledge: How the Numbers Came Up for Whitman," *New York Times*, 29 January 1995.

19. "Whitman Warms to Clinton Rebuff," *Asbury Park Press*, 21 January 1995.

20. C. Whitman interview, 9 January 1996.

21. "Whitman to Speak to Nation," *Asbury Park Press*, 20 January 1995.

22. C. Whitman interview, 9 January 1996.

23. Peter Verniero, interview with author, 19 January 1996.

24. Author's notes.

25. Verniero interview, 19 January 1996.

26. Whitman budget address text, 23 January 1995.

27. New Jersey State Assembly Democratic release, 23 January 1995.

28. "Budget's Losers Display a Touch of Resignation," *New York Times*, 24 January 1995.

29. "GOP Answers Clinton With Call to 'Revolution of Ideas,' " *Los Angeles Times*, 25 January 1995.

30. C. Whitman interview, 9 January 1996.

31. State of the Union coverage, ABC News, aired 24 January 1995.

32. "GOP Makes Short Work of Clinton's Long Speech," *Washington Times*, 25 January 1995.

33. Ibid.

34. "Whitman's Lower Tax Message Beamed to U.S.," *Asbury Park Press*, 25 January 1995.

35. Editorial, *Atlanta Journal and Constitution*, 25 January 1995.

36. "Whitman Steals Show at Governor's Meeting," *Bergen Record*, 31 January 1995.

37. Shaw interview, 22 January 1996.

38. John B. Judis, "Hot Toddy," *The New Republic*, 13 February 1995.

39. "Shocking! Howard's Rest Stop," *Asbury Park Press*, 27 January 1995.

40. Ibid.

41. Ibid.

42. Ibid.

43. Stern, *Miss America*, 458.

44. Author's notes.

Chapter 12   Reality Check

1. "Tax Men Want a Cut From Coupons," *Asbury Park Press*, 22 January 1995.

2. "GOP Tests Whitman in Year 2 of Tax Cut," *Asbury Park Press*, 8 May 1995.

3. Whitman interview, 4 December 1995.

4. J. Whitman interview, 4 February 1996.

5. C. Whitman interview, 25 January 1996.

6. Golden interview, 23 January 1996.

7. "A Gentlewoman's Challenge to Newt's Republican Revolution," *London Independent*, 9 April 1995.

8. "Whitman Angers Black Leaders, Illegitimacy Remark Reopens Old Wounds," *Asbury Park Press*, 14 April 1995.

9. "The Governor Says She Is Sorry for a Comment on Black Males," *New York Times*, 14 April 1995.

10. Whitman Angers Black Leaders, Illegitimacy Remark Reopens Old Wounds," *Asbury Park Press*, 14 April 1995.

11. Ibid.

12. David Wald, "Whitman's Racial 'Misstatements' Keep Piling Up," *Star-Ledger*, 23 April 1995.

13. "Whitman Calls for Welfare Forums," *Asbury Park Press*, 25 April 1995.

14. "Whitman Has Trouble With Race," *Asbury Park Press*, 7 May 1995.

15. Sabato interview, 26 December 1995.

16. "Gingrich Aide in 'Black Sex Game' Storm," *Daily Mail* (London), 15 April 1996.

17. "Made for the White House," *Guardian* (London), 7 March 1995.

18. *On the Record,* New Jersey Network, aired 21 April 1995.

19. Gualberto Medina, interview with author, 19 January 1996.

20. Aron interview, 29 December 1995.

21. *On the Record,* New Jersey Network, aired 21 April 1995.

22. "Whitman Trip to Left Coast a Right Move?" *Asbury Park Press,* 27 April 1995.

23. Ibid.

24. Ibid.

25. "California Trip Highlights GOP Divisions," *Asbury Park Press,* 30 April 1995.

26. Whitman Nixon Library Speech Text, 27 April 1995.

27. "California Trip Highlights GOP Divisions," *Asbury Park Press,* 30 April 1995.

28. Ibid.

29. "Whitman Tells Conservatives Don't Fight on Social Issues," *Asbury Park Press,* 29 April 1995.

30. *Inside Politics,* Cable News Network, aired 18 May 1995.

31. "Sale of Whitman Videos Fuels Political Critics," *Asbury Park Press,* 25 August 1995.

32. New Jersey State Senate Democratic release, 26 April 1995.

33. New Jersey State Assembly Democratic release, 29 June 1995.

34. "Whitman Gets What She Wants," *Asbury Park Press,* 28 June 1995.

35. Democratic Assemblywoman Loretta Weinberg speech text, 26 June 1995.

36. "Whitman, Pen in Hand, Slashes Income Tax Again," *Asbury Park Press,* 5 July 1995.

37. "Whitman Puts Image on Line," *Asbury Park Press,* 18 July 1995.

38. "Weathering the Storm of Dissent," *Asbury Park Press,* 6 July 1995.

39. J. Whitman interview, 22 December 1995.

40. "Weathering the Storm of Dissent," *Asbury Park Press,* 6 July 1995.

41. *Inside Politics,* Cable News Network, aired 7 July 1995.

Chapter 13   The Sweep of History

1. "Gov. Whitman Plays King For a Night," *Asbury Park Press,* 7 July 1995.

2. *Larry King Live,* Cable News Network, aired 6 July 1995.

3. "GOP Raises $4 Million at $1,000 a Plate Governor's Ball," *Asbury Park Press*, 17 September 1995.

4. "GOP Hopes For 'Christie Coattails,' " *Asbury Park Press*, 5 October 1995.

5. "Warchest of GOP Padlocking Opponents," *Asbury Park Press*, 5 November 1995.

6. "GOP Medicaid Plan Tough Call For Governor," *Asbury Park Press*, 21 September 1995.

7. "Gingrich Defends Medicare Proposals to N.J. Seniors," *Asbury Park Press*, 13 October 1995.

8. "Whitman and Newt: So Far, and Yet So Near," *Asbury Park Press*, 29 October 1995.

9. Ibid.

10. Ibid.

11. "2 Sides Crow Over Results, But Failed to Defeat Apathy," *Asbury Park Press*, 9 November 1995.

12. Ibid.

13. "Whitman Holds Off Backing Dole," *Asbury Park Press*, 29 September 1995.

14. Ibid.

15. C. Whitman interview, 25 January 1996.

16. Ibid.

17. "Whitman Backing Dole," *Asbury Park Press*, 10 December 1995.

18. Ibid.

19. C. Whitman interview, 25 January 1996.

20. Shaw interview, 22 January 1996.

21. Hooks interview, 7 February 1996.

22. DiFrancesco interview, 29 December 1995.

23. C. Whitman interview, 25 January 1996.

24. B. Kenny interview, 21 December 1995.

25. "Family Values As an Issue in the 1996 Elections," Federal News Service, 17 November 1995.

26. "Whitman to Dole: I'm Off V.P. List," *Asbury Park Press*, 28 March 1996.

27. Ibid.

28. Jennifer Preston, "Dreams of Washington Remain Dreams, For Now," *New York Times*, 31 March 1996.

29. "Whitman Seeking Role in Selling Moderates," *Trenton Times*, 17 October 1995.

30. Verniero interview, 19 January 1996.
31. B. Kenny interview, 21 December 1995.
32. Leo Klagholz, interview with author, 3 February 1996.
33. Author's notes, 13 November 1995.
34. C. Whitman interview, 25 January 1996.
35. Salmore interview, 22 December 1995.
36. John Engler, interview with author, 6 February 1996.
37. Hodes interview, 11 December 1995.
38. Roy Romer, interview with author, 4 February 1996.

Index